IN SEARCH OF THE *Split* SUBJECT

In SEARCH *of the* SPLIT SUBJECT:

Psychoanalysis, Phenomenology, AND THE NOVELS OF *Margaret Atwood*

SONIA MYCAK

ECW PRESS

CANADIAN CATALOGUING IN PUBLICATION DATA
Mycak, Sonia
In search of the split subject : psychoanalysis,
phenomenology, and the novels of Margaret Atwood
Includes bibliographical references.
ISBN 1-55022-269-4

1. Atwood, Margaret, 1939–   – Criticism,
interpretation, etc. 2. Splitting (Psychology)
in literature. I. Title.

PS8501.T86Z7 1996   C813'.54   C95-932538-7
PR9199.3.A7827 1996

Design and imaging by ECW Type & Art, Oakville, Ontario.
Printed by Imprimerie Gagné, Louiseville, Québec.
Distributed in Canada by General Distribution Services,
30 Lesmill Road, Don Mills, Ontario M3B 2T6.

Published by ECW PRESS,
2120 Queen Street East, Suite 200,
Toronto, Ontario M4E 1E2.

ACKNOWLEDGEMENTS

The present book grew out of a doctoral dissertation undertaken in the School of English at the University of New South Wales in Sydney, Australia. The ideas were developed over a number of years and were presented by the author at various conferences including the following:

The national conference of the South Pacific Association for Commonwealth Language and Literature Studies (SPACLALS) held at The University of Wollongong, Australia, in February 1990: "Margaret Atwood's Life Before Man: The Prehistory Paradigm and the Repressed Feminine."

The biennial conference of The Association for Canadian Studies in Australia and New Zealand (ACSANZ) held at The University of New England, Australia, in July 1990: "The Dynamics of Exchange and Consumption in Margaret Atwood's *The Edible Woman*."

The biennial conference of the Association for Canadian Studies in the United States (ACSUS) held in Boston, U.S.A., in November 1991: "(M)other and Daughter: The Construction of Subjectivity in Margaret Atwood's *Lady Oracle*."

The biennial conference of The Association for Canadian Studies in Australia and New Zealand (ASCANZ) held at the Victoria University of Wellington, New Zealand, in December 1992: "Split and Sutured Subjectivity: A Reading of Margaret Atwood's Novels."

The annual conference of the British Association for Canadian Studies (BACS) held at Cambridge University, U.K., in March, 1993: "The Decentered Subject in Margaret Atwood's *Bodily Harm*."

The biennial conference of the Association for Canadian Studies in the United States (ACSUS) held in New Orleans, U.S.A., in November 1993: "Margaret Atwood's *Cat's Eye*: Mimesis and the Construction of Reality."

The 28th Congress of the Australian Universities Language and Literature Association (AULLA) held at The University of New England, Australia, in February 1995: "Imagination and the Imaginary in Margaret Atwood's *Life Before Man*."

The author would like to thank the editors of the *Canadian Review of Comparative Literature* for permission to reprint her article "Divided and Dismembered: The Decentred Subject in Margaret Atwood's *Bodily Harm*."

TABLE OF CONTENTS

INTRODUCTION

This book is a close reading of six of the novels of Margaret Atwood in the light of psychoanalytic and phenomenological theories, with a view to exploring an aspect of Atwood's work well recognized but not adequately accounted for: the divided self. It begins with the premise that there is an identifiable "I" in Atwood's work: the voice of a narrator/protagonist who may be difficult to characterize, but who nonetheless becomes familiar to anyone reading more than one of Atwood's novels. While there is a strong sense of there being "somebody" about whom each novel is written, and this very "self" should be a focal point for analysis, there is an equally strong sense that this "self" is neither integrated nor whole. And while critics acknowledge both the consciousness of the protagonist and its attendant divisions as significant aspects of Atwood's work, neither has been examined with the kind of theoretical precision warranted by their importance. To date, critics have either paid the divided self nominal attention, or have seen the division as effected through characterization, as evidence of a conflict within Atwood herself, as an element of the narrative, as a psychological barrier to be overcome, or as a motif to be interpreted through paradigms of feminist, nationalist, postcolonial, or postmodern thought. This has, in effect, meant that the divided self has been subsumed into other approaches and its significance both as a recurrent motif in Atwood's fiction and as a crux of contemporary literary and philosophical theory has been negated.

In the belief that understanding the divided self is crucial to understanding Atwood's work, this book is a detailed theoretical investigation into the ways in which, within a number of the novels — *The Edible Woman, Lady Oracle, Life before Man, Bodily Harm, Cat's Eye*, and *The Robber Bride* — identity is dislocated, alienated, splintered, and split. My analysis excludes *Surfacing* and *The Handmaid's Tale* for reasons explained in the appendix, but interprets the six named by drawing upon a number of key concepts that characterize the work of psychoanalytic and phenomenological theorists, notably: specular identity formation, familial relations and connections with the maternal, the role of the Imaginary, symbolic exchange, the mimetic construction of reality, dynamics of spatial location, signification, and enunciative positioning. By using these concepts, the recurrent motifs that characterize Atwood's work are explained by way of a critical method that allows for new interpretations of the novels.

Margaret Atwood's novels are preoccupied with the self. By this I mean that each novel explores the impressions, thoughts, and emotions that constitute a person's being. Human nature, character, and consciousness are paramount; foremost are the questions of who one is at a particular time in a particular situation and what is intrinsic to the identity of an individual. As one critic has noted, Atwood's characters undertake journeys that are "descents into the obscure regions of the self" (Rainwater 26). This is most often effected through the creation of a single protagonist whose focalizing perspective and narrative voice organize the plot, and a thematic concern with the developing consciousness of that protagonist. As Francis Mansbridge points out, the protagonist occupies "the spotlight on center stage" throughout each of Atwood's novels (107), making the notion of identity and the self worthy of attention regardless of critical intent.

While critics readily acknowledge that a desire to explore the self inspires Atwood's work,[1] they admit even more readily that that self is neither singular nor straightforward. Speaking of the protagonist of *Lady Oracle*, Susan Maclean states that "Atwood plays havoc with notions of identity," making the novel a veritable "whirligig of identity" (189). Maclean bases her argument upon the constantly transforming personae that characterize the protagonist. In this she concurs with Nora Foster Stovel who writes that "Margaret Atwood's novels all centre on the quest for identity, as each Janus-headed heroine struggles to integrate her splintered personae" (50). Certainly, within the novels characters are presented in successive and varying states of consciousness. The result is a kind of continuum of disconnection, wherein each protagonist may be positioned from a vague sense of dislocation and alienation, to "a feeling of dispossession, of absence from one's self" (Maclean 184), to a position in which the "hold on the self is only tenuous" and "her mode of existence is tentative, provisional" (183).[2] What in some instances remains an underlying sense of estrangement culminates in others in dysfunctional behaviours, multiple personalities, and complete psychological disintegration — characteristics that are, by now, the calling cards of the Atwoodian protagonist.

Quite simply stated, critics agree that the self portrayed in Atwood's fictional world is a self that is divided. Sherrill Grace, for example, argues that the ironic exploration of self is "a constant Atwood theme," and that "The closest Atwood comes to resolving the paradoxes of self and perception is in terms of duplicity" (132). For Grace, the message behind Atwood's work is a kind of psychological imperative to accept duality within the process of living, leading her to conclude that "Atwood explores the concept of duplicity thematically and formally. . . . Duplicity, then, is a touchstone in her art" (3). Maclean makes the point that "Atwood has always been intrigued by the concept of the double . . ." (188). Analysing *Lady Oracle*, Maclean maintains that "As the novel progresses, it becomes increasingly evident that man himself is duplicitous. The Dr Jekyll/Mr Hyde dichotomy is developed as a fundamental trait of human nature" (190). Stovel argues that Atwood uses mirror images and reflections of doubles to "symbolize her theme of self-definition" (50). Mansbridge identifies a number of related themes that all bespeak a division of sorts: the relationship of humanity with nature, the conscious and the instinctual, physical reality and fantasy, the mind and the body, and man and woman.

For many critics, duplicity "as a basic stratagem of existence" (Maclean 196) is seen to structure characterization within Atwood's novels. Roberta Rubenstein maintains that "most of [Atwood's] central characters experience themselves as internally divided" (*Boundaries* 65). In Rubenstein's survey, the protagonists of both *The Edible Woman* and *Lady Oracle* experience themselves as "acutely self-divided" (70); the three central characters of *Life before Man* "also manifest internal division" (73); and in *Bodily Harm*, ". . . Atwood illustrates that each person contains several 'stories' which must somehow be synthesized for coherence of personality" (101). Similarly, Lucy M. Freibert contends that the protagonist of *Lady Oracle* is another version of the "divided self" that Atwood developed in *The Edible Woman* and the "I" of *Surfacing* (24).

For at least two critics, the divided self is more than a thematic or narrative preoccupation — it is no less than the author's muse. Stovel argues that Atwood uses mirrors to reflect "the concept of duality," both of which are "central to Atwood's art" (50). According to Grace, "For Atwood the dynamic of violent duality is a function of the creative act. . . . She is constantly aware of opposites — self/other, subject/object, male/female, nature/man — and of the need to accept and work within them. To create, Atwood chooses violent dualities, and her art re-works, probes, and dramatizes the ability to see double" (134).

Given, then, that the divided self is often mentioned in critical appraisals of Atwood's work, it is appropriate to question how it is interpreted and to what conclusions critics are drawn. There are a number of ways in which the divided self, as recurrent motif of Atwoodian fiction, is utilized in critical accounts of the novels. First, there is what may be termed the perfunctory use of the divided self, where it is mentioned in passing without explication or where it is mentioned as being one aspect of the text rather than being the focal point of analysis. Examples of this include Sharon Wilson's account of *Bodily Harm*, which discusses Atwood's use of camera images in the novel and concludes by reference to the camera's ability to "dramatize the fragmented self" (145), and Marilyn Patton's scant allusion to *Bodily Harm* as being "a fragmented text that replicates the fragmentation of identity and of the world" (161).

Second, there is the approach that focuses upon the dynamics of division between characters. Glenys Stow's comparative analysis of *The Edible Woman* with the work of Lewis Carroll discusses what Stow calls "pairing" or "mirroring." This is a narrative strategy in which the hero and heroine are each split into two characters (Marian and Ainsley form one pair, and Len and Peter form a parallel couple) and protagonist and secondary characters Marian and Duncan also mirror each other. Similarly, Susan E. Lorsch confronts "the diffusion and multiplicity of personality" (464) that characterizes the protagonist of *The Edible Woman* by alleging that Duncan becomes a projection of Marian's self, her double,[3] and a symptom of her psychological breakdown. As "mirror" or "shadow" self of Marian, Duncan is seen to function as "a male externalization of part of Marian" (472). Ildiko de Papp Carrington similarly sees Duncan as being Marian's double, whereby they "share identical attitudes" (75) both physically and psychologically. In an approach in which she compares Atwood's novel with Joseph Conrad's *The Secret Sharer* in the belief that both works share thematic and narrative concerns, Carrington's underlying premise is that it is by correlating "Conrad's doubles" (81) with those of Atwood that *The Edible Woman* will be best understood.

Accounts that see one character as being a functional part of another draw upon a duality that is fully dependent upon characterization and that is essentially an intersubjective phenomenon. Furthermore, in Carrington's account, not only are the roles of the characters allegedly defined but through this ". . . Atwood's ultimate purpose in writing her novel" (74). With this we are brought to the third way in which the divided self is dealt with: critical practice that begins with scrutiny of the novel but ends with an analysis of the author.

Atwood is seen by Carrington to be one of a number of contemporary writers who split their ego and personify the conflicts in their own mental life by creating characters who are duplicitous. At this point, the novel is seen to be driven by "the terrible psychological tension" generated by the insistent question in Atwood's own mind: "Who am I?" (Carrington 83). In this context, the fictional construction of Marian and Duncan performs a kind of "exorcism" (84) by which the author is able to master the anxiety of her own identity crisis, and the resolution of Marian's inner dualism is seen to be the resolution of Atwood's own conflict. In this kind of author-centred approach, Carrington is not alone. Lorraine McMullen, for example, sees Marian and Ainsley as functioning in contrast to each other and in turn reflecting conflicting attitudes within Atwood herself. Similarly, Maclean argues that ". . . Atwood has repeatedly stressed that she is not the protagonist of her novels. However, this does not mean that the characters do not, at some level, represent some fragmented aspect of her own self" (195). In her analysis of *Lady Oracle*, Maclean contends that just as Joan's characters are projections of various facets of her personality, so it seems that Atwood's characters may very well be projections of her self. "It is Atwood, working through the medium of the novel itself," continues Maclean, "who is the real Lady Oracle" (196).

Interpreting dynamics of division as a kind of literary or narrative strategy may be quite rightly considered as an approach in itself, and it is the fourth way in which the divided self has been accounted for. Jayne Patterson, for example, aims for a stylistic analysis of language in *The Edible Woman*. However, inspired as she is by the aim of examining the development of Marian's personality, her task necessitates a look at "the split voice" (151) of the narrative. Meanwhile, Linda Hutcheon, in examining narrative structures in Atwood's work, argues that two thematic poles structure *The Edible Woman*. For Hutcheon, the narrative elements are ordered through contiguity with one or the other of the poles, and thus dichotomy becomes an organizing principle of the novel ("From Poetic").

13

Less concerned with narrative structure, the fifth way in which the divided self has been explained is the tendency for the literary critic to psychologize, to reason that the division evident within the novels is a function of the mind and indicative of the mental state of the reader. The result is a focus upon integration and wholeness rather than division as such, whereby it is hoped that the initial fragmentation will eventually be replaced by a unified sense of self and identity.[4] Denise E. Lynch, for example, analyses *Bodily Harm* as being a novel that is "personalist," by which she means that the plot allows for the "restructuring" of a "unified self" (47) by breaking down boundaries and forging "a vision of wholeness" (46). In this, the plot has a unifying effect and is constituted by its purpose of developing a "personalist consciousness" (48).

A similarly "integrative vision" (*Boundaries* 55) is evident in Rubenstein's work. Here each narrative is seen to be concerned with ego boundaries — merging and splitting, engulfment and separation — so that a cluster of psychological issues is ultimately clarified for the protagonist as she comes to understand her relationship with her parents (particularly her mother), a man, or both. "In each instance," writes Rubenstein, "the structure of the narrative mirrors the central female character's self-division and, later, her movement toward psychological integration" (*Boundaries* 100). Similarly, for Grace, duality is not in itself negative. What is destructive is our tendency to polarize experience, to affirm one perspective while denying the other. For Grace, Atwood's message is that duality should be accepted rather than denied. In this way, there will be "The possibility of affirmation through 'choosing a violent duality' . . ." (134).

On a more theoretical note, the last of the ways in which the divided self is dealt with in critical accounts to date is its inclusion within other schools of thought. The feminist approach, for example, may acknowledge the split self but it is immediately subsumed within issues of sexual difference. Rubenstein's work is an excellent example of this. She aptly makes the point that "The inner division that afflicts nearly all of Atwood's protagonists can be understood as a manifestation of a female's conflicting possibilities in patriarchy" (*Boundaries* 78). Broadly speaking, in this approach the self that Atwood is seen to be concerned with is undeniably a female one. In what Rubenstein identifies as narratives of female discovery, development, and crisis that demonstrate a "concern with women's lives in patriarchy" (111), Atwood is seen to be dramatizing issues of boundary and separation, "giving us new insight into central psychological and ideological themes in female experience" (116). Furthermore, the divisions within female identity are seen to be "recast on the level of cultural ideology as well as personal psychology" (84). As a result, the divisions within the female self evolve into a metaphor for the wider divisions between self and other and self and society, and what is otherwise individual automatically becomes both cultural and ideological.[5]

Elsewhere, the motif of the split self is subsumed into postcolonial interpretations of Atwood's work, whereby the estrangement of the self becomes the estrangement of a postcolonial society from its origins and its colonizing power. In Ken Goodwin's appraisal of *Bodily Harm*, "revolution is a symbol for the divided self" (114). Here decolonization is expressed in terms of individual humanity, and revolution confuses both the boundaries between self and other and the protagonist's sense of identity. With a similar focus upon cultural difference, the divided self is often subsumed into a nationalist approach that sees Atwood's fiction as being primarily Canadian. "Duality is a fact of our national character," writes Grace, and she notes that "Atwood portrays the contemporary national dilemma" (133). This is seen to involve not only a thematic preoccupation with a divided Canadian national identity, but a positioning of the author within a distinct literary tradition in which ". . . Atwood shares her interest in duality . . . with writers like Robertson Davies and Sheila Watson" (134).

On yet another theoretical note, Hutcheon accounts for the dynamics of division within Atwood's work by foregrounding them in theories of postmodernism, in particular the opposition between art as product and art as process (*Canadian Postmodern*). For Hutcheon, the tensions of the mind/body polarity that structure *The Edible Woman* are the tensions that can be found everywhere in Atwood's work, and they duplicate the postmodern contradiction between the written product and the act of writing. Hence, in Hutcheon's opinion, Atwood "does not . . . try to 'overcome dichotomies creatively.' She needs them; her art derives its power and meaning from those very postmodern contradictions" (*Canadian Postmodern* 157).

The divided self is, then, an aspect of Atwood's work well recognized. Notable also is the fact that the divided self has become the mainstay of contemporary philosophical debate. As Elizabeth Grosz points out, the decentring of identity effected by philosophers such as Nietzsche, Marx, Freud, and Lacan is tantamount to no less than "an intellectual revolution" (*Jacques Lacan* 1) in the face of a prevailing Cartesianism. Quite simply stated, after the work of these theorists, the "I" of Western consciousness would never again be the same. It would never again be central, in control, fully conscious, and secure in its own knowledge. In the words of Lacan, "For a long time thinkers, searchers, and even inventors who were concerned with the question of the mind, have over the years put forward the idea of unity as the most important and characteristic trait of structure" ("Of Structure" 190). However, continues Lacan, "The idea of the unifying unity of the human condition has always had on me the effect of a scandalous lie" (190).

The divided self, then, by way of poststructuralist thought, has become a crucial element of contemporary philosophical theory. It is also crucial to an understanding of Atwood's work. It is my contention that a marriage of the two — of contemporary theory and Atwood's work — will result in the most articulate rendition of the Atwoodian self, a way of reading recurrent motifs, and new interpretations of the novels. Hence this book: a close reading of Atwood's novels in light of psychoanalytic and phenomenological theories with a view to investigating and explaining the divided self. It is my belief that psychoanalysis has the greatest theoretical potential and allows for the complexity necessary for a highly developed account of human existence and of the self. As Ellie Ragland-Sullivan notes in a slightly different context, "no simple method or historical rendering will account for a subject who is centered in different orders simultaneously but contradictorily" ("Seeking" 53). And while I do not take issue with Grosz's objections to psychoanalysis on the grounds of its alleged phallocentrism, I concur with her on the point that psychoanalysis provides "arguably the most sophisticated and convincing account of subjectivity" (*Jacques Lacan* 3).

My reasons for also drawing upon the work of certain phenomenological theorists revolve around an attempt to enhance rather than detract from the complexity of the issues raised. For while psychoanalysis theorizes a self, that self is a subject of perception, and it is my belief that phenomenology best explains the way a person perceives. That is, while psychoanalysis addresses the ways in which an "I" is constructed, phenomenology investigates the ways in which that "I" relates to the world. In this, the theories are compatible, and together they provide an excellent framework from which to explore the issue of the divided self, and from which to read Atwood's work.

The application of psychoanalytic principles to Atwood's fiction should not be altogether unexpected in terms of critical practice. On occasion, critics will raise the issue of the unconscious, based on the fact that many of the protagonists seem not to be in full control of their lives or actions. Maclean, speaking of *Lady Oracle*, writes that "Joan's internal conflict may be viewed as a division between the conscious self, the world of reality, and the unconscious self, the world of fantasy" (184). Perry Nodelman maintains that in reading *The Edible Woman*, what the reader witnesses is "a convincing description of the 'subconscious' workings of Marian's mind" (81). Also speaking of *The Edible Woman*, Mansbridge states that "The novel portrays an awakening of the unconscious demands..." (108) of the protagonist's body. For Frank Davey, the novels involve "a descent to an underworld that affirms the instructive value of the Freudian unconscious" (*Margaret Atwood* 163).

Periodically, critics will incorporate elements of the psychoanalytic approach into their own work. Elsewhere, Davey writes that the structural divisions in *Surfacing*, *The Edible Woman*, and *Lady Oracle* "reflect Atwood's gradual development of a psychoanalytic perspective throughout the three novels" ("*Lady Oracle*'s Secret" 213). By this he means regressive fantasies, transferences, and projections from childhood experiences that plague the protagonist, and a pattern of catharsis whereby unconscious forces are made conscious and neuroses lose their power. Hutcheon's analysis of *Life before Man* seeks to understand Lesje's fantasy life as functioning according to the principles of the psychopathological symptom ("Reading Atwood's"). Her preliminary statement that psychoanalytic thought has taught about the symbolic properties of unconscious processes and of the significance of apparently haphazard associations (43) is preparatory for later characterization of the daydreaming as being Freudian in nature, and having a "childish regressive and escapist tendency" (49) that functions largely as an exercise in wish fulfilment. Barbara Godard draws upon psychoanalytic theory in interpreting *Lady Oracle* as being a tale of the archetypal feminist quest. Psychoanalysis and especially the unconscious are, in Godard's account, conscripted for the feminist project, the aim of which is the self-actualization of women based upon a recognition of unconscious forces and mythical archetypes lodged in the psyche. With this, a theory of the unconscious is pointed toward the reclamation of a primeval female existence.

Shannon Hengen's discussion of Atwood's *Two-Headed Poems*[6] is perhaps the most significant of these accounts, as it relies totally upon a psychoanalytic framework. Like Godard's account, Hengen's is underwritten by an identifiably feminist focus. In justification of a Lacanian approach, Hengen acknowledges that she is "reacting to what frankly disappoints me in much of [Atwood's] work" (36), a response motivated by what is arguably Atwood's antifeminist stance: the fact that the women are "disappointingly mute," "sexy but desperate characters" (37) who interact primarily with men and remain isolated and helpless. Inspired by the work of Jane Gallop, Hengen introduces the element of sexual difference in order to "analyze Atwood's women in relation to Lacan" (37). With this, she introduces the issue of gender identification both to Atwood's work and to Lacanian theory, using Lacanian concepts to liken the experiences of the fictional characters to "the psychotherapeutic setting" (37) in which women regress and emerge changed. The result is the potential for a positive outcome — both for Atwood's heroines and in terms of the wider psychoanalytic model — for a new kind of gender identification effected through a different kind of specular experience. With this, Hengen concludes her account with an assertion that *Two-Headed Poems* ends with an implied belief that "a new speech" (40) for women is possible, a nontraditional family relation in which the girl will look to the adult woman for an identity with newly found freedom.

Eleonora Rao's work *Strategies for Identity* shows the most recent and, to date, most extensive use of psychoanalysis in interpreting Atwood's work. Sharing a concern for selfhood and the decentred nature of identity, Rao's study of the poetry and prose prioritizes the notion of the ego as "inconsistent and in constant process" (xvii) in that Atwood's work is seen to be "a fundamental exploration of heterogeneity" (xii). The notion of the subject and subjectivity to which Rao refers is named as being a category of "a linguistically based psychoanalysis" utilized because "this theoretical framework provides useful insights for an understanding of Atwood's portrayal of subjectivity" (xvii). However, her use of psychoanalytic theory as a tool of interpretation remains undeveloped, nestled amid three other aspects to the argument.

The first of these is a focus upon narrative, whereby Atwood's use of different genres and intermingling of narrative forms is seen to express heterogeneity at the level of the construction of the text. With this, the "composite character" (vi) that Rao identifies as being characteristic of Atwood's work becomes an issue of genre and literary production, and the "heterogeneity" she speaks of is understood as "the bringing together of disparate and conflictual elements that stem from different generic domains" (xii).[7]

The second of the aspects alongside which psychoanalysis is positioned is the claim that the epistemological and ontological concern with heterogeneity and a high degree of self-reflexivity positions Atwood's work as being postmodernist. With this, the discursive nature of reality that marks Atwood's work is seen to effect a "postmodern multiplicity" (Rao 174) and, as is characteristic of postmodernist fiction, the novels are seen to be calling for "a re-evaluation of heterogeneity, alterity, multiplicity and difference" (xviii). "In particular," continues Rao, "they expose the danger of thinking in terms of binary structures" (xviii). Now characterized as being preoccupied with the limitations of traditional Western thought, the texts are seen to achieve "the reformulation of oppositions" (xviii).

This opening of binary structures is said to have "a liberating effect" because, rather than being "paralysed" by the loss of Cartesian unity, the texts are seen to "indicate an attempt to devise a strategy to live within this predicament" (Rao 174). In this, Rao's argument appears to impute an agenda or intention to the works: a directive for action that can and should be found by the reader of the text. This becomes more apparent in Rao's contention that ". . . Atwood's texts show an attempt to re-think heterosexual relationships and to reformulate them according to a logic that defies systems of male definitions" (xxiv), and it is here that the third aspect to her argument — an identifiably feminist focus — comes to the fore.

In keeping with a feminist perspective, Rao sees Atwood as investigating the "ideological construction of subjectivity" (174). Women are seen to be "particularly contradictory subjects" (174) marked by a greater degree of division, while male figures are seen to repeatedly attempt to control and fix reality due to the absolute and unitary nature of masculine logic. For Rao, the female personae are portrayed as being comfortable with disorder in accordance with their "more flexible structures of being" (xxii), and duplicity is "a female strategy" (xviii) that enables characters to survive in a world that does not recognize their needs. In general, Rao is concerned with notions of subjectivity as being either masculine or feminine and thus her focus is on "the emphasis placed by recent psychoanalysis on the importance of gender and sexual ideology" (xxii). With this gendered perspective, psychoanalysis is drawn away from being the primary focus for analysis, as indeed it is by Rao's concern for narrative and postmodernist strategy.

It seems, then, that the accounts that have drawn upon psycho-analysis either use the terminology in a somewhat perfunctory manner, or employ the psychoanalytic model for a specific aim or with ideological intent. As a consequence, within these accounts the issue of the divided self has not been addressed with the kind of detail that it warrants. Even if it is acknowledged that divisions such as the split between fantasy and reality, the unconscious and the conscious, the mind and the body, and so on, reflect a fundamental division in the protagonist's identity,[8] there remains a certain inarticulateness as to the origins, consequences, and nature of this "sense of double-ness" (Maclean 190). My own interpretation of the novels seeks to use psychoanalytic theory in an exacting and systematic fashion with no agenda other than to explore fully the way in which the divided self is evident in Atwood's work.

While I rely upon the work of certain psychoanalytic theorists, I am reluctant to position myself as being a psychoanalytic literary critic as such. This is because it is my intention to use the terms and thematics of the theory rather than the methodology to explicate the texts. Meredith Anne Skura has written of a necessary focus upon process if psychoanalytic criticism is to be true to its clinical roots. Outlining five models of criticism that include the most traditional to the more contemporary use of psychoanalysis, she states that "all of them ultimately derive . . . from different aspects of the psycho-analytic process" (5), and thus to talk about literature in this way is to "draw on examples of psychoanalytic exchanges in the clinical situation" (6). Of her own work she has written: "My own emphasis is not on the *theory* but rather on the *process* of psychoanalysis. . . . My emphasis on process draws attention to psychoanalysis as a method rather than as a body of knowledge, as a way of interpreting rather than as a specific product or interpretation" (4–5), and in this she joins some of the most influential psychoanalytic critics of today.[9]

Skura's stress upon psychoanalysis as being dynamic rather than informative, the fact that she is interested "not so much for what it reveals about human nature . . . but for the way in which it reveals anything at all" (5), is at odds with my own approach, which draws upon psychoanalytic theory for its philosophical, ontological insights in understanding and interpreting a text. Certainly, psycho-analysis functions in a therapeutic context by invoking certain interpersonal relations between analyst and analysand and thus in practice is transferential; however, outside the clinical setting, it provides explanations for certain actions, and in theory establishes models and patterns according to which human behaviour may be explained. While a transferential model of reading practice marks a more contemporary use of psychoanalysis and is heralded by some as being either most appropriate[10] or definitive[11] of a psychoanalytic approach, it is the nontherapeutic function of the discipline upon which I call: psychoanalysis as a school of thought that theorizes psychological and psychical life.

The interpretive distance, then, between my own approach and one such as Skura's extends to a delineation between myself and psychoanalytic literary practice in general. I neither accord with the earliest school of critics who, in analysis of the text, were led to psychoanalysis of the author,[12] nor to consequent schools of thought that privilege the machinations of the reader's psyche allegedly effected when he or she engages with the text.[13] Nor do I concur with the most recent uses of psychoanalysis and critics who, as Richard Feldstein and Henry Sussman describe, are "more interested in language, the page, and the textualization of the mind that lends itself to literary production and analysis" (2). Here critical interpretation of the text is marked by an insistence on language predicated upon a Lacanian focus on the significatory status of the subject. As James Mellard states: "It is the working of language — between the analyst and analysand, the author and the text, the reader and the text — through all those verbalizations (case history, fantasy, dream, transference) that permits the final possibility of literature's being an allegory . . . of the psychoanalytic process" (62). I, on the other hand, am more like those critics whom he describes as "those who prefer to 'use' theoretical structures for the reading of specific, sometimes recalcitrant, always concrete pieces of literature" (ix). My intent is to explicate a particular text, not the psychoanalytic process itself. That is, it is my intention to use psychoanalytic theory to understand each of Atwood's novels (and account for the interpersonal relations between characters, the setting, characterization), not the novel to illustrate psychoanalysis in practice. My allegiance, then, is not to psychoanalysis as such but to whatever best explains the split self within the text. For this reason, at times it becomes appropriate to draw upon the work of phenomenological theorists in what amounts to a kind of interlacing of approaches in textual interpretation.[14] This is a conscious attempt to open each text for analysis with both respect for its specificity and acknowledgement of the complexity of the theorized self.

While my approach does not position the literary text as "an allegory of the psyche's fundamental structure" (Ragland-Sullivan, "Magnetism" 381) and thus does not necessarily coincide with contemporary modes of psychoanalytic literary criticism, it does nonetheless draw upon the work of psychoanalytic theorists in its reading of Atwood's fiction. This perhaps warrants some explanation as to my own critical method.

First, my interpretation of each novel is informed by key notions and concepts well accepted within psychoanalytic thought. While ideas such as the oedipal complex, the unconscious, the ego, the symbolic, the Imaginary, and the like have become the maxim of the psychoanalytic critic, they remain open to idiosyncratic use on the part of critic and theorist alike. In acknowledgement of this, and in deference to the magnitude of the field, I have included a glossary that consists of a set of key terms. These terms encapsulate the very underpinnings of my argument, the notions upon which my interpretation rests, and because of this the glossary precedes the discussions of individual texts. Defining them attempts to show their genesis as theoretical constructs and my use of them, and in doing so bespeak some of my own methodology.

If certain theoretical assumptions mark my account as psychoanalytic, so too do a number of critical ones. The first of these is a belief in retrospection, the practice of interpreting the fictional "present" in light of its "past." Psychoanalysis is by definition a discourse of reminiscence, as behaviours and symptoms occurring in the present are analysed according to what is believed to have happened at a much earlier time. The result is that meaning is conferred, constructed in the light of presumed early infantile experience. In much the same way as analytic discourse acts to construct meaning by including elements not immediately accessible, so too does my reading of Atwood's work impute meaning to the text. In this, my approach is not unlike the more traditional schools of critical practice that seek metaphorical, symbolic, or allegorical meanings in their exposition of theme. In much the same way as the analyst looks to make sense of a situation presented through circumscribed dialogue, I try to make sense of fictional events, times, places, and thoughts, and suggest an interpretation that is credible given the parameters of the text. This may mean, however, interpretations that reach beyond the obvious "common sense" significance of a particular event, character, statement, or setting. It may be argued, as at least two critics have done, that Atwood's work lends itself particularly well to analysis of this type.[15] And it is perhaps at this point that an approach that is "conservative" in that it is a close reading becomes contentious by generating meanings otherwise nonexistent and opening the significance of the text beyond its manifest scope. In order to counteract critical audacity informed by psychoanalytic assumption, in interpreting Atwood's work I try to remain faithful to the text by supporting statements with actual textual evidence. This is in accordance with a belief that while external influences can and should be brought to the text, and that no text need stand in isolation in terms of theory, interpretation, or reading practice, the aim of this book is to elucidate the novels above all else.

Analysing the texts in this fashion means a concentration upon the protagonist and peripheral figures, and in this sense my work may be seen to coincide with one of the more traditional uses of psychoanalysis within critical practice. My focus is undeniably upon characterization and an interpretation that is both illustrative and speculative. This is arguably one of the most obvious uses of psycho-analysis given its concern for the individual under analysis, yet as Skura points out, "Character analysis . . . has a bad reputation" (29). Skura herself speaks fairly disparagingly about the alleged appli-cation of theories of unconscious motivation to characters as if they were real people, quoting New Critical claims that this involves a "misreading" (30) of literature because the characters are not analys-able personalities but determined solely by the requirements of the text. Meanwhile her own (more recent) objection lies in what she sees as the critic imitating the analyst, treating the manifest story too much like the raw material of an analysis (32).

My own belief is that character analysis is a perfectly respectable form of literary criticism and, in terms of the current project, highly appropriate given Atwood's own emphasis on character and protag-onist. Perhaps it should even be seen to be a necessity given the tendency for Atwood to be regarded as working primarily within the confines of realist fiction, producing characters who are conven-tional and commonplace.[16] In any case, I take heart in Skura's admission that "It is still as true for us as it was for Freud that the psychoanalytic truths in literature must be referred to truths of character . . ." (31), and her further statement that "Character analysis . . . provides a vital meeting place for psychoanalysis and literature . . ." (33). Further to this, I regard her point that character analysis raises problems to do with both the nature of psychoanalytic statements and the nature of literary interpretation[17] as an inadvertent comment upon just how fruitful character analysis can be. Indeed, Skura notes that "Interest in the unconscious existence of literary characters has led to questions about just where character, or the 'self' is located ..." (31), and I would hope that my own work does exactly that.[18] Meanwhile, her view of character analysis as problematic because the "mind" that is being analysed is "a mind located ambiguously between the people mentioned in the text and the speaker himself" (32) is in my opinion a welcome enigma — a fascinating ambiguity well suited to our contemporary, poststructuralist awareness of the text.

While a number of Skura's justifications as to why "we have no basis for psychoanalyzing the characters" (38) could and perhaps should be contested,[19] at this point in this introduction I turn to a brief discussion as to why the said interpretation is of use. If, as Jessie Givner maintains, "One of the most persistent arguments in Atwood criticism is that her works are structured by duality and binary opposition" (56), what then can analysis in terms of psychoanalytic and phenomenological theories achieve, and why is the current project necessary? First, while critics mention and, most often, take for granted "the duplicity theme" (Maclean 190) within the novels, no one has yet chosen to explore the dynamics of division in a manner that is systematic and with theoretical precision and rigour.

Second, interpretation in light of psychoanalytic and phenomenological theories allows for analysis not so much in terms of the self but in terms of the subject. With this, "subject" no longer refers to a person as such, but to subjectivity as a process of identity, ego, or self formation. Subjectivity becomes a signifying stance effected by the intervention of the phallic third term into an otherwise dyadic relationship with the mother. It is a position of enunciation subsequent to both oedipal resolution and specular identification of the self. It is a symbolic position through which the subject participates in social and circulatory networks of exchange.

The psychoanalytic subject is by definition divided; and this new emphasis upon the subject rather than the self allows for a widening of the concept of division otherwise seen in criticism to date. As a consequence, identity now becomes alienated through specular misrecognition, placed "elsewhere" through spatial positioning, and split through signification owing to the subject's enslavement to desire and the metonymy of the signifier. With this, the self is divided both within the psyche as well as intersubjectively and these divisions may be expressed by way of the psychopathological symptom. In short, with psychoanalytic and phenomenological theories, the divided self becomes the decentred subject; and the ways in which identity is dislocated, estranged, barred, or fading is broadened as it may be applied to Atwood's work.

Third, as a consequence of the more precise theoretical use of the term "subject" and its attendant forms of division, the specificities of each novel may now be respected and accounted for with new insight. Previously, there was a tendency for the novels to be levelled in a kind of comparative approach that saw the same divided self surface in all or a number of the texts. While I acknowledge the recurrent nature of many of the motifs, this book attempts to foreground the split subject in the very characteristic that differentiates each novel from the others. Thus, in my analysis of *The Edible Woman*, split subjectivity is contextualized within issues of exogamous exchange because the novel is overtly concerned with marriage and the social contract. In my analysis of *Lady Oracle*, the split subject is explored in light of the dynamics of maternal symbiosis and separation because the novel is marked by the protagonist's relationship with her mother. The striking feature of *Life before Man* is the fantasy life of one of the characters, and hence for this particular novel the imagination and the Imaginary become points of entry for analysis of the split subject. *Bodily Harm* is distinct in its international setting and its focus upon the construction and dissemination of knowledge. For this reason, in regard to this particular text, the split subject is contextualized within issues of positionality, both spatial and significatory. Given the preoccupation with artistic imitation and creation in *Cat's Eye* and the repetition of forms, my analysis explores split subjectivity from the point of view of mimesis and the construction of reality. And my account of *The Robber Bride* draws out the various conflicts that inform both plot and characterization and interpret them in light of aggressive relativity so that they gain significance by being seen to illustrate the necessary relations between self, other, and object. It is because of this attempt to respect the specificity of each of the novels and provide as detailed an analysis as possible that this book is organized in a way that allows each novel a chapter of its own.

Absent from the list of novels to be analysed are *Surfacing* and *The Handmaid's Tale*. This is due to a decision that, while a framework of psychoanalytic and phenomenological theories best accounts for *The Edible Woman, Lady Oracle, Life before Man, Bodily Harm,*

Cat's Eye, and *The Robber Bride*, there are more appropriate ways of reading the remaining two, both of which differ significantly from the others in terms of form. This is further explained in the appendix.

NOTES

[1] Sherrill Grace, for example, writes that "Atwood's theory of art is closely linked to her views on the nature of the self and human perception" (2).

[2] Maclean uses these terms in assessing the protagonist of *Lady Oracle*.

[3] Of course, other critics also discuss the function of doubles in the novel. Nora Foster Stovel sees Ainsley as being "a reverse mirror-image" of Marian, while the two dolls are mirror images that symbolize the conflicting aspects of her character (52).

[4] While this kind of approach may appear to coincide with a psychoanalytic one because of its focus upon the psyche and its apparent use of terminology such as "the ego" or "the unconscious," it should be noted that theoretically this approach is similar to what is widely known of as "ego-psychology," a school of thought that is theoretically contrary to the poststructuralist focus of recent psychoanalytic theory. This is because ego-psychology depicts the ego as an agent of synthesis and integration and in clinical practice works toward achieving a unified identity and whole sense of self by focusing upon conscious determinants in the psyche.

[5] Elsewhere, for example, Rubenstein speaks of the protagonist of *Bodily Harm* as having a "double . . . denied self" that is "the form of her deepest recognition of submission to male power" ("Pandora's" 132).

[6] While the scope of this book does not include poetry, I refer to Hengen's work because it is one of the most significant accounts of Atwood's work in terms of psychoanalytic theory.

[7] The result is that "This study starts with an analysis of how Atwood's fiction can be located at the 'interstices of genres' and traditions" (Rao xiii).

[8] Hutcheon, for example, states that the split between her unconscious and conscious reflects "a deep split in Elizabeth herself" ("Reading Atwood's" 45).

[9] Shoshana Felman, for example, in an article that appeared in the seminal special issue of *Yale French Studies* (1977), writes of her reading of *The Turn of the Screw*: "The question underlying such a reading is thus not '*what* does the story mean?' but rather '*how* does the story mean?' How does the meaning of the story, whatever it may be, rhetorically take place through permanent displacement, textually take shape and take effect: *take flight*" (119).

[10] Peter Brooks exemplifies this in his argument for a psychoanalytic methodology that is "textual and rhetorical" over and above "methodologically disquieting" thematic readings (335).

¹¹ James Mellard writes: "A psychoanalytic theory of interpretation finally rests on a theory of a textual unconscious, an unconscious that is shared by both text and critic, one mediated by language, of course, but one created between text and critic (as between analysand and analyst) in a process like the analytic transference" (5).

¹² Within this approach, the work of fiction essentially becomes a figment of the author's unconscious, a manifestation of his or her own unconscious discourse, introducing to the text a biographical element and status as psychopathological symptom. My own approach allows for what I consider to be a productive autonomy from both the author's intention and her psyche, finding all the material for interpretation within the text, regardless of whether Atwood herself intended these meanings to be there.

¹³ Within this approach, it is the transformation of the reader's unconscious wishes and demands that is of paramount significance, and reading effects a kind of identity formation in the mind of the reader. While my approach is weighted toward the reader's response in that it is essentially an interpretative stance, it is not modelled upon the transference relationship between analyst and analysand that makes of the novel the kind of narrative transaction otherwise seen in the therapeutic setting.

¹⁴ It is for this reason, also, that I refer freely to the work of Lacan while not considering myself a "Lacanian" and draw upon his theories of subjectivity without making use of what Mellard aptly names "a Lacanian poetics" (44).

¹⁵ Maclean makes the point that "The works of Margaret Atwood are mines of many levels. Although characterized on the surface by clarity and accessibility, they often suggest ambiguous possibilities" (179). Similarly, Davey declares that "Atwood's work is . . . ideally suited to a criticism which discounts declared meaning, which looks instead for sub-languages of syntax, vocabulary, literary structure, imagery, and symbol" (*Margaret Atwood* 162).

¹⁶ While a critical tendency to interpret all of Atwood's novels according to genre or ideological stance (quest romance, feminist, Marxist, postcolonial, nationalist) tends to reduce the characters to players in a predetermined field, so too does categorization of the novels as dealing primarily with social realism. Critical response to *Life before Man* provides the most overt example of this. Gayle Greene quotes Atwood herself as saying that *Life before Man* has "limited appeal" because it is a "mainline social novel" ("*Life before Man*" 65). While Greene herself goes on to reclaim the novel as being powerful and worthy of critical attention, she admits in her opening paragraph that "Many readers have responded to the novel with a lack of enthusiasm like Atwood's own" (65). Given the subject matter, the fact that "Externally nothing much happens. . . . The action is unremarkable" (66), classification of the novel as working within the confines of realism is not in itself inappropriate. However, such a classifi-

cation runs the risk of overlooking the subtlety and psychological dimension of the characters and their fictional world by implying that both are pedestrian and prosaic. Look, for example, at Davey's appraisal: "The characters here take few risks, refuse the deconstructive cathartic act — refuse to smash objects or relationships, or to descend into madness or exile. Their insights into themselves are thus restricted to conventional language, to the rational, and are never transmitted to their irrational selves, to the pre-linguistic underground of their biological energies" (*Margaret Atwood* 85). My own account, on the other hand, will strive to show the opposite: that the daily lives of the protagonists are anything but mundane because their actions are underwritten by a psychical life that predates ego awareness of the self, oedipal resolution, and conscious control.

[17] Skura writes of character analysis that it provides a vital meeting place for psychoanalysis and literature "where problems in interpretation arise with particular force and clarity. These problems have to do with the nature of both psychoanalytic statements and literary interpretation . . ." (33).

[18] Certainly, Skura's mention of the fact that "heretofore uninteresting or 'inappropriate' parts of the text have come to be seen as aspects of character portrayal" (31) is clearly evident within my own methodology. However, I disagree with a later comment by her — "The self lies not in a locatable scene with characters . . . but in a nonspatial, temporal play between scenes, and even in a changing narrative stance" (57) — being used to imply that character analysis is in some way invalid. Surely "the self" that Skura speaks of can lie in any one or all of these places so that recognition of one need not exclude the significance of the other. Surely this "self" that lies in between the narrative is not by definition more important than the "I" of characterization, and character analysis need not be discarded just because it deals with the more "simple" manifestation of identity.

[19] While space does not permit a full discussion, some of the more important points are as follows. Skura bases her argument upon an assumption that analysis of the character is and should be analysis of the character's unconscious mind. Yet psychoanalysis encompasses more than theories of the unconscious (look, for example, at object relations, specularization, or theories of the gaze), and thus character analysis can accommodate much more. As Skura herself says, "The discovery of the unconscious is not the same as the discovery of psychoanalysis" (34), so why then should character analysis be limited to "the actuality of living with unconscious forces" (38)? In this context, I believe that Skura's statement that "Shakespeare's schema and Freud's theoretical map of the mind resemble each other more than either of them resembles unconscious experience . . ." (38) need not be used as a disclaimer but rather as an affirmation of the potential of character study. Second, in keeping with her allegiance to the reality

of the lived unconscious experience as an index of judgement, Skura bases much of her argument upon the contention that "The unconscious experiences which psychoanalysis traces are less coherently organized than even the most horrible and irrational passions in any poetic schema" (38). With this she takes Shakespeare as an example, stating that all irrational behaviour is externalized in a fictional world that explains what the characters do. In other words, she contends that "Shakespeare's characters live out their dramas in contexts which explain and even justify their behaviour, and that real, unconsciously shaped acts cannot be explained in this way" (49). I would contest the idea that a real unconscious act (whether it surfaces in the analyst's office or interrupts daily life) should be defined or seen to be authentic according to its degree of "messiness," and I wonder also whether a text needs to be measured against such standards of reality (on "the kind of unconscious experience on which analysis is based" [38]). The other point that needs to be made is that even if Shakespeare made his characters so explicable, not all fictional figures are. Indeed, Atwood's protagonists are marked by their irrationality, and a certain amount of conjecture is a prerequisite for understanding their at times odd behaviour. Skura herself writes of the real unconscious experience that "the unconscious motive is always present in some form, however bizarre or disowned, and always provides the analyst with cues to its presence" (40). Perhaps Shakespeare's characters lack such indiosyncracies, but Atwood's novels seem to be full of them. Skura also contends that in the fictional world the explanation for a character's behaviour "lies in the context, not in some additional unseen shaper of the will, and certainly not in offstage, never-mentioned past events" (40). While the Shakespearean protagonist may be fully located in the present, Atwood's fictional world is altogether different. Here the narration of a character's present-day life is interspersed with fragments of the past; chapters are juxtaposed in a way in which chronological time is manipulated, and the events or relationships of adult life are contextualized within memories of infantile experience and the incidents of childhood. Finally, Skura makes the point that "The unconscious the poets discovered is not only irrational but often something which destroys ordinary selfhood; it is more an un*self*conscious than an unconscious . . ." (35). In the context of Atwood's fiction, which is preoccupied with disintegrating identity, this is even more reason to study the characters in depth, especially seeing as contemporary psychoanalytic theory is so articulate as to the decentred nature of the ego and the conscious "I."

GLOSSARY OF TERMS

Castration complex

The castration complex is a Freudian[1] term describing a stage in the child's development connected with the perception of anatomical difference. It describes the fear of loss of the male genital organ, and as such has specific processes and differing consequences for the boy and the girl.

The castration complex is thought to begin when the boy sees the female genitals for the first time. At this point, he realizes that the organ he values so highly need not necessarily accompany the body. This comes either before or after having heard specific threats of dismemberment, usually a result of the little boy having been caught masturbating by an authority figure, an activity that predominates in this early phase of infantile sexuality. Meanwhile, the boy has been taking the mother as love-object, an aim that has been accompanied by the danger of punishment. The sight of female lack together with the threat of dismemberment now leads the boy to interpret the potential punishment for desiring the mother as entailing the possible loss of his own genital organ. Motivated by extreme anxiety, the boy now relinquishes his desire for his mother. This in effect means that for him, the oedipal complex ends; in fact, it is usually entirely destroyed through complete repression of the incestuous desire.

While Freud believes it is not unusual for a little boy caught masturbating to be told by a caretaker that his member will be cut off, and he maintains that castration was quite possibly a reality in the primeval time of the human family ("Paths" 416–18), he stipulates that the danger of dismemberment is not a matter of reality. While the castration is never likely to occur, what is decisive is the fact that the danger is one that originates from outside the child, and is a fear that the child believes in (Freud, "Anxiety" 119). For the boy, the threat of castration will be the most powerful motivating force in his subsequent development. It is not only the strongest motive for repression but for the formation of neuroses as well (119).

For the girl, the castration complex has a different progression. It too begins with the sight of the other's genitals. However, while the young girl perceives anatomical difference, it is Freud's contention that she perceives the significance of her own lack, and feeling disadvantaged, begins to envy the boy his member. While she does not submit to this readily, retaining for some time both the wish to obtain a penis and the belief that this is possible, eventual acceptance of the lack initiates feelings of resentment and hostility toward the mother. She now holds the mother responsible not only for her own lack, but that which she perceives to be her mother's castration. The girl's object-choice had been love of the phallic mother; hence, with the discovery of the mother's castration, she now relinquishes her as object. Consequently, with the wish for the penis that her mother has refused her, she turns to her father whom she expects can give her what she wants. In the course of normal development, this wish for the penis is eventually replaced by the wish for a baby. However, the turning point resides in the fact that with the turning away from the mother and turning toward the father, the girl has entered her oedipal complex.

While for both sexes the castration complex results in the termination of the attachment to the mother, in the case of the girl, rather than terminating the oedipal complex, it begins it. Furthermore, while girls do have a castration complex, they do not have the fear of being castrated that motivates the boy (Freud, "Anxiety" 119). Hence, the girl retains the oedipal longing for an indeterminably long time, and it is never fully resolved. For Freud, this results in a superego that is ill-formed, which in turn means less capacity for sublimating desire into cultural pursuits. It results also in a lesser sense of justice and the predominance of narcissism, vanity, and shame. This adds to the envy and jealousy that already plays a greater part in the mental life of women because of original feelings of penis envy.

This traditional Freudian account of the castration complex has since been built upon by a number of psychoanalytic theorists. Feminist theorists such as Luce Irigaray have questioned what they regard as being a phallocentric bias in his account, while Stephen Heath may be seen to extend it, questioning the sexually specific consequences of castration ("Difference"). Other theorists have broadened the concept to place it in the context of an entire series of traumatic experiences that are characterized by loss or separation from the maternal or from an object (the loss of the breast in breast-feeding and weaning, for example, or of faeces in defecation) (Laplanche and Pontalis 57). The concept of the detachable part of the body that was once a part of the self but is now an object that is other to it features in Lacan's formulation of the *objet a*. While this too functions primarily at the level of the gaze, it takes on a new role in the constitution of subjectivity by being a symbol of lack, of the phallus, and of desire (Lacan, *Four Fundamental* 103–05).

The widening of the concept of castration into a general one of separation and admittance of otherness allows for its investigation in light of the symbolic or discursive aspects of subjectivity. Heath names the function of castration as being the term of a production of symbolic as well as sexual division ("Difference" 110). In his account, the symbolic force of castration is the revelation of lack, which is a metaphor of the division of the subject, cut, as it were, by the signifier ("Notes" 52). The causation of the subject through castration now takes on an enunciative function, evident in Kaja Silverman's formulation of signification as being a castration involving the loss of the object and hence the loss of what was once part of the subject. Quoting Leclaire, she defines castration as being the break with the Real induced by language (9). For Kristeva, the discovery of castration is one of two thetic points that posit not only the subject but the act of signification. In her account, castration detaches the subject from the mother, but in doing so it makes the phallic function a symbolic one, now leaving the subject able to transfer presymbolic drive energy and motility onto the symbolic order (*Revolution* 46–51).

Desire

Desire is the metonymic dynamic of signification, effected through the intervention of the third term and the introduction of lack and absence. It is the dynamic of endless substitution via the symbol; it heralds the endless deferral and unattainable grasp of the referent effected through the introduction of the signifier. Through desire, the individual embarks upon an endless and unfulfillable quest that forevermore structures him or her as a subject, and as wanting. Desire is a Lacanian term, which, as Elizabeth Grosz points out, is one element in a libidinal trilogy. As such, it becomes clear only in the context of the associated concepts of need and demand.[2]

Need is the term used to describe the universal and constant requirements of human existence (food, shelter, warmth, et cetera). It is a dynamic that deals with the obtainment of real, tangible objects. Dictated as it is by organic insufficiency and physiological necessities, need is instinctual. In itself, it is short lived. However, it is based upon the presumption of a reliable and available source of satisfaction. Eventually, this assumption is transformed through Imaginary and symbolic systems of meaning, and need becomes transformed into the dynamics of demand and desire.

When needs are represented through signification and their satisfaction is substituted by representation, need becomes a demand. Demand is the dynamic whereby the subject consciously asks for the concrete objects that would have fulfilled a need. However, by correlating these objects with signifiers, the individual is asking not only for the specific objects requested (objects of nourishment or warmth, for example), but is demanding things that cannot be given (full acceptance, the referent, total satisfaction, et cetera). Demand thus bears upon something other than the satisfactions it calls for, and in doing so it annuls particularity and asks for absence or presence. Thus, it is operative by way of an ambiguity in that demand always has two objects: the spoken object that is the thing demanded, and the unspoken that is the call to the other to whom the demand is addressed.

Demand is always formulated through language and, predicated upon absence, is fundamentally insatiable. By definition, it is always addressed to an other, constituting the other as already and always possessing the ability to satisfy demands. Thus, the instinctual aspect of need is now replaced by a social function, whereby the subject asks for and either does or does not receive from the other. However, demand requires affirmation from the other to such a degree that only Imaginary union would suffice. In fact, the other to whom the demand is addressed is the Imaginary (m)other, or the image of the counterpart in the mirror, and the object of demand is always an Imaginary object. This in effect means that demand transcribes need within a dyadic dynamic and becomes the representation of Imaginary relations of the self with the object and the other.

In the gap or margin that separates need from demand, Lacan posits the concept of desire. It is that which is evoked by any demand beyond the need that is articulated in it. While both need and demand may be satisfied, desire can never be.

Like demand, desire is intersubjective in that it is a dynamic always directed toward others. However, desire is effected through the intervention of the phallic third term and the post-oedipal repression of incestuous love for the mother. Through the mechanism of repression, desire marks the infant's entry into the sociocultural order. It is the very hallmark of the subject and the underlying principle of all forms of production. Connected as it is to repressed wishes deemed unacceptable, desire is caught in the nexus between the conscious and the unconscious. In this sense, it has a distinctly intrasubjective functional aspect. Consequently, while desire has the freedom to effect signification and symbolic law, it is free to subvert or interrupt the conscious discourse of demand.

The infant's development from need to demand to desire is congruous with a movement from the Real into the Imaginary and symbolic. If need is characterized as being of the realm of the Real, and demand is the dynamic of the Imaginary, desire should be conceived as being their symbolic counterpart. In fact, desire is the structural principle by which the symbolic functions. Desire introduces the subject to a system of symbolization that is broader than the dyadic relation of demand and allows for the exchange of a third term and consequent infinite signification. It is operative through the general model of metonymy and is the very structure of language. As such, it is predicated upon lack and absence and is unfulfillable and insatiable. It also privileges the place of the other, now elevating it to an omnipotence through which the subject is subjugated, and the other, as locus of want, lack, and speech, becomes absolute. In this sense, the desire of the subject is the desire of the other.

Drive

Drive is a term generally accepted as denoting flux in libidinal energy, or a kind of tension or physiological charge directed along neuronal pathways within the body.

For Freud, the drive has a source (a kind of biological stimulus or urge), an aim (to eliminate tension at this source), and an object (which is responsible for the satisfaction of this aim) ("Three Essays"). However, other theorists have qualified the distinction between the physiological and psychosomatic by seeing the drive as being operative through the biological pathways traced through the body by needs or instincts. Grosz, for example, sees the drive as being a form of corporeal mimicry of the biological need, whereby the two are linked metonymically. Within this account, for example, hunger is a need and its object is milk (*Jacques Lacan* 50–81). Orality is a drive and, through association, its object is the breast. In this model, the drive borrows the sites and techniques of satisfaction generated by needs and instincts to develop its own modes of psychosexual satisfaction. In this sense, it is a second-order system based upon first-order needs.

This conceptualization of the drive bespeaks the issue of the regulation of the body. Initially, the infant's drives are not ordered by erotogenic zones; they circulate freely and in a state of disorder. Thus dominated only by the quest for pleasure and satisfaction, the drives are polymorphous perverse. The sexual instinct, for example, initially lacks a specific aim or object and is not yet directed toward genitalia as such. It becomes subordinate to the genital zone and aimed at intercourse only when the infant has undergone a number of developmental stages, such as the phallic phase and the resolution of the oedipal complex.

The somatic aspect of the drive may be broadened to explore the body's earliest significatory stance. Kristeva investigates the coupling of libidinal cathexes with signifiers in what amounts to the individual's earliest attempts at representation. The drive undergoes stases whereby its forwardly directed impulse is provisionally arrested and marks out discontinuities in materials such as voice, gesture, and colour. Differences and similarities are thus coded in phonic, kinetic, or chromatic terms; and these articulations are able also to provisionally connect the zones of the body to objects in the external world. These are a kind of presyntactical relation that are prior to the acquisition of language. Eventually, they become operative in the very signification of the subject (Kristeva, "Subject" 23). In this context, subjectivity is effected through the investment of drives into a series of signifiers (forms, colours, organs, words) that begin by representing the specific drive, but eventually signify other meanings and relations. This investment of drive energy in and through external objects is a structuring of drive facilitations that positions the subject within corporeal, natural, and social boundaries. However, while ordering the subjective space, the drive process simultaneously retains the potential to subvert any stable position. The sudden interruption of drive charges are most likely to occur at textual and artistic moments, when the confines of both the subject and society are challenged and transformed (Kristeva, *Revolution* 102–03).

Ego

The ego is a concept that combines common usage of the term as being the image one has of oneself or the act of being one's own person, with an accepted use in psychoanalytic theory as being one agency among others functioning within the psyche.

Freud's formulation of the ego spans decades and differing approaches and is hence one of the most complicated concepts to chart.[3] Most useful is his conception of the ego as having the form of an amoeba, as being a kind of reservoir of libidinal energy from which energy is cathected onto objects in the external world at the same time as energy is being absorbed back from them. This means the ego is constantly changing, and that its form is determined by the charge of libidinal energies, and at whom and what they are directed. In this context, the ego consists of a series of identifications and images that are introjected, incorporated, and projected, through which libidinal energy is invested, transferred, and cathected.

In this, the ego is the interaction of physiological drives and neuronal impulses with the objects, images, and relations of the external world. It is a play of internal causation and external influence and is operative on both inter- and intrasubjective levels. As a mechanism of self-actualization, the content of the ego is the conscious data the individual has about him- or herself; the qualifiable, knowable information that rightly or wrongly characterizes a self to the self. As such, it is an agency of self-definition that exists in dynamic relations with other agencies functioning within the psyche.

Lacan takes up the Freudian ego insofar as he bases it upon a concept of libidinal economy ("Some Reflections"). Following Freud, Lacan assumes that a decisive psychical action has to take place to constitute an ego-identity;[4] and in his account, the genesis of the ego lies in mirror-stage specular identity formation. This being the case, while the ego constructs an image of unity, permanence, and substantiality for the individual, it is in actual fact marked by all the misrecognition and alienation inherent within the reflected specular image.

The Lacanian ego is one determined by relations with the other. Prone to the forces of desire, it is above all signifying. Constituted by a process of subjectification at the hand of the signifier, the ego now becomes a consequence of the metonymy of its signification

(Lacan, "Subversion" 307). In this, it is placed on the side of the symbolic; and while "ego" need not necessarily be used synonymously with "subjectivity," it is nonetheless true that neither can exist without the other.

While the ego may be seen to date, chronologically speaking, from the advent of the mirror-phase of infantile development, it may further be characterized as being a post-oedipal phenomenon. That is, it is put firmly in place with the repression of oedipal wishes and object choices, after which it acts as a kind of censoring mechanism that blocks wishes now deemed unacceptable. This implies an ego actively engaged in self-actualization that is both dynamic and conflictual in defence against the forces of the unconscious. As a formation of consciousness, the ego is placed on the threshold of a splitting that marks the position of the subject. This may be seen to echo the other forms of separation effected by an agency that bespeaks division even while it attempts to construct unity; namely, its foundation upon systematic misrecognition and the fraudulent construction of reality, and its functioning through oppositions between self and other and subject and object.

Imaginary

The Imaginary[5] is Lacan's term for one of the three orders of existence (the other two being the symbolic and the Real) through which the individual negotiates for him- or herself a subjective stance.

The Imaginary is based on the relationship with the image. In this, it is to do with form and semblance and the formation of images or concepts not necessarily immediately present to the senses. However, its use differs from the conventional sense of the word in that it is based upon a relationship with the counterpart and the narcissistic formation of a self-image in light of identification, introjection, and projection with and of the other.

While there is some speculation whether the Imaginary should be seen as being anterior or posterior to the mirror phase, Grosz maintains that the mirror stage initiates the child into the two-person structure of Imaginary identifications, inaugurating also a dependence upon images and representations for its own forms or outline (*Jacques Lacan* 48). While the Imaginary introduces alterity into a narcissistic situation, and is in a sense the negotiation of otherness into a representation of the self, it locks the infant into a form of duality from which he or she is unable to participate in wider symbolic exchange of a third term.

Imaginary captation is a drive toward unity and fusion and the dyadic relation between self and mother. For this reason, it may be seen to be pre-oedipal. However, while it may be seen to be functioning at its fullest up until the resolution of the oedipal drama, it should be conceived as existing simultaneously alongside the other two orders, influential upon the identity and position of the subject well into adulthood. Furthermore, it is likely to surface in adult life in certain privileged moments (Grosz, *Sexual Subversions* xviii).

Mirror Stage

The mirror stage is the term used by Lacan to describe the developmental stage instrumental in the formation of the ego ("Mirror Stage" 1–7).

Somewhere between six to eighteen months of age, the infant will recognize his or her reflection in a mirror. The response will be one of triumphant jubilation, in an apprehension of the self through identification with the image (or imago) in the mirror. This imago now mediates the relation of the infant to his or her own body; however, it is from the earliest moment based on an untruth. This is because the imago appears to the child in the form of a gestalt or totality of form that is discordant with his or her actual lived experience, which is one of motor incoordination and a bodily experience of fragmentation due to the foetalization or specific prematurity of the human infant at birth. In addition, the imago is inverted or reversed through the symmetry of reflection, and there is imaginary triumph in anticipating a degree of muscular coordination and control that the infant has not yet actually achieved.

Thus, while this specular moment creates a sense of self for the infant that is in fact the earliest formation of the ego, it is an agency based on *méconnaissance* or misrecognition. The discrepancy between the image and the actual lived experience structures the ego from this moment on, and forever, as alienated. From this point on, the infant may proceed through the castration and oedipal complexes to become a subject; however, this subjectivity is now destined to be decentred and in constant pursuit of an illusory unity that lures the subject away from his or her actual self.

The mirror phase is an investment of libidinal energy in relation to the body image that is essentially narcissistic. It also allows for spatial captation, positioning, and externalization of the subject, and the lure of the gaze. It introduces to the infant an otherness within and external to itself. Because of this identification with the image of the other, the specular moment inaugurates a primordial jealousy or aggressivity that foreshadows future social relations.

Oedipal Complex

The oedipal complex is a Freudian term[6] to describe the progression and transference of the incestuous wishes of infantile sexuality, coined from the legend of King Oedipus, which dramatizes the two extreme wishes of the son — to kill his father and marry his mother.

The boy's earliest sexual aim is the incestuous desire for his mother. However, with the emergence of the castration complex, the fear of dismemberment makes the boy abandon the mother as primary love-object. In deference to the father, and in exchange for the anticipation of later satisfaction of his wishes, his desire for the mother is repressed and the unconscious formed. At this point, the boy's oedipal complex is resolved. In the normal course of events, it almost immediately dissolves. With the acceptance of paternal law comes the formation of the superego as agent of paternal authority and subsequent entry into the cultural order of society.

For the little girl, the primary love-object is also the mother. However, because of her acceptance rather than fear of castration, she abandons her desire for her mother amid resentment and hostility toward her. Rather than wishing for union with the mother, she now identifies with her. In the usual course of events, the girl thus relinquishes her active aims (and her clitoral masturbatory activity), accepting the feminine stance and the passive aim of wanting to be wanted by the father. At this point, she is driven by wanting the father's penis — a wish eventually replaced by the longing for a baby. Taking the father as the love-object, she will eventually transfer this desire for the father outward and onward to other men. However, at this stage, acceptance of paternal authority paves the way for the formation of the superego, which is destined to be weaker than the boy's. This is due to the fact that, with the advent of the castration complex and abandonment of mother as love-object, the girl's oedipal complex only just begins. Unlike the little boy, whose oedipal complex ends with castration, the girl remains within the oedipal drama for an indeterminate length of time. In fact, Freud stipulates that it is never fully or adequately resolved, leaving the girl with an ambiguous relationship with the maternal that stretches well into adulthood. This further complicates a situation in which already the oedipal situation is long and difficult, as the girl needs to change her erotogenic zone and her object when adopting the appropriate feminine (vaginally oriented) sexual stance — both of which a boy retains, because his transference develops naturally from the phallic phase of sexuality in which he is already immersed.

In accordance with his revision of Freudian theory in the light of structuralist and linguistic analyses, Lacan broadens the traditional formulation of the oedipal complex in a move away from the psychobiological slant given it by Freud. First, Lacan associates the incestuous desire for the mother directly with another of Freud's mythical motifs — the primeval murder of the father by the tribal horde of sons ("Oedipus Complex"). To the oedipal drama, Lacan brings the concept of kinship, whereby the relinquishing of the mother as love-object initiates a substitution for her, and the exogamous exchange of women becomes the founding principle or law of society. With this, he takes the incest taboo away from the level of the individual and emphasises its function as the structural principle of the entire social contract.

Through kinship structures, then, the transition from the natural to the cultural order is operative (Lacan, "Function" 66). However, given that the desire for the mother has been replaced by a symbol, Lacan's account brings to the oedipal drama a particular slant — one concerned with signification. Indeed, he states clearly that the paternal authority or law of the father is identical with an order of language (66), so that the exchange contract that structures society consists not only of the traffic of women but of nomenclature.

The dynamic of symbolism is imaged and effected through the intervention of an external third term that interrupts the incestuous link between mother and child and introduces desire into what has previously been a dyadic equation. This third term is of the order of the paternal and is imaged as the phallus. Lacan's formulation of the phallus replaces anatomical significance with symbolic meaning, making it the privileged and ultimate signifier in this advent of desire and circulatory exchange ("Signification"). The phallus images castration, as its detachability images division. As signifier, it functions as the object that is in itself vacant and devoid of meaning but is exchangeable. As such, it positions the subject within a network that is above all symbolic, now making him or her both signifying and signifiable.

The fact that the phallus functions as a signifier means that it is positioned in the place of the other, and likewise positions the subject in a position of otherness. This brings to the fore the fact that Lacan's formulation of the oedipal complex makes it a drama situated in the field of the other (*Four Fundamental* 204), as the dyadic mother-infant relationship is opened into a triadic one capable of admitting alterity.

Real

The Real[7] is a Lacanian term that designates concrete existence prior to the division effected through the third term, and outside the realm of signification. The Real is material in that it occupies space, weight, and motion; it is corporeal in that, for the infant or individual, it is by necessity experienced through the body. As such, it is the natural order, where there is not yet difference or division. Being of a presignifying nature, the Real stands in opposition to language and representation. It is the residue extrinsic to the procession of signifiers. It is the order of the referent and it is full and complete since the signifier has not yet brought absence.

With the assumption of an enunciative position and entry into the symbolic order, the Real is foreclosed to the individual who is now a fully functioning subject. For this reason, the Real is easily perceived as being chronologically prior to the assumption of speech. However, it is important also to conceptualize it as being a register that never ceases to exist, but is merely inaccessible and unavailable directly to the individual once he or she is positioned as a subject. From that moment on, the Real may only be inferred; for while it is itself beyond symbolic description and Imaginary perception, it can only be imaged through them. It is at this point that the Lacanian Real differs from conventional notions of reality, for reality as it is known to the subject is merely an interpretation or, more precisely, multiple, arbitrary interpretations of the Real.

Symbolic

The symbolic[8] is a term introduced by Lacan to designate one of the three registers in which the subject is caught and constituted.

The symbolic order is the very structure of the social contract. As such, it is the order of exchange and circulation, not only in terms of kinship and exogamy but with regard to symbols and signs. As such, the symbolic is the order of language and signification and the register of representation and discourse. It is effected through the entry of the external third term, which allows for nomenclature both of the self (through use of the personal pronoun and first or surnames) and the naming of objects and experiential relations by way of substitution via the symbol.

As the order of the signifier, the symbolic is the realm of difference and opposition and presence predicated upon absence. It is a pre-established order that exists prior to any one individual. Furthermore, it is the signifier, produced in the field of the other, that makes manifest the subject of its signification. That is, the structure of the subject is discontinuity with the Real, and this is effected through the signifier, which represents the subject for another signifier (Lacan, "Subversion"). In this way, the subject is positioned as signifiable as well as signifying. For this reason, the symbolic order is the register that most fully determines the subject. For while it is true that the subjective stance is an interaction of all three orders (symbolic, Imaginary, and Real), it is only when the individual takes up his or her rightful place in the sociocultural and signifying order that he or she attains full subjectivity.

The symbolic may be seen to be post-oedipal in the sense that it functions under paternal law, or the name of the father. It requires repression of incestuous wishes for union with the mother, and is operative under the entry of the phallic third term that introduces desire, is agent of exchange, and regulates the circulation of the sign.

Symptom

The symptom is the expression of an unconscious wish previously repressed and its interruption into conscious life by way of a dream, daydream, fantasy, slip of the tongue, et cetera. The traditional Freudian formulation of the symptom[9] stipulates that the precondition for its existence is that a mental process has not come to an end, and thus seeks expression and admission within the psychical life of the individual. The symptom is a form of wish fulfilment, whereby it is a regression to an earlier time and a substitute for what did not happen at that point. The fixations that motivate the creation of a symptom always revolve around the activities and experiences of infantile sexuality and the objects of childhood that have been relinquished. Symptoms create a substitute for the frustrated satisfaction by means of a regression of the libido to earlier times, which involves a return to earlier developmental stages of object-choice.

While Freud's account sees the pathology of symptoms as being a perfectly normal part of mental life, it does imply the concept of an opposition on the part of the conscious mind toward the unconscious wish now deemed unacceptable. This resistance or censorship is termed repression and it emanates from the constraining forces of the ego. Thus, symptoms represent not only the repressed but also the repressing forces that share in their origin and are evidence of a conflict between psychical agencies.

The same processes that belong to the unconscious play a part in the formation of symptoms — namely, condensation and displacement. Through the primary processes, the unacceptable wishes are able to surface within conscious discourse in the form of a compromise. This compromise formation emerges as an overdetermined and distorted derivative of unconscious libidinal wish fulfilment. As such, it abandons its relation to external reality, and may not only be consciously incomprehensible as a means of libidinal satisfaction, but appear fully ambiguous, with meanings engaged in mutual contradiction. While apparently incongruous, the symptom will always be regulated by its own internal logic.

In keeping with his revision of Freudian psychoanalysis in light of linguistic and semiological theories, Lacan's concept of the symptom[10] is one that brings to the fore its discursive aspects. For Lacan, the symptom bespeaks a conflict that is, above all, symbolic. Representation is driven out of conscious discourse but is inscribed in other ways: in the natural functions (hysteria and neuroses), in archival documents (childhood memories, myths, legends), and in semantic evolution (vocabulary and use of language). The symptom is the signifier of a signified repressed from the consciousness of the subject. However, it is speech functioning to its fullest, for not only is it structured like a language (as indeed the unconscious is) but it is fully operative as the discourse of the other. Since the symptom is the unconscious other speaking to the self, the signifying material of the symptom is none other than the disintegration of the imagined unity of the subject, fictionally constructed through the agency of the ego. Hence, the symptom points not only to the intersection of the different orders of existence but to the intrasubjective splitting that structures subjectivity.

Unconscious

The unconscious is a repository of signifiers, both visual and auditory, that are repressed at the oedipal moment when incestuous desire for the mother is no longer perceived to be acceptable by the ego. Such an account is in accordance with Freud's formulation that what is unconscious in mental life is also infantile and is the initial, primitive part of psychical life ("Archaic Features"). The wishes, fantasies, and images of the unconscious are thus likely to be tainted by the primary physical drives, and the egotism, narcissism, and incestuous choice of love-objects of early infantile sexuality.

The original nucleus of images, wishes, and fantasies is in itself not subject to chronological time or to a truth factor. This is a point Lacan stresses when he states that what happens in the unconscious is inaccessible to contradiction, to spatiotemporal location, and to the function of time (*Four Fundamental* 31). Freud further explains that the unconscious pays no attention to the demands of external reality and seeks to satisfy pleasure rather than be regulated by the reality principle to which the ego is subject ("Paths" 413).

Unconscious wishes attract to themselves other signifiers throughout the subject's life. This is in accordance with Laplanche and Leclaire's definition of the unconscious as having an elementary layer or ballast of signifiers that are put in place during primal repression. It concurs also with Grosz, who states that the original mnemonic trace inscribed at the moment of primal repression attracts other traces through signifying or linguistic relations, and these later repressions constitute the bulk of the unconscious (*Jacques Lacan*).

The moment of repression instigates a division between the subject's unconscious and conscious discourse, with the former interrupting the latter periodically and unpredictably in the compromised form of the psychopathological symptom (dreams, hallucinations, fantasies, et cetera). Unconscious wishes are constantly striving for expression; as Freud states, the repressed wishes and desires have a strong upward drive or an impulse to break through into consciousness ("Dissection"). At certain moments, through the mechanisms of the primary processes, they do, gaining access to conscious discourse in condensed and displaced forms. Through these manifestations, the wishes are able to discharge libidinal energies and transfer cathexes onto representatives that have slipped past the censoring function of the ego and are thus free to surface in compromised form in conscious thought or language.

There are two important issues within this account. The first is that this characterizes the unconscious as being a system,[11] with its own contents, aims, and mechanisms (Freud, "Archaic Features" 249). The second is that this characterizes the psyche as being dynamic.[12] By this, what is meant is that the unconscious now becomes a system that is in direct and continual conflict with the ego, a system that is in a constant state of resistance due to the striving of the wishes to obtain immediate satisfaction. As Freud himself notes, the ego and the conscious do not coincide; and the ego, which originally put the repression into force, strives forevermore to maintain it ("Dissection").

Freud's formulation of the psyche as being a dynamic struggle between systems means that the human psyche is subject to particular forms of division. Thus, Lacan speaks of the function of the cut, gap, or rupture in subjectivity, and states that the unconscious is always manifested as that which vacillates in a split in the subject (*Four Fundamental* 28). Since unconscious discourse is other to conscious discourse, the unconscious itself functions as a form of intrasubjective alterity.

[1] Except when otherwise stated, this account is drawn from Freud's "Femininity."

[2] The following account is drawn from three of Lacan's essays ("The Signification of the Phallus," "The Subversion of the Subject and the Dialectic of Desire in the Freudian Unconscious," and "The Direction of the Treatment and the Principles of Its Power") and Grosz's rendition in *Jacques Lacan* (59–67).

[3] The debate is too lengthy to chart at present, but Laplanche and Pontalis (130–43) give an account of the development of Freud's usage of the term, as does Grosz in *Jacques Lacan* (24–31).

[4] A point Freud makes in "On Narcissism: An Introduction."

[5] Throughout this book, "Imaginary" is written with an uppercase "I" in order to differentiate between Lacanian use of the term and conventional usage.

[6] Taken from "The Development of the Libido and the Sexual Organizations," "Anxiety and Instinctual Life," and "Femininity."

[7] Throughout this book, "Real" is written with an uppercase "R" in order to differentiate between linguistic/psychoanalytic use of the term and conventional notions of reality.

[8] Throughout this book, although "symbolic" is a Lacanian term, it is written in lowercase because it is considered common usage within theoretical discourse.

[9] The following account is taken from "Resistance and Repression" and "The Paths to the Formation of Symptoms."

[10] The following is taken from Lacan's "The Function and Field of Speech and Language in Psychoanalysis" and "The Freudian Thing."

[11] Freud makes this point many times. It is stated clearly in "The Dissection of the Psychical Personality."

[12] Again, this is a Freudian term.

CHAPTER ONE

The Edible Woman:

The SPLIT SUBJECT *as* AGENT *of* EXOGAMOUS EXCHANGE

My account of *The Edible Woman* (*EW*) begins with the thematic assumption that the novel is, above all, a statement about social relations and the reproduction of culture. This approach is based upon a theoretical assumption that there are key dynamics by which society is founded — dynamics of circulation, consumption, and commodification, and relations of marriage, sex, and signification. However, in constituting society, these processes, all of which are symbolic, also create the subject; thus, the individual is able to take up his or her appropriate position in the marital, signifying, and exchange economy that underlies social organization. Thus, society and any individual subjective position within it are mutually constitutive; while Marian's identity is structured by the various dynamics that underlie the symbolic order, she too reproduces these dynamics by taking part in them. Thus, Marian's self both constitutes and is constituted by society.

While the founding moments of society and the subject are symbolic, they are also divisive, creating an individual whose identity is by definition alienated and discordant with itself. It is my belief that the recurrent images of disunity that characterize the protagonist and her fictional world, and the evident dissolution of her sense of self, may be best explained by uniting a focus upon her multiple and fractured identity with a focus upon the social commentary that is so important an aspect of *The Edible Woman*. In this way, the issue of the split subject, which this novel shares with the other novels, is examined in its specificity and as it pertains to this particular work.

My interpretation of the novel approaches it from four angles. The first is an explication of marital and exogamous relations and the constitutive and destructive effect they have upon the protagonist's identity. In this, I argue that Marian's engagement is posited as being crucial to the formation of her ego-identity, that exogamous relations between the sexes are one of the ways in which the individual is placed within the social network and takes up an interactive role. However, I also aim to show that Marian's relationship with one man — Peter Wollander — effects a disintegration of her sense of self that foreshadows the potentially destructive consequences of the marital contract.

At this point, my account attempts to illustrate, by way of key incidents and self-characterization on the part of Marian, the gradual yet systematic deterioration of the protagonist's identity. In this, I join other critics in discussing events such as the office Christmas party, Marian's intoxicated identification with the rabbit-cum-toilet-roll, her flight through the streets of Toronto, her experience of Peter's party, and her dreams. While it is well acknowledged that these events are indicative of a disintegrating personality, my account differs from those of other critics by analysing them with a view to psychoanalytic notions of the ways in which the psychical agencies function. This is an extension of the basic theoretical underpinning of my approach: namely, the belief that a combination of structural anthropological and psychoanalytic ideas can best account for the action of subjectivity within its sociosymbolic milieu. In response to hypothetical questioning as to why these particular frameworks are most appropriate, it would have to be said that Lévi-Straussian notions of exchange in terms of kinship and exogamy best explain why the sociosymbolic order is a marital one. Meanwhile, Freud's formulation of the oedipal complex and consequent masculine and feminine positions accounts for sexual relations as they are internalized within the psyche of the individual, and then are able to be played out, firstly on the wider familial level and finally on the widest social one. Finally, Lacan's emphasis upon subjectivity as a signifying entity that is imaged through the exchange of words, appearances, and looks, best explains why the positioning of the subject within the sociosymbolic order makes the self an alienated one.

The issue of exogamy and its relation to the positioning and maintenance of Marian's identity is most overtly expressed through her relationship with her fiancé. However, it is equally important to account for her relationship with the other man in her life. Within my account, Marian's liaison with Duncan takes on significance as a sexual interaction that becomes significatory in meaning. This in effect means seeing Duncan as having a functional capacity as the external term of exchange, and the vacant signifier that has no content in itself but is decisive in determining whether or not a subject is positioned as such. Duncan is not as overtly threatening to Marian and appears positively innocuous in comparison to Peter. However, not being able to offer her marital status, his surname, or his children in exchange for interaction with her body, he is also unable to offer her an actual position within the exogamous and sociosexual network. Thus, he threatens her with both relegation to the asymbolic and a positioning within a pre-oedipal dynamic that would flavour their interaction with maternal connotations and leave her with an indecisive stance within the post-oedipal sexual arena.

Discussion of the proprietary aspects of the exogamous contract introduces the second angle of my approach. Intentionally avoiding allocation of blame and yet recognizing Marian's position as being one that is sexually specific, I turn to analyse the processes of commodification by which Marian is made into both consumer and commodity. Acknowledging the processes of commodification and consumerism upon which the novel is based, I look by way of illustration at incidents such as Marian's experience at the beautician's, her reaction to supermarkets, and her employment as a market researcher. In this, my account does not stand alone and may not appear to differ from critical accounts that precede my own. However, where my interpretation does differ is in its attempt to explain these processes of commodification in terms of the individual subjective stance, rather than contextualizing them purely in general terms of social exploitation. That is, rather than viewing the dynamics of consumption as being forms of patriarchal or capitalist exploitation effected at a communal level, my account seeks to relate the dynamics of commodification to the construction of an individual subjective stance, thereby exploring the way in which identity functions as a negotiation of the individual with the (symbolic) system. It does this through introducing Hegelian dynamics of master and slave as an explanation of the way in which consumption allows for the negotiation of individual identity, while simultaneously underwriting the wider contract upon which society is founded. From this point, it is theoretically appropriate and textually practical to move toward an analysis of Marian's inability to eat, which is perhaps the most obvious thematic and narrative device within the novel and the third angle from which I approach *The Edible Woman*.

Analysis of Marian's inability to eat in the light of intersubjective dynamics of master and slave and the symbolic circulation of commodities connects her anorexia to her position within exogamous networks of exchange. However, it also points toward the fact that corporeality underwrites the symbolic contract, and the fact that the oral drive, which is largely a corporeal function, may also function as an introjection of other sorts. In this context, I argue that Marian's self-imposed starvation becomes the symptom of an inability to circulate within exchange and a regression to the asymbolic. Thus, analysis of the anorexia is taken from the personal plane to a social or symbolic one in a play of power between self and other.

My account does not focus at length upon illustrating the anorexic dynamic that structures the three parts of the novel, as this has been adequately covered by almost all critical accounts to date. It does, however, see Marian's inability to eat as an example of the way in which the body is involved in the symbolic. This in effect means seeing the body as signifiable, and in this case, as the signifying material of the psychopathological symptom. In light of Marian's anorexia as being a literal fading of her self, this leads to the fourth angle of approach — symbolic sacrifice — and the conclusion both of the novel and of my account.

Drawing upon Lacanian theories of disunity and alienation integral to the subjective specular experience, I suggest that the cake-lady becomes a prototypical image of the fragmented body that for Marian has surfaced in what had been a systematic collapse of ego-identity, but which is, in Lacanian terms, an ever-present dynamic effective in the maintenance of a subjective position. However, the fragmented body that underwrites the alienation of the specular also invests the image with an aggressivity, drawing upon and perpetuating the relativity between self and other. With this, the cake-lady crystallizes not only the intrasubjective division of the imaginary body image, but also intersubjective dynamics of master and slave.

The interaction here between the personal register and the collective, social one brings to the cake-lady a symbolic dimension that transcends the usual critical boundaries of interpreting the cake as being little more than a metaphor of Marian's psychological well-being. For within my account, a close reading of the conclusion provides a new interpretation of the cake-lady, one that does not focus primarily upon the positive or negative message of the episode (which most critics to date have done) but that sees it functioning primarily as a kind of totemic meal. Drawing out the significatory significance of food, Marian's position, and dynamics of circulation and substitution, my interpretation contextualizes the ritual cake-cutting within the very inauguration of the symbol. With this, my initial aims of exploring the ways in which the social contract is founded and the effects it has upon the subjective stance of the individual are satisfied in a way that is fully reconcilable with an ending that for most critics is ambiguous and remains problematic.

* * *

In *The Edible Woman*, we are introduced to a young woman named Marian MacAlpin who leads a conventional life, involved with conventional people. She has all that is socially acceptable — job, friends, and fiancé — and yet traversing across and undermining her respectable lifestyle are the various dynamics that are constitutive of her subjectivity, and that threaten to unravel the threads of her identity.

In light of the fact that the novel seems to explore the dynamics of the social contract, Marian's ego-identity may be seen to be structured by the various dynamics of exchange that underlie the symbolic order. Social anthropologists and psychoanalysts alike have identified the kinship system whereby women are exchanged in marriage, along with the consequent traffic in nomenclature and symbolic gifts, as being the founding moments of society that mark the division of the cultural world from the natural one.[1] The structure that governs marital, linguistic, and other forms of symbolic exchange is the structure that in turn governs the constitution of the subject, and is formalized in the psychic formation known to us as the oedipal complex. The resolution of the oedipal complex on a personal or familial level marks the internalization of the incest taboo that functions on the social level. This in turn raises a number of issues: the split between the unconscious and the conscious, the alienation of the subject through the act of signification, the exchange of pre- for post-oedipal desires, and consequent forms of production involving objectification — all of which may be seen to affect the subjective status of the protagonist in *The Edible Woman*.

Marian's contractual agreement to become Peter Wollander's wife is one of the more overt ways in which she is positioned within the circuit of symbolic exchange. Her attitude toward her forthcoming marriage is, above all, practical. She speaks of the need to "run a well-organized marriage," so much of which is "a matter of elementary mechanical detail" (*EW* 102), and sees herself as taking on a role that needs to be fulfilled in order to have a normal life: "Of course I'd always assumed through high school and college that I was going to marry someone eventually and have children, everyone does" (102). The oedipalization of desire through an acceptance of castration and compensatory yearning for childbirth is, within the psychoanalytic model, the most appropriate resolution for the dilemma facing the pre-oedipal girl[2] and signals a successful assumption of femininity that will allow her to take her place within the circulation characterizing the symbolic order. Indeed, Ainsley seems to have consciously acknowledged this as "she's convinced that no woman has fulfilled her femininity unless she's had a baby" (157); and while at first Ainsley appears intent on subverting the conventional societal contract whereby she must marry in order to satisfy her desires, her actions eventually echo Clara's dutiful submission to the oedipal edict in the reproduction of the necessary domestic infrastructure.

In terms of the symbolic identity that is assumed by the individual entering the social order, what is necessary is the oedipal exchange of desires and a consequent psychic restructuring in realignment with the paternal. This is evident within Marian's experience of the office Christmas party. Here, amid plates of chocolate brownies and sponge cake, the men safely isolated on another floor so that it's "just all us girls here together" (163), the congregation of ladies who "could have been wearing housecoats and curlers" (166) function as the epitome of conventional feminine domesticity. In between the office gossip and the Orange-Pineapple Delight, Marian's sense of discomfort slowly increases, and we witness a number of interesting dynamics. The first of these is the fact that Marian and the three "office virgins" have nothing to exchange save their chairs: "they had no children whose cuteness could be compared, no homes whose furnishings were of much importance, and no husbands, details of whose eccentricities and nasty habits could be exchanged" (163).

Their positions within the spatial organization of the scene are at this point interchangeable, and this may be indicative of the fact that they have no currency of their own through which to engage within a market economy specifically theirs. Irigaray has noted that the only way women can achieve status as traders is to circulate their children, at which time they themselves will be positioned outside the system. She further states that women are invariably reduced to some common feature whereby they resemble each other, and that their value lies not in any relation between them but in a standard that remains external to them ("Women"). Emmy, Lucie, and Millie are plainly reduced to their availability, through which they share relations of equivalence predetermined by the system of exogamy; without the necessary maternal status, they are able to circulate only words. Clara, by comparison, no longer needs language, as she sinks more and more into "the vegetable stage" that is pregnancy (*EW* 130). Her regression into the maternal space that Kristeva characterizes as being a foreclosure of symbolic capacities "beyond discourse, beyond narrative, . . . beyond figuration" ("Motherhood" 247), described by Marian as Clara becoming "sentient and sponge-like . . . being absorbed in, or absorbed by, her tuberous abdomen" (*EW* 130), is echoed in their inability to exchange even thirty minutes' worth of conversation (127).

The most striking feature of the office Christmas party is the gradual deterioration of subjective identity within what is a purely feminine environment. There is an emphasis upon corporeality as Mrs. Gundridge is described: ham-like thighs, rolls of fat pushed up by her corset, porous cheeks, and dimpling jowls. The other ladies, too, become nothing more than "dune-like contours of breast and waist and hip" (167), abounding in fluidity only just contained within their bodily limits. Dynamics of introjection and expulsion characterize the ladies' interaction, hinting at the corporeal subject dominated by drive energy: "the continual flux between the outside and the inside, taking things in, giving them out, chewing, words, potato-chips, burps, grease, hair, babies, milk, excrement, cookies, vomit, coffee, tomato-juice, blood, tea, sweat, liquor, tears, and garbage" (167). The kinds of condensed and displaced drive energy and their objects usually abjected in the acquisition of a speaking position surface here to render the boundary of the body indistinct, and threaten to dissolve Marian's own ego-boundaries: "she was one of them, her body the same, identical, merged with that other flesh that choked the air in the flowered room with its sweet organic scent" (167). The transitivism[3] that attests to the merging of self with other aligns her momentarily to an Imaginary prespecular continuity and characterizes the undifferentiated feminine as being a threat to symbolic identity. This incident prefigures a time when she herself becomes "afraid of losing her shape, spreading out, not being able to contain herself any longer" (219). At that point, her solution is to look toward her engagement ring as the "protective talisman that would keep her together" (218). Here, too, the necessary shift in oedipal desire is evident as Marian turns toward the phallic: "she felt suffocated by this thick sargasso-sea of femininity . . . she wanted something solid, clear: a man" (167), and she heightens the castrating effects of separation by "clenching her body and her mind back into her self like some tactile sea-creature withdrawing its tentacles" (167).

While the undifferentiated feminine poses a threat to symbolic identity, post-oedipal castrated femininity plays a role in its maintenance. Such ambiguity is further heightened by the fact that the exchanged objects are Imaginary in form but symbolic in function (Gross, "Lacan" 21). As such, they perform not as icons with significance that is self-evident, but are themselves empty of any meaning other than a differential value given them by a circuit that predates their individual emergence. Exchange must be a reciprocal act between two subjects, yet the specificity of each person need not be respected as it is the circuit as a whole that confers meaning rather than any individual connections within it. At some level, Marian senses this lack of distinctness that characterizes her identity and role within such a system. She reacts with anxiety on hearing about the Pension Plan that is obligatory, a system within which she gives money in return for social security: "It wasn't only the feeling of being subject to rules I had no interest in and no part in making. . . . It was a kind of superstitious panic about the fact that I had actually signed my name, had put my signature to a magic document which seemed to bind me to a future so far ahead I couldn't think about it. Somewhere in front of me a self was waiting, pre-formed . . ." (21).

Her panic regarding nomenclature is perhaps indicative of her being caught in the concatenated net of symbolic exchange. Being prone to the signifier that always anticipates meaning through the mediation of an entire significatory system and imposes itself upon the subject who is moulded by the structure of language (Lacan, "Signification" 284; "On a Question" 181; "Agency" 153), she is, in more ways than one, predetermined. Yet as the novel progresses, the identity that awaits her becomes more and more unstable as she threatens to regress to a formless state: "The alarm clock startled me out of a dream in which I had looked down and seen my feet beginning to dissolve, like melting jelly, and had put on a pair of rubber boots just in time only to find that the ends of my fingers were turning transparent" (*EW* 43).

The psychopathological symptom is the interruption of repressed unconscious material into conscious discourse, in this case by way of a dream. Here an iconic representation of the corporeal body not able to be contained within distinct boundaries attests to a certain fragmentation reminiscent of prespecular Imaginary existence. The pre-mirror-stage child is not yet defined within a physically limited space, and its organic insufficiency promotes an anarchic, formless existence. It is thus significant that in response to her dream, Marian "started towards the mirror" (43), perhaps in an attempt to take comfort in the thetic[4] moment whereby the ego is established by way of identification with a unified specular image.

Slowly but surely, such disintegration of Marian's ego-identity becomes linked to her contractual agreement to marry Peter. The incident that she herself names "the powder-room collapse and the flight" (77) is the occasion on which their engagement is formalized, and may be seen to function as another symptom of regression. There is no doubt that Marian, while intoxicated, is driven by unconscious forces, as she herself admits: "It was my subconscious getting ahead of my conscious self, and the subconscious has it own logic" (101). Locked in the bathroom of a hotel bar, she identifies with a roll of toilet paper that she perceives to be a hunted rabbit "waiting passively for the end" (70). Preempting this association are her hallucinatory images of Peter's hunting trip, which he has been describing in somewhat bloodthirsty detail. Predatory images of the gaze of a camera lens are intertwined in such a way that they hint at specular involvement: "Peter was talking at full speed to Len about the different methods of taking self-portraits: with reflecting images in mirrors, self-timers that let you press the shutter-release and then run to position and pose" (70–71).

Peter's representation of his own image through the projection of the gaze is a fundamental mechanism reminiscent of the mirror-stage when an exchange of looks constitutes and is constituted by the subject. His enthusiasm for the "teleconverter" (71) may signal the way in which the observing subject is eventually transformed into the object of the look, as through the portraiture, he himself becomes the object of his own gaze. But the gaze is also the dynamic through which the subject is externalized and positioned within the spatio-temporal grid of the other; and this use of the scopic drive to ground an ego-identity is evident in Peter's use of Marian as an object underpinning his own location. In her own words, she was "a stage-prop; silent but solid, a two-dimensional outline. He wasn't ignoring me . . . he was depending on me!" (71).

Her response to her objectification in this way is one of paranoia in the psychoanalytical sense. Laplanche and Pontalis define paranoia as being a delusion of persecution that retains ideas of reference but with no weakening of the intellect and no tendency toward deterioration (296). Marian's belief that she is being hunted is explicable through her own associations and is only a momentary lack of conscious control. However, it is noteworthy that her panic-stricken flight through the streets and Peter's pursuit of her is characterized by the imagery of a hunt and ends only with an accepted proposal of marriage. At the very moment she commits herself to being Peter's wife, she finds herself being imaged in the presence of the other, admitting that ". . . I could see myself, small and oval, mirrored in his eyes" (83). The alienation of being caught in the specular exchange of looks is evident when she finds herself "gazing into a multitude of eyes," in which his stare is described as being "intent" and "faintly ominous" (82).

It is significant that this dynamic is one that will eventually characterize their relationship. Some time later, Marian tells how "Lately he had been watching her more and more" (149), especially while they were in bed. Peter's gaze now becomes sexually specific, with Marian's body as its object: "he would focus his eyes on her face . . . then he would run his hand gently over her skin, without passion, almost clinically, as if he could learn by touch whatever it was that had escaped the probing of his eyes" (149). Laura Mulvey describes the scopophilic drive as "taking other people as objects, subjecting them to a controlling and curious gaze" (59). While Peter uses Marian in this way as an object of libidinal stimulation by way of sight, the detachment is indicative of the separation of his own erotic identity as subject from that of Marian's, upon whom he gazes. This distancing of himself and his reliance upon tactile perception may have something to do with the fact that the woman displayed for the enjoyment of the male gaze as scopophilic fetish, while producing pleasure, also evokes an anxiety that is none other than the repressed distress of the original castration complex (Mulvey 64). Here lies the ambiguous nature of the gaze that is sexualized and fundamental to the construction of male subjectivity. Little wonder then that Marian senses a dynamic that she finds threatening and that "made her uneasy" (149).

Another incident foreshadowing the disintegration of Marian's identity in the face of entry into the marital economy is the party that Peter organizes, which she is obliged to attend. The gathering is obviously intended to function according to the rules of symbolic exchange, whereby words and desires are being traded, somewhat like "The peanuts and potato chips and other things [that] were circulating from hand to hand . . ." (233). Further association with post-oedipal dynamics and Marian's proposed entry into the exogamous network is made evident when Peter puts an arm around Marian's waist and undoes the zipper on her dress, suggestively anticipating their future sexual encounter. This is heightened by the fact that the scene is dependent upon the encounter of femininity with masculine desire: Clara and Joe are discussing the identity of married women, the office virgins are manoeuvring to entice Leonard Slank, and when Ainsley appears there is a general upsurge of male attention directed toward her. Even the spatial ordering of the scene is dependent upon sexual dynamics whereby territories are allotted according to marital status and availability. It is within this highly charged atmosphere that Marian's sense of self starts fragmenting, as she stares into the full-length mirror in the bedroom to examine her profile but "couldn't grasp the total effect: her attention caught on the various details . . . the fingernails, the heavy ear-rings, the hair. . . . She was only able to see one thing at a time" (229). It is crucial that specular identification with one's own body image in the form of a gestalt replace the experience of the body-in-bits-and-pieces (Lacan, "Some Reflections" 13), the undivided image then becoming a key structural formation without which no ego can exist. But here, Marian is left asking: "What was it that lay beneath the surface these pieces were floating on, holding them all together?" (229).

The perceived threat to her identity culminates in her paranoid reaction to the camera that Peter aims at her in an attempt to capture her image: "Her body had frozen, gone rigid. She couldn't move, she couldn't even move the muscles of her face as she stood and stared into the round glass lens pointing towards her" (232). . . . "he raised the camera and aimed it at her; his mouth opened in a snarl of teeth. There was a blinding flash of light. 'No!' she screamed. She covered her face with her arm" (244).

For Freud, female paranoia was specifically linked to the mechanics of the male gaze and the fear of being photographed in a compromising situation.[5] Mary Anne Doane sees female paranoia as being the problematic wherein male violence is expressed through the voyeuristic gaze (*Desire* 125), so that what begins as the desire to be gazed upon is transformed into a fear of being looked at, or a fear of the apparatus that systematizes that process of looking ("Caught" 206). Marian sees Peter as "a homicidal maniac with a lethal weapon in his hands" (*EW* 246), and she flees from the party after having hallucinated a sinister scenario in which her absence accompanies a Peter whom she cannot recognize. In her work on films of the 1940s, Doane names the risk of not knowing one's husband well enough as being a common motif that conceals "the more fundamental terror of non-differentiation and the eclipsing of subjectivity" within an exogamy that reinforces, at the social level, the oppositions constitutive of identity (*Desire* 147). Hence, Marian's threatened subjectivity may now be seen as accompanying her place within the marital contract, and in particular her assumption of the post-oedipal feminine role that will allow her to circulate in networks of exchange. Indeed, Doane maintains that the paranoid stance is a feminine one that corresponds not to a pathological state but to a normal condition in the case of the female who is, in an attempt to be feminine, constantly on display (*Desire* 126–43). Textual reference to the fact that Marian's delusions are symptomatic of the exhibitionism expected of a woman within the economy of exchange centres upon her masquerading in makeup and seductive clothes that mark her as a "target" (*EW* 244) for paternal desire. Wearing the kind of dress she would normally never wear, she is described as being "Egyptian-lidded" and having the "outlined and thickly fringed eyes of a person she had never seen before" (222). In performing the feminine role, she also constructs for herself a mimetic identity "walking carefully inside her finely-adjusted veneers" (229). In fact, Duncan's response to her new appearance is indicative of just how artificial an image she has constructed, as he cries: "You didn't tell me it was a masquerade. . . . Who the hell are you supposed to be?" (239).

Such artifice designed to make oneself the object of desire also signals a fixation upon the bodily surface that now becomes the threshold between the corporeal and the imaged, and acts as a kind of insertion into the symbolic order. It, too, is an entry into society that is dependent upon a series of exchanges. Peter's exchange of a bachelor life for married responsibilities reflects upon the compensatory mechanism whereby his once-relinquished oedipal desires are now rewarded by a maternal substitute. His superego is likely to be strengthened as he takes up his rightful place under paternal law, but Marian, in exchanging her oedipal desires, stands to lose not only her name but any stable identity of her own.

Marian's other entry into the sexual arena also proves to be a threat to her sense of self, albeit in quite a different way. While Peter is a lawyer who spends his life structuring contracts (57) and is the epitome of social conformity, Duncan is a man who offers her nothing and "wasn't threatening her with some intangible gift in return" (183). Furthermore, Duncan's subjectivity is likely to "evaporate" next to a man such as Peter, with whom he is afraid to be in the same room (239). His threatened specular identity may be seen to be represented by his destruction of the mirror because "I got tired of being afraid I'd walk in there some morning and wouldn't be able to see my own reflection in it" (139).

Duncan's reluctance to leave his flatmates who, he readily admits, take the place of his parents (146, 201) hints at an unresolved oedipal dilemma whereby he avoids taking the place allotted to him under symbolic law. He himself admits he has an affinity with the amoeba (201), which has the ability to perpetually change shape, on the grounds that "Being a person is getting too complicated" (201). This is in direct contrast to Peter, whose obsessive need to wash (58, 61) and preoccupation with neatness (88) implies a "mortification of the flesh" (62) that attests to abjection[6] and his need to mark the threshold of a stable enunciative position through the expulsion of anything unclean or disorderly. Peter is, after all, the man who "never shed[s]" (146); with this he tries to exist in defiance of corporeality in his attempt to delineate himself from others.

Duncan, too, is threatened by flesh but not for the reason of ego-affirmation. In fact, his hatred of anything corporeal seems to be connected to his desire to not be positioned at all, to very simply not take up space. Walking with Duncan in the snow, Marian fears that he will vanish or sink beneath the surface; indeed, fantasizing about his favourite place, he admits: "I wouldn't like tropical islands at all, they would be too fleshy. . . . But in the snow you're as near as possible to nothing" (263). Duncan's unconscious response to the corporeal takes the form of a flight into the "labyrinth of words" (140). An eternal graduate student writing and rewriting term papers, he proclaims himself "a slave in the paper-mines for all time" (97), caught in the metonymy of signification that is no less a form of production than the commodity that finds itself in any of the "used car graveyards" (143). The model of signification as an incessant sliding of the signifier with only a momentary anchoring point at which time it temporarily hinges to a signified is evident when Duncan describes his fellow students as being people who can never attain any permanence in their knowledge: "The thing is, they repeat themselves and repeat themselves but they never get anywhere, they never seem to finish anything" (95). And the fact that, like any other cultural pursuit, intellectual work is, in fact, miming a referential reality that is no longer accessible is implied when he states: "Words . . . are beginning to lose their meanings" (96). Indeed, Duncan's existence is marked by duplicity, from the moment he and Marian meet during the Moose Beer survey, at which time he refuses to answer in a way that is not fraudulent (54, 99), to the time he refers to himself as a changeling that was switched for a real baby at birth. He himself cautions her against placing any faith in the content of what he says, warning her that "the trouble with people" is that "they always believe me" (140). It is, however, at the point at which he describes himself as being "very flexible" because he is none other than "the universal substitute" (145) that his symbolic function as phallic signifier is finally made clear.

The phallic third term has no content in itself but merely attracts meanings by way of its migratory function. In light of this, the absence of any permanent significance in Duncan's words may be seen to be indicative of the figurative and metaphorical role he now plays. The paternal signifier is, ultimately, the object exchanged and that which is circulated within any symbolic act. Duncan may now be seen to have lost his individual subjective stance through his becoming a vacant position in the circuit of exchange.

While the phallic signifier has the castrative effect of initiating post-oedipal desire and consequently engenders the division of the subject through the act of signification, there is a certain ambivalence in its attempt to substitute for the lack it has introduced. Duncan represents this ambiguity by using his relationship with Marian as a way to reach the Real. While consciously committed to the lure of the signifier, his hope is that through Marian he will gain access to that realm that is foreclosed once an enunciative position has been taken: "I'd like something to be real. Not everything, that's impossible, but maybe one or two things. I mean Dr Johnson refuted the theory of the unreality of matter by kicking a stone, but I can't go around kicking my room mates. . . . Besides, maybe my foot's unreal anyway. . . . I thought maybe you would be. I mean if we went to bed" (201–02).

When they do finally have intercourse, it is interesting to note that he strips her of any mimetic identity she may have constructed by specifying that she wipe off her makeup. It is not coincidental that he touches her as if he were "ironing" her, an act that, up until this point, has characterized his need to escape from the intellectual (95). For Duncan, the act of ironing and the objects he straightens out are a type of fetish. Within the psychoanalytic model, fetishism functions as a disavowal of maternal castration and a mechanism through which the subject can gain access to signification but simultaneously retain the pre-oedipal attachment to the mother. Hence, it is not surprising that their sexual encounter has maternal connotations whereby Marian assumes a foetal position and he admits to having tried to do the same (254). This is reminiscent of the episode in the museum when Duncan takes Marian to meet his "womb-symbol" (187). It is an Egyptian mummy that has caught his fascination, and there is speculation as to whether it is, in fact, a child. At this point, his reaction parallels the response she sensed when they first met, when she suspected that his actions had been calculated to evoke "a mothering reaction" (99) and "she realized with an infinitesimal shiver of horror that he was reaching out for her" (188). It is not coincidental, then, that soon after, in the museum coffee shop, he makes his intentions clear, saying: "You know, I think it might be a good idea if we went to bed . . ." (189).

For Kristeva, the maternal is a function without a subject, a space that lacks agency. It is the site of a splitting between the organic and the social, and the threshold between the natural and cultural orders ("Motherhood"; "Maternal Body"). Duncan's search for a relation to the maternal body through Marian endangers her enunciative position; through him, she risks being positioned on the side of the asymbolic and being relegated to the order of the referent extrinsic to the procession of signifiers. This threat to her sense of self is paralleled by Duncan's overwhelming self-absorption, his tendency to "direct the conversation towards the complex and ever-fascinating subject of himself" (184). His ability to protect himself at the expense of her well-being is revealed by his imminent rejection of her (257), and the fact that he devours with serious intent the cake that comes to represent her identity (281).

The consumption of Marian and her commodification are well imaged throughout the novel. On an interpersonal level, her engagement to Peter allows him to enjoy "private property rights" (227) in their relationship, evident in the fact that "Now that she had been ringed he took pride in displaying her" (176). On a wider collective scale, Marian, like most women, is also subject to social forces that act to objectify her. The advertisement with the seminaked girl in a grass skirt and flowers alongside a sign giving a price (175) is evidence of this dynamic. So too is Marian's experience at the beautician's, which explicitly links femininity to her treatment as "a slab of flesh, an object" (209). One of many in an assembly line of ladies, her overriding sensation is one of being "inert" and "half-etherized" (210, 211), as she asks: "Was this what she was being pushed towards, this compound of the simply vegetable and the simply mechanical?" (210).

According to Irigaray, such appropriation is sexually specific and the result of an exchange system whereby women become "products" or "merchandise" under paternal law (*This Sex* 84). Subject to this system, the commodities are not in themselves specularizable, but become materializations of abstract human labour that function as the mimetic expression of masculine values (*This Sex* 170–91). This may well explain why Marian walks straight into a department store, and her recent experience is juxtaposed with images of household goods. It may also explain why her head is compared to a cantaloupe (*EW* 83), and other women are described in terms of resembling vacuum cleaners (64) and cold porridge (48).

While the commodification of Marian is undeniable, it is important to remember that the kinship system is, as Gayle Rubin points out, a "production" in the most general sense of the term. With this, property rights are not exclusive to one individual and all people and objects are molded and transformed (176–77). Indeed, Marian enjoys certain proprietary rights over Peter, evident in "the sense of proud ownership" (*EW* 146) she feels toward her acquisition: "I could feel the stirrings of the proprietary instinct. So this object, then, belonged to *me*" (90). This parallels the other ways in which she is forced to take responsibility for being a consumer. In the supermarket, she resists the temptation to reach out and grab anything that catches her eye; however, she admits to herself that "You had to buy something sometime" (172). And within her job as a market surveyor, she actively traffics in the exchange of commodities. Analysis of her Moose Beer questionnaire reveals a number of circulatory relationships. To begin with, the survey, by definition, relies on the idea of swapping answers to questions in return for better products. A potentially infinite exchange of words circulating in endless metonymic procession is hinted at by the fact that Marian herself is given a pamphlet by the Christian temperates in exchange for her questions. And Duncan's free association in response to key phrases of the advertisement reveal primary processes of condensation and displacement,[7] whereby gym shoes and jockstraps lead to swallows shot through the heart, and literary allusions to *Titus Andronicus* are inspired by a glass of beer. However, her role within the symbolic economy takes on a sexualized tone when one of the more obliging participants lurches toward her with suggestive intentions (47–48). The anticipated exchange of words for her body is also implied when Duncan stipulates that he will only cooperate if she follows him into his bedroom (51).

Marian's status as both commodity and consumer may seem on the surface to be somewhat contradictory. However, the fact that she partakes in, and in some ways initiates, the transactions that ultimately result in her own commodification are not, in fact, irreconcilable. As Doane explains, "Irigaray's theory of the woman as commodity and the historical analysis of the woman's positioning as consumer — as subject rather than object of the commodity form — are only apparently contradictory" (*Desire* 23). Doane situates the female subject as being "the prototype of the modern consumer," but believes her objectification can only be understood if the absoluteness of the division between subject and object is rethought (23).

In analysis of *The Edible Woman*, reconsideration of this relationship between subject and object is most appropriate in the light of the Hegelian master-slave dialectic. This is the conflict in which the coexistence of two self-consciousnesses can only be solved by the destruction of one of them; and it is a dynamic that Lacan situates as being not only at the base of subjective identity but at the very heart of the exchange system: "the most developed forms of the production of consumer goods, shows that it is structured in this dialectic of master and slave, in which we can recognize the symbolic emergence of the imaginary struggle to the death in which we earlier defined the essential structure of the ego" ("Freudian Thing" 142).

John Fiske also links consumerism to a kind of battle when he defines shopping malls and the variety of shopping that takes place in them as "key arenas of struggle" (14). Although he places this conflict in the context of ideological struggle, he also believes consumption offers the individual certain forms of control over social relations and socially derived meanings of the self (25). The consumption of products thus takes on a specifically symbolic dimension whereby the subject not only gains access to culturally produced meaning systems but is able to exert some influence over the meanings that such systems produce: "commodities are not just objects of economic exchange; they are goods to think with, goods to speak with" (31). In this analysis, the struggle inherent within the dynamics of consumption touch upon the very foundation of the social contract and the construction of individual subjectivity. Shopping, like other significatory systems, relates the individual to the social order; however, by allowing for specific differences in the way in which each consumer manipulates the system, consumption also allows for a negotiation of individual identity (34–35).

Returning to the Hegelian definition of symbolic identity as being the dynamic whereby the object is subordinated to the demands of the subject in its constitution, it is necessary to examine not only Marian's role within social economies, but her developing inability to eat. As her own subjective position becomes threatened, she finds herself steadily becoming unable to kill and consume that which is other: "She was watching her own hands and the peeler and the curl of crisp orange skin. She became aware of the carrot. It's a root, she thought, it grows in the ground and sends up leaves. Then they come along and dig it up, maybe it even makes a sound, a scream too low for us to hear, but it doesn't die right away, it keeps on living, right now it's still alive. . . . She thought she felt it twist in her hands. She dropped it on the table" (178). Her difficulty in eating an egg signifies her own subjective involvement in the dynamic, and attests to the fact that at some level she is now identifying with the positions of both master and slave. Earlier she had placed herself on the side of the object and feared becoming like the uncooked egg that had lost its boundaries (99). Now she tries to be the subject and exert some power over the soft-boiled egg on the breakfast table (161).

Marian recognizes the entire dynamic as being some type of psychopathological symptom, acknowledging that her conscious mind plays no part in the decision (152). However, when she begins to speak of her own body with a detachment that gives it total control, she intimates a level of regression that manifests itself primarily at a corporeal level: "She was becoming more and more irritated by her body's decision to reject certain foods. She had tried to reason with it, had accused it of having frivolous whims, had coaxed it and tempted it, but it was adamant. . . . [I]t simply refused to eat anything that had once been, or . . . might still be living" (177–78). Something has been repressed from the discourse that normally structures her conscious subjectivity and transferred by way of the oral drive onto a bodily function. In light of Grosz's point that the word may be driven out of concrete conscious discourse and transfer its significance through drive energy onto a corporeal reality ("Lacan" 27), we may see the repressed term in Marian's symptom as being the symbolic gift normally circulated in exchange. It is for this reason, then, that at around this time Marian begins to abstain from the usual trafficking: "she no longer felt like giving anybody anything. She felt even less like receiving . . ." (169).

Other images also link Marian's anorexic inability to eat with the circulation of commodities. The new canned rice pudding, for example, had previously featured in the social circuit by being the subject of a taste test at Seymour Surveys. It later appeared at Clara and Joe's dinner party, thereby playing a role in the domestic economy. It now becomes completely inedible as Marian is unable to see it as a product to be consumed (203).

Further extending the symbolic dimension of the symptom, which at this point includes her role as commodity and consumer and her inability to be active in the Hegelian dialectic, Marian's anorexia may also be connected to her exogamous function in the circuit of exchange. In fact, her inability to introject the very food that constitutes her as a subject surfaces for the first time when she watches Peter make himself "feel a little more human" (152) at the expense of a dead cow. He is described as being "pleasantly conscious of his own superior capacity" (152) as he devours his steak. This is significant in light of the fact that other incidents have shown their relationship to constitute a threat to her subjectivity, and one can assume that he will be using her as well as beef to bolster his own identity.

At the point at which she finally can eat nothing (257) and is in danger of a literal fading of the self, she orchestrates an event in which the various dynamics of introjection that have threatened her can be externalized once and for all. She bakes a cake in her own image and offers it to those who have "eaten" her in other ways. Choosing sponge cake because its sentient nature is most appropriate, she begins with a blank, featureless body and constructs an identity step by step. At one point, "her creation gazed up at her" (270) in a dynamic reminiscent of the infant's search for an image reflected off the mother. However, when the cake-lady smiles back at her "glassily" (273), there is no doubt that she functions as a specular image for Marian.

The cake motif whereby Marian is symbolized as being the "edible woman" is not altogether unexpected in terms of narrative development. It has, in some ways, been foreshadowed by the dolls who stare blankly at her from their position on the top of her dresser. In their exchange of glances, we witness a type of specular inversion in which Marian "saw herself in the mirror between them" (219) as though she were inside them both, looking out at the empty image of herself. This momentary lack of specular unity has been preceded by an experience in the bathtub in which Marian's recognition of her own body is an acknowledgement of her multiple and dissipating self: "How peculiar it was to see three reflections of yourself at the same time. . . . All at once she was afraid that she was dissolving, coming apart layer by layer like a piece of cardboard in a gutter puddle" (218).

This sense of fragmentation and the alienating experience of having identified a body "somehow no longer quite her own" (218) is fundamental to the mirror-stage formation of the ego as Lacan describes it. In his account of the identificatory process whereby the infant recognizes his or her own image, the apparent unity visually introjected is in discordance with the actual bodily experience that is one of organic prematurity. The *méconnaissance*[8] specific to this dynamic is expressed in what Lacan terms "imagos of the fragmented body" that are images of mutilation, dismemberment, dislocation, devouring, and even "the doll torn to pieces" ("Aggressivity" 11). Lacan's stipulation that the fragmented body surfaces in the symptom only when the subject begins to display a level of disintegration ("Mirror Stage" 4) is relevant to an analysis of the cake-lady that sees her dismemberment as being symptomatic of what has been the gradual collapse of Marian's ego. Furthermore, the experience of the body-in-bits-and-pieces and systematic misrecognition invests the specular image with a certain aggressivity, an aggressive stance in which the subject is placed in both rivalry and simultaneous dependence upon the other. This aggressive relativity is not only involved in all kinds of regressive behaviour ("Aggressivity" 24), but is fundamental to the master-slave relationship ("Subversion" 302). In this sense, also, the cake-lady functions as the epitome of all those dynamics that have previously threatened Marian's identity. That is, the aggressive intention crucial for ego-formation and the Hegelian dialectic, whereby there exists a contest of wills, is succinctly expressed when she says to Peter, "You've been trying to destroy me, haven't you?" (271), and again when she hands Duncan a fork with which to attack the carcass.

From the time she begins to construct her effigy to the time when "the image was complete" (270), the conscious determination with which she composes a body, face, and arms, and fills in the details implies the autoscopic process whereby an image in gestalt replaces that which has previously functioned as a pointille. Further to this, the cake-lady may also be seen to function as a type of "imaginary anatomy" (Lacan, "Some Reflections" 13) whereby Marian's ego takes the form of a body image introjected as a kind of psychical map. The imaginary anatomy is a cultural construct whereby the body takes a subjective position from which to regulate perception, while simultaneously being positioned as an object accessible to the other. This raises the issue of aggressivity and its role in the construction of the social contract. In terms of the cake motif, the symbolic aspect of the edible woman may be understood in the context of the very first expression of the aggressive intention through dismemberment: namely, the myth of the sacrificial meal as it is described in Freud's *Totem and Taboo*.

The myth of the primal horde in which the brothers devoured the Father and in doing so appropriated both his status and his name is seen to be the earliest ritual of incorporation that commemorates the beginning of society. The totemic meal has the exogamous function of replacing oedipal rivalry with a social contract based on kinship structures, but it is reliant upon a fundamental statute that predates the imposition of symbolization: the act of sacrifice. In Kristeva's account,[9] the act of sacrifice establishes not only the symbol but its entire order. By focusing violence onto a specific victim, the act displaces presymbolic tumult onto the symbolic order at the very moment that order is being founded. The murder is ambiguous in function, being both destructive and regulatory; and sacrifice, rather than unleashing violence, shows that representing it is enough to stop it and concatenate an order. Given that the site in which the violence is confined becomes the signifier, the victim becomes the very first symbol; and sacrifice represents the exclusion inherent in any sociosymbolic contract — namely, the death of the referent.

The same sacrificial structure takes different forms according to the relations of production that are specific to a given culture (Kristeva, *Revolution* 76). In the context of the various dynamics that have threatened Marian's subjectivity up until now, it is appropriate that she should offer herself in the form of food as the sacrificial object. The ceremonial flavour of the episode is evident in the way in which she kneels in front of Peter after having come "bearing the platter in front of her, carefully and with reverence, as though she was carrying something sacred in a procession, an icon or the crown on a cushion in a play" (271). And the fact that sacrifice reveals the symbolic to be founded upon a rupture with corporeality is evident in the way in which she is torn, limb from limb. However, the totemic meal is a socially sanctioned form of consumption that safeguards against other more chronic forms of pathology. It is a ritual way in which the social norm may be maintained without danger to any individual or threat to the collective group. Perhaps this explains why Duncan's response, while stern, poses no real threat, and why Peter does not even partake of the game. As Kristeva puts it, "The whole system is merely a play of images" (*Revolution* 76) exemplifying the structural law of symbolism. This is further evident in Marian's naming of herself as "a substitute" (*EW* 271), which is indicative of the fact that the sacrificial object, regardless of form, reiterates the structure of the symbol (Kristeva, *Revolution* 75). Thus, if there is to be a murder in the realm of the referent, it need not coincide with the death of Marian; and this representation of the covenant that founds the sociosymbolic order need not in any ultimate way endanger her.

Marian's own reaction is an interesting one in that "She plunged her fork into the carcass, neatly severing the body from the head" (273). Perhaps this is indicative of the consenting nature of a sacrifice that is, above all, contractual. In any case, her ability to distance herself from her sacrificial image supports Kristeva's point that the sacrificed, while giving a part of him- or herself, prudently sets another part aside (*Revolution* 75–76). Perhaps it is the part of her that has been kept in reserve, which may now surface to reestablish her identity.

At this point, Marian seems stronger than ever before, and the totemic meal, in its function as resolution of the novel, shows her return to a safe subjective position. She is able to assume an enunciative position once more, thinking of herself "in the first person singular again" (278). She has made a decision about her role in the marital economy and is able to renounce Duncan as well as Peter. She is able to eat once more, proud of herself for having conquered a piece of steak. And she is able to accept her own inclusion in the network of power relations whereby each individual protects him- or herself at the expense of the other. Her conversation with Duncan traces a maze of Hegelian dynamics in which her part positions her once more in the system of exchange:

"Peter wasn't trying to destroy you. . . . Actually you were trying to destroy him."

I had a sinking feeling. "Is that true?" I asked.

. . . "But the real truth is that it wasn't Peter at all. It was me. I was trying to destroy you."

I gave a nervous laugh. "Don't say that."

"Okay," he said, "ever eager to please. Maybe Peter was trying to destroy me, or maybe I was trying to destroy him, or we were both trying to destroy each other, how's that? What does it matter . . . you're a consumer." (280–81)

In the introduction to *The Edible Woman*, Atwood names "symbolic cannibalism" as having been the preoccupation that inspired her writing of the novel. The gradual disintegration of Marian's identity, whereby she is subject to forces that effect her dislocation, her fragmentation, even her dismemberment, raises a number of issues of division: the alienated specular image, the split between unconscious and conscious discourse, the barring of the pre-oedipal from the symbolic, and the exclusion that underpins a signifying position. In turn, these explain the ways in which Marian is enmeshed in networks of exchange and consumption and a domestic economy that lies at the very base of the sociosymbolic contract, and explains her individual subjective position within it.

[1] Lévi-Strauss, Rubin, Irigaray ("Women"), and Lacan ("Freudian Thing" 142; "Agency" 148).

[2] Freud, in "Femininity," postulated that for the girl there were three options for the resolution of the oedipal complex: normal castrated femininity (the preferred and most common result), the assumption of a masculinity complex, and sexual inability or frigidity.

[3] Lacan refers to pre-mirror stage "infantile transitivism," whereby the child is unable to differentiate between self and other. The example Lacan puts forward is of the child who strikes another but reacts as if he had been struck, or the child who sees another fall but reacts as if he had fallen ("Mirror Stage" and "Aggressivity").

[4] This is a Kristevan term, as outlined in *Revolution in Poetic Language*, that refers to two experiences that constitute the subject: the mirror-stage and castration.

[5] I refer here to Freud's "A Case of Paranoia Running Counter to the Psychoanalytical Theory of the Disease," as it is explained by Doane in *The Desire to Desire*.

[6] This is a Kristevan term, as outlined in *Powers of Horror*, that refers to the dynamic by which the subject attempts to retain his or her subjective position by delineating a body and reacting with horror to anything that is abject and threatens its distinct boundaries. In the context of the characterization of Peter, Kristeva's point that the abject which is loathed usually takes the form of bodily waste is significant, as is her point that abjection is an inability to deal with the corporeality of human existence.

[7] Condensation is a Freudian term that refers to the process whereby the libidinal energies of a number of associated ideas or images are invested in one single image. Displacement refers to the process whereby the libidinal energy invested in one image or idea is transferred to another image that may appear to be unconnected but is associated in some way.

[8] Misrecognition.

[9] The following account is drawn from *Revolution in Poetic Language* (72–83).

CHAPTER TWO

Lady Oracle:

The SPLIT SUBJECT *and* DYNAMICS *of* MATERNAL SYMBIOSIS *and* SEPARATION

My account begins with what opens the novel and what is arguably a preoccupation in terms of its narrative development: death. It is my contention that suicide and the construction of one's own death haunts not only the fictional life of Joan Foster but the thematic concerns that underpin the entire novel. Furthermore, it is my belief that the structuring influence death has upon the protagonist and her story signals not only a kind of narrative commitment to the protagonist's conscious desire to cease to exist, but may be seen to be indicative of the psychic necessity to negotiate one of the most fundamental principles of life: the death drive.

With this initial assumption, then, that the death instinct drives not only Joan but subjectivity itself, Freudian and Lacanian theories and textual evidence culminate in an analysis that brings to the fore the relationship between the death drive and discourse. This is in full accordance with the symbolic nature of Joan's supposed suicide, and the fact that it is constructed through the manipulation of words and images. However, given the highly ambiguous and paradoxical nature of a drive that compels the subject to annihilate him- or herself, the influence that symbolic death has upon the protagonist's life may be interpreted as being indicative also of the problematic nature of Joan's sense of self. It is not long before the divided and alienated nature of Joan's identity becomes clear, and it is this that my account proceeds to analyse in detail.

The theoretical base upon which my argument rests is that of Kristevan semiology and psychoanalytic formulations of the self. There are a number of reasons why this is appropriate. First, because Joan's personality and characterization is striking in its division. Second, because the subjective stance is an enunciative one. And third, because both are underwritten by the discursive aspects of the death drive. Kristeva's formulation of the semiotic and symbolic aspects of subjective existence accounts perfectly for all three, and provides an excellent framework within which to analyse the ways in which they are illustrated in the text. Generally speaking, there are four ways in which semiotic energies may be seen to surface within the novel, and it is these that structure not only the fictional life of the protagonist but my account of it.

Broadly speaking, the first of these is the disintegration of Joan's ego-identity into multiple personalities, personae, and names that come to represent the behaviour of many selves. At this point, my account becomes descriptive, illustrating by way of excerpts from the text the way in which the protagonist is characterized by duplicity and division. This much my account has in common with those that have preceded it. However, after having catalogued the various descriptions of Joan's splintered identity, I then analyse them in the context of Lacanian ideas of specularization and the narcissistic imaging of the self, both of which are instrumental in the formation of subjectivity. As a consequence of analysis in the light of psycho-analytic theories of the self, the dissenting voices of Joan's manifold personalities and the destructive effects of this division are accounted for with new precision. For Joan's fractured existence is no longer seen as an idiosyncratic phenomenon, but as a function of the alienation that by definition plagues subjective identity. In an attempt to preserve the specificity of Joan Foster's life and world, my account remains close to the novel, basing its assertions upon textual evidence. However, in a simultaneous attempt to contextualize the incidents within a wider interpretative stance, I choose to analyse them in terms of the ambiguity and estrangement that marks not only these particular events but all subjective experiences of the self. This involves the assumption that it is no coincidence that the character of Joan Foster is marked by disjunction; it further implies that, having devoted critical attention to the ways in which the protagonist systematically illustrates the fate of each and every subject, a psychoanalytic model will most suitably account for dynamics otherwise not focused upon.

Beginning with the dynamics of mirror-stage specularization and the ways in which these are illustrated within the novel, my account comes to rest upon Joan's relationship with the other form of the intrasubjective identification that in her case is indicative of alienation: the imaginary anatomy. Brought thus to the issue of the body, one is brought also to the relationship between the protagonist and her mother, on the grounds that it is through the maternal that corporeal identity is ordered and marked. Positionality as a function of familial structure through which the libidinal expenditure of the child is filtered brings to the fore Kristeva's concept of the chora, and the related dynamics of orality and anality. Psychoanalytic formulations of these are well suited to accounting for Joan's problematic relationship with food. Like no other, the psychoanalytic model is able to account for the ambiguity that marks the oral- and anal-aggressive drives, and hence explain the contradictory nature of Joan's actions, which work simultaneously toward constituting and destroying her identity.

Most critics agree that Joan's relationship with Mrs. Foster is of paramount importance within the novel. What is often absent, however, is a detailed exploration of it that does not negate the complicated and highly ambivalent nature of their connection. Drawing upon the work of a number of psychoanalytic theorists, my account explores in detail the relation between mother and daughter that haunts the characterization of both women. This means addressing the issues of separation and symbiosis. However, any negotiation of Joan's identity eventually involves a negotiation of her mother's, a point well made by the detail in which Mrs. Foster is characterized throughout the novel. Hence, my account turns toward Mrs. Foster and the reflected division that marks her appearance in the mirror, her attempts at self-imaging through masquerade and disguise, her captation within the interplay of masculine and paternal desire, and her role within the maintenance of the social and symbolic contract.

What becomes evident is that the mother's displaced sense of self has an irrevocable effect upon the daughter. Nowhere is this more evident than in the episodes in which Mrs. Foster "visits" her daughter. My account is alone in interpreting the motif of the astral projections as involving a negotiation of choric space. With this I discuss the visitations in terms of the positioning of both mother and daughter within a dynamic defined solely by their relationship. The result is that subjective identity now becomes a matter of spatial variation and displacement, and both Joan and her mother are seen to be locked in a kind of territorial dispute. Because of the privileged role orality and corporeality play in negotiating choric space, this struggle between mother and daughter is expressed primarily through the attempted control, on both their parts, over Joan's body. As a consequence, Joan begins to assert herself by way of abjecting her own body through an immersion in anorexic dieting; and the resulting weight loss, in the context of its functioning as an attempt at detachment from the maternal, initiates her entry into the sexual arena of masculine desire.

Initially, Joan's foray into the world of men implies an externalization of the self via the gaze of desire. However, soon it is seen to effect a certain dislocation within her self, emphasized by the duplicitous nature with which she conducts her affairs. Parallels are seen to exist between Joan and the men with whom she is in amorous attachment, as the Polish Count, the Royal Porcupine, and even Arthur are revealed in their duplicity. All the men with whom Joan becomes involved are shown to have artificially constructed identities, and while this is a source of comic humour and characterization in the novel, it also raises the issue of representation of and within the self in the context of the dynamics of desire. It is at this point that the ambiguity that cloaks the characterization of Joan's father begins to take on special significance. Assuming that an adequate resolution of the oedipal drama is necessary both for the transference of desire and its investment within the economy of the signifier, Joan's relationship with Mr. Foster is seen to function as a play of maternal presence over paternal absence. This is a dynamic that is seen to influence Joan's ability to connect with the men in her life, and account for the element of discursivity that underwrites all of Joan's interactions with men.

In light of the psychoanalytic model through which Joan's affairs have been read, sexual and amorous interaction with men now implies the assumption of an enunciative position. Both require a renunciation of the attachment to the maternal; and with this, love becomes a negotiation of symbolic demands over and above oedipal desires. Joan's experiences with Fraser Buchanan are seen to support this contention, as it is argued that he is operative in her life as agent of exchange, signification, and societal positioning. What has been at issue here is the negotiation of sexual activity in the face of significatory desire, and with this my account turns toward Joan's

74

writing of costume Gothics as a form of textual practice that further sheds light upon the enunciative status of the subjective stance.

What is immediately apparent is the fact that Joan's authorship structures her life with the kind of duplicity we have come to expect. However, more importantly, textual practice like Joan's bespeaks the very issue of subjectivity itself. In an interpretative stance that draws upon Kristeva's formulation of signifying practices, previous allusions to the death instinct, the maternal, the oral, and the anal are brought together in an interpretation that sees Joan's writing of Gothic romance as functioning in terms of semiotic and symbolic textual process. As such, the protagonist's authorship now becomes a renegotiation of the choric relationship. The "automatic writing" incidents and the construction of a fictional fantasy world thus become operative as a form of regression to the archaic maternal space and reinvestment of that energy into adult symbolic existence. The threat of symbiotic union with the mother is made clear and then echoed through the interchangeable identities of Joan and her fictional characters, and the mimetic construction of textual realities. Meanwhile, discussion of the psychopathology of the texts — the processes of condensation and displacement that mark them — reveal the primary processes that underlie the protagonist's investment in textual practice.

Psychoanalytic formulations of the symptom accord them qualities of wish fulfilment as well as those of subversion. Hence, within my account, the protagonist's drive to write implies a compulsion for some type of resolution. It is my contention that what underlies Joan's artistic endeavours is an attempt to create a new position for herself, a position that does not negate the maternal but nevertheless assures her a symbolic identity. Arguing that this, in fact, occurs, my argument concludes, as indeed does the novel — for Joan finally reaches a point of insight concerning her relationship with her mother and decides to set aside the costume Gothics, return to Canada, and resume her life.

* * *

Lady Oracle (*LO*) is a novel in which all direct action is dependent upon the protagonist's staging of her own death. Joan Foster's clever construction of her own apparent annihilation dominates the structure of the novel. It continually propels, then harnesses, dramatic action, after which the remainder of the text takes the form of a cluster of mnemonic flashbacks that are organized around the elaborate deception. Given that the supposed suicide plays so important a role in the narrative, what then does this reveal about the consciousness of the protagonist? And what are the psychical consequences of having a death wish as the most influential factor that structures life?

Freud posited the death drive as one of the most fundamental principles of psychical life, an instinct that finds its expression in the day-to-day life of a subject through a kind of self-destructiveness, and "which cannot fail to be present in every vital process" ("Anxiety" 140). In his account, the death wish is the attempt of every living organism to return to an earlier state of being,[1] which, in the last instance, would be a complete reduction of tensions to the level of the inanimate. Freud proceeds to divide instincts into two groups: those that are "erotic," thereby seeking to combine more and more living substance into greater and more unities, and death instincts, which oppose this effort and "lead what is living back into an inorganic state" ("Anxiety" 140). The concurrent and opposing interaction of these two instincts, each of which has its own specific aim, is, in Freud's formulation, the secret of life itself. However, it allows for a somewhat complicated dynamic whereby live matter is at danger from its own internal causation, and libidinal economy takes on the function of innoculating the destructive instinct by directing drive energy toward object relations with the external world. These factors point first to the inherently self-destructive nature of subjectivity, and second to the connection of the death drive with symbolic discourse and signification.

The relationship between discourse and the death wish is explicated clearly by Jean Laplanche and Serge Leclaire when they state that "language, like the unconscious, is primarily and indissolubly linked to the surfacing of the death-drive in so far as the latter remains precisely that foundation of the world of desire" (171). Speaking of desire, which "crawls, slips, escapes" (Lacan, *Four Fundamental* 214) through the metonymy of the signifier, Lacan also raises the issue of the annihilation of the subject within object relations situated by way of signification in and through the field of the other. He does this by making the point that the original and most fundamental object that the subject offers to the other when positioned post-oedipally within the circulation of words is, in fact, "his own disappearance": "The first object he proposes for this parental desire whose object is unknown is his own loss — *Can he lose me?* The phantasy of one's death, of one's disappearance, is the first object that the subject has to bring into play in this dialectic, and he does indeed bring it into play . . ." (214).

Thus, death may be seen not only as a decomposition in the context of corporeal existence but in terms of signification; in the latter instance, death means not only the total expenditure of libidinal energy but a dissolution back into the Real whereby the bar between sign and referent is dissipated.[2] In this, death would seem to be the absence of representation, and the death instinct the movement in which, in the hope of returning to an earlier state of being, drives interrupt signification, reinvesting the metonymy of desire usually pointed toward and positioned within the other back onto the pre-oedipal and narcissistically invested body.

Further focusing upon the implications of the death instinct as a form of internal causation constitutive of subjectivity, it may also be said that entry into the signifying realm of the symbolic induces a form of death, evident in the establishment of the barrier between the shifting chain of signifiers and the Real. As Lacan notes, the initial and fundamental splitting, without which no subjective position may be held, is, in fact, one based upon an annihilation of that very subject: "at every moment he constitutes his world by his suicide, and the psychological experience of which Freud had the audacity to formulate, however paradoxical its expression in biological terms, as the 'death instinct' " ("Aggressivity" 28). It is this association of death with the endless deferral of signification that allows Joan's words to take on special significance. Commenting on the discursive construction of her death through written reports in the newspapers, she says: "I'd been shoved into the ranks of those other unhappy ladies, scores of them apparently, who'd been killed by a surfeit of words" (*LO* 313). And she highlights the funereal dimension of the signifier when she notes the commentators "spewing out words like flowers on a coffin" (314).

The ambiguity concerning death and the subject's drive toward it are the type of paradoxical notions Kristeva capitalizes upon in her piece "The Father, Love and Banishment." Here, she plays with the idea of death as being the annihilation of the mother, the abjecting of the maternal preempted by identification with the Imaginary father and effected by the oedipal entry of the phallic third term. In this case, her use of death also revokes the murder of the primal father[3] instrumental in the founding of society, where the corpse of the father itself becomes waste the sons expel through the anal-aggressive expression of maternal absence in the signifying moment of Fort-Da.[4] In these accounts, it is death that allows for the moment of narcissism, the realization and acceptance of castration, the entry of the phallic third term, and the subsequent transference of the other onto an endless movement of desire linked to the object and relayed through the signifier — all very necessary developments if the not-yet subject is to be constituted as one and escape the realm of psychosis. However, Kristeva also characterizes the symbolic order of signification as being funereal for the oedipal daughter who has turned her gaze toward the paternal and accepted as her fate the alienating name and law of the father. For her, banishment, on the one hand, implies exile from the maternal; however, on the other hand, if directed toward the symbolic, it becomes a chance for escape from the fixed meaning in which she would otherwise become trapped. Kristeva's call for women to flee the order of paternal signification by banishing themselves from it allows us to focus upon Joan's self-imposed exile with a new perspective. In the context of Kristeva's assertion, Joan's flight from the societal and therefore symbolic order she is familiar with in Canada to one in Italy, in which she is alien and "didn't know the words" (312), may be seen to be an unacknowledged attempt to flee the ego-identity that has been discursively constructed for her. In light of this, the subversive nature of her actions is highlighted when her supposed drowning is seen to be a suicide and hence an act of free will. And the paradoxical trappings of death and the drive toward it in the case of the oedipal daughter is made clear as she states ". . . I pretended to die so I could live, so I could have another life" (315).

If we accept that the subject-in-process is actually one regulated, if not structured, by the death drive, then we may take the novel's narrative concern with the protagonist's "suicide" to be an invitation to delve more closely into the status of her enunciative position and thus the very construction of her subjectivity. We soon learn that in both areas her existence is divided and problematic, and, further developing the link between the death drive and consequent disturbances of the symbolic, we may choose to interpret the manifest content of the protagonist's life within a framework of Kristevan semiology. With this, the focus would be upon a silent production that traces a mark prior to the appearance of circulatory speech and the exchange of meaning. Similarly, that which structures the subject in division — namely, the threshold between the primary and secondary processes, the unconscious and the conscious, and the maternal and the paternal — would become the focal point of analysis.

These forces register the interaction of the conflicting energy charges of what Kristeva has termed the "semiotic" and the "symbolic." In her account,[5] the symbolic refers to the intersubjective realm of representational activity, which is made possible through the securing of an enunciative position and constituted under the auspices of the other. It is the order of social regulation and signification, whereby denotation, or the designation of an object, is accompanied by the displaced subject of enunciation so that a predicative function may mark the spatiotemporal and vocal positioning of the subject. The semiotic, on the other hand, refers to the presignifying bodily elements of existence expressed as rhythmic, gestural, or intonational behavioural structures that predate conscious corporeal control and are eventually harnessed and represented within regulatory language. The semiotic refers to the anarchic circulation of polymorphous perverse[6] drive energy that animates the infant, and the inscription of impulses across the body that form a site on which earliest vocalizations can be traced, allowing phonemic elements to be produced when primary processes connect signifiers to psychosomatic functioning. The forces of the semiotic, while mostly contained and redirected through the thetic moments of the mirror-stage, castration, and the oedipal complex, remain forever highly subversive. They are sure to keep the subject in a state of unpredictability, to interrupt and disrupt the symbolic order and the stability of the ego-identity at certain "privileged" moments otherwise seen to be instances of neurosis and psychosis, of religious ecstasy, and of art and poetry. Although the semiotic predates spatiotemporal positioning and any division between subject and object, it can only be conceived retrospectively by the speaking subject as a purely hypothetical presignifying moment that once lay chronologically anterior to but now traverses the symbolic, introducing negativity through an instance Kristeva calls a "second-return."

Noting that all such semiotic distortions of the symbolic order attest to a residue of the death drive, the influx of which no thetic phase could ever fully contain (Kristeva, *Revolution* 102–03), we are reminded once more of our protagonist, for whom the return of the semiotic trace in post-oedipal adult figuration features in four specific configurations. Within the domain of subjectivity, the upheaval of the symbolic and sudden appearance of semiotic energies takes the form of what may be seen to be unconscious symptoms. This refers first to moments of psychosis in which Joan's singular ego breaks down and her sense of self fragments into multiple identities, a process reinforced through her various experiences with specularization. Second, it refers to the sightings and visitations on the part of her mother, who follows her across continents and years, supposed incarnations of her spiritual aura that take the form of psychotic hallucinations. These not only shed light upon the difficult relationship between Mrs. Foster and her daughter, but are connected with Joan's complex relationship with food as transitional object[7] in the process of maternal separation. Third, within the domain of signifying and textual practices, Joan's second-return semiotic surfaces in her construction of a fantasy world inspired by her writing of Gothic romance fiction. Her choice of the historical novel as genre allows for an unconscious turning of her gaze back to a time that predates any she can consciously remember, which in turn echoes the lack of conscious corporeal control with which she produces her other artistic endeavour — a volume of poetry she writes through the spiritualist method of "automatic writing." Finally, the complex web of semiotic drives and energies is evident within the love relationships onto which she transfers earlier cathexes once directed toward the mother as primary love-object. In this context, her relationship with her father is significant, as is her affair with the Royal Porcupine and her encounter with Fraser Buchanan.

Joan's division into manifold personalities that are not only discordant with each other but perform different behavioural functions is illustrated early in the novel. We are introduced to Joan, the middle-aged ex-librarian who is overweight and painfully shy, a recluse who writes costume Gothics and is horribly allergic to anything signalling exposure to the outside world (33). This is an identity she constructs for herself consciously and discursively while she functions as an author, and it contrasts markedly with the Joan who arrives in Italy, sporting a new hair colour and style and a new personality: "a sensible girl, discreet, warm, honest and confident, with soft green eyes, regular habits and glowing chestnut hair" (184). Of course, the woman to whom we are introduced in Terramotto is busy concealing the remains of what she calls "my former self" (19). Burying a green garbage bag with her wet clothes, so that ". . . I could start being another person, a different person entirely," she conducts her own kind of funeral: "The clothes were my own, I hadn't done anything wrong, but I still felt as though I was getting rid of a body, the corpse of someone I'd killed" (20).

From this point, we go on to meet the rather sedate Joan who is married to the politically correct and angst-ridden Arthur and is rather reluctantly engaged in a life of political activism; and we stumble upon the obese Joan "who looked like a beluga whale and never opened her mouth except to put something into it" (74). No sooner do we come to know this asexual fat lady than the desperately thin Joan enters the stage, taking handfuls of diet pills and laxatives as she negotiates the sexual arena, desperately hiding her past from the men who now find her attractive. These identities exist in addition to the teenage Joans, one of whom is sullen and weepy, taking refuge in dark movie houses, virtually comatose at times; the other of whom is a "swell kid" who plays volleyball, is active in school clubs, and is everybody's favourite, the girl who scored an entry in the yearbook that called her "Our happy-go-lucky gal with the terrific personality!!! . . ." (93). She is not unaware of the somewhat anomalous nature of her existence, speaking of herself as "a sorry assemblage of lies and alibis, each complete in itself but rendering the others worthless" (211); and the desperately driven nature of her disjointed life is highlighted when she fears that "If I brought the separate parts of my life together (like uranium, like plutonium, harmless to the naked eye, but charged with lethal energies) surely there would be an explosion" (217).

Her anxiety in contemplating a prospective unity of self may be seen to be a function of the highly alienated and decentred nature of subjectivity, which is structured, as Lacan has pointed out, by way of organic prematurity, bodily experience of fragmentation, intro-jected misrecognition, and permanent alienation. In his account of the developmental phase instrumental in the formation of the ego, the infant reaches out toward the external world, forging Imaginary relations with it by introjecting a reflected imago: "We have only to understand the mirror stage *as an identification*, in the full sense that analysis gives to the term: namely, the transformation that takes place in the subject when he assumes an image" ("Mirror Stage" 2). The importance of incorporating what Lacan has called the "salutary imago" ("Aggressivity" 18) reflected in the mirror is clearly evident in the initiation ceremony that Joan undergoes to join the Brownies:

You then had to close your eyes and be turned around three times, while the pack chanted,

Twist me and turn me and show me the elf,
I looked in the water and there saw . . .

Here you were supposed to open your eyes, look into the enchanted pool, which was a hand-mirror surrounded by plastic flowers and ceramic bunnies, and say, "Myself." The magic word. (61)

While the endeavour seems to be one in which Joan is searching for her self, there is a distinct emphasis on cultural dependence effected through the signifying voices and presence of figures representative of a definitive social order. This is, perhaps, illustrative of the fact that while the imago is the forerunner of the way the subject will see him- or herself in the future, it is, as J. Laplanche and J.B. Pontalis point out, the "prototypical figure which orients the subject's way of apprehending others" (211). In their account, the imago functions fully as an acquired set of Imaginary representations that are procured through a familial and social network. This bespeaks the issue of the subject's relationship with him- or herself in simultaneous existence with those of others, and is hinted at in Joan's encounter with the Brownies, which now becomes reminiscent of the myth of Narcissus[8] gazing at his own reflection in a pool of water.

Within the psychoanalytic model of the self, narcissism has the rather ambivalent status of being necessary for the individual to be able to constitute a relationship with and for him- or herself, yet it is potentially dangerous if the subject becomes overly self-reliant. Freud's earliest accounts conceptualize narcissism as a mode in which the subject's ego recathects itself while withdrawing cathexes from external objects ("On Narcissism"). This absence of object relations in conjunction with an ego turning in upon itself in self-reflexivity comes close to a psychotic condition that by necessity must be overcome if the subject is to take up a rightful and interactive position in society. However, Freud does maintain that since the ego does not originate as an organic unity, a new psychical action must initiate some level of narcissistic investment by which the ego may take itself as an entirety. Thus, as Laplanche and Pontalis succinctly state, "we must inevitably make the period of infantile narcissism's dominance coincide with the formative moments of the ego" (256). At this point, Lacan's formulation of the mirror-stage as the "erotic relation, in which the human individual fixes upon himself" ("Aggressivity" 19) comes into play, making the libidinal self-investment a state of inter- rather than intrasubjectivity. Now the "narcissistic passion" (21) evident in the amorous captivation of the subject by his or her reflected image functions as the internalization rather than repudiation of a relationship with the outside world.[9] Joan's ritual search for herself in the handheld mirror surrounded by the voice of society illustrates this very point — that while subjectivity is constitutive of a permanent libidinal cathexis of the ego, drive energy should never be completely withdrawn from the other if the subject is to find that magic word "I."

From the specular moment on, then, the subject is destined to reexperience him- or herself through relations with the other, a situation that engages the subject in a delicate play of self gratification and the demands of the other. For Joan, narcissistic self-appraisal in the face of conflicting mandates from those around her means that she is in a chronic and perpetual state of self-doubt. When one of her lovers accuses her of being unfaithful, she says: "I'd always found other people's versions of reality very influential and I was beginning to think that maybe he was right, maybe I did have a secret lover" (160). Her doubting of her own perception of herself and inability to define her own identity hints not only at the inevitable positioning of the ego within the locus of the other, but at an inadequate narcissistic relation with the self, whereby she seems unable to accept any ideas about herself that have their origins in her own ego. This seems to result in an ever-widening discrepancy between the person she thinks she is and the one that those around her perceive. Thus, she herself admits: "When I looked at myself in the mirror, I didn't see what Arthur saw" (214).

While this highlights the conflictual nature of the dynamic between self and other, such estrangement from one's own self may also be seen to be illustrative of the particular form of alienation that Lacan defines as being specific to mirror-stage formulation of the ego. In his account, specularization is marred by the internalization of a fictional imago "in which the human individual fixes upon himself an image that alienates him from himself" ("Aggressivity" 19). It is the discrepancy between the reflected image of a unified and self-controlled body and the actual lived experience of corporeal disarray that is fundamental to the specular moment and that structures the subject as forevermore divided. In Lacan's own words, "What I have called the *mirror stage* is interesting in that it manifests the affective dynamism by which the subject originally identifies himself with the visual *Gestalt* of his own body: in relation to the still very profound lack of co-ordination of his own motility . . ." ("Aggressivity"

18–19). The discordance between the real organic insufficiency caused by prematuration of the infant at birth and the reflected image of a controlled self results in the particular form of misrecognition that defines human subjectivity, so that it is upon the *"méconnais-sances* that constitute the ego, the illusion of autonomy to which it entrusts itself" (Lacan, "Mirror Stage" 6) that the ego-identity will be based. While this state of affairs "symbolizes the mental per-manence of the I," at the same time "it prefigures its alienating destination" (2).

The alienation that marks human subjectivity and its relation to specular identity formation is well illustrated throughout the novel in Joan's encounters with mirrors. The distorting mirrors at the Canadian National Exhibition reflect alien images of a self recogniz-able as her own but wider or thinner or longer than the one she is accustomed to. The experience is one that is undoubtedly threaten-ing, as she admits: "I found those mirrors disturbing" (90). However, even more distressing are the occasions when Joan's physical appear-ance belies the person she actually is. Having run away from home and fled to a downtown hotel, she tells of how ". . . I stood in front of the full-length mirror on the back of the bathroom door and examined myself . . ." (137). Here, the schism between external image and internal experience is heightened because this time she barely recognizes herself: "my face was that of a thirty-five-year-old housewife with four kids and a wandering husband" (137). This estrangement of self from self is soon displaced onto her relations with others, so that those around her also fail to recognize her: "People used to say to me, 'You don't look at all like your photo-graphs,' and it was true, so with a few adjustments I'd be able to pass [my husband] on the street one day and he wouldn't even recognize me" (24).

Indeed, Arthur does fail to recognize a photograph of Joan in which, in an interesting reversal of the specular gaze, the fat lady in the image stands squinting at the camera, peering through the lens, returning the stare. This inversion signals a problematic relationship between image and corporeal reality, evident also when she speaks of her body as "shucked-off" and "empty as a mongoloid idiot's" (91). This experience of heterogeneity between Joan and her body may be interpreted as being a failure in the coding of what Lacan terms the "imaginary anatomy," which is the subject's own pro-jection or internal registration of his or her body. It is an intrasub-jective and identificatory process, reliant, as Lacan points out, on a narcissistic investment in the self: "the cerebral cortex functions like a mirror, and . . . it is the site where the images are integrated in the libidinal relationship that is hinted at in the theory of narcissism" ("Some Reflections" 13).

A number of interesting features characterize Lacan's account of the body image. The first is that the projected image functions in discordance with actual biological reality, and is instead structured by cathexes of libidinal energy that are wholly dependent upon what Elizabeth Grosz terms "morphological" (*Jacques Lacan* 43–47) or psychosocial rather than anatomical constraints.[10] Drawing upon clinical evidence of the phantom-limb phenomenon and segmental anaesthesia, Lacan stipulates that the imaginary anatomy follows its own laws of logic and is structured through networks of drive energy that are channelled along lines of cleavage. The result is a kind of selective coding of the shape of the body that regresses to a pre-specular existence when the body was not yet regulated or subject to any form of cohesion. For this reason, the imaginary anatomy is a function of "the body in bits and pieces" (Lacan, "Some Reflections" 13), a fact well illustrated when Joan admits that she can only deal with her body image if she conceptualizes it in segments: "I didn't usually look at my body, in a mirror or in any other way; I snuck glances at parts of it now and then, but the whole thing was too overwhelming" (*LO* 121).

The other interesting feature of Lacan's account of the psychical registration of the body is that "It all happens as if the body-image had an autonomous existence of its own" ("Some Reflections" 13). This autonomy of the body image that is freed from the constraints of biological and anatomical reality may be seen to manifest itself in Joan's inability to manage the images of herself that surface despite her best attempts at repressing them. The photograph of herself with Aunt Lou taken at the Canadian National Exhibition is a perfect example of the image over which she has no authority:

"Is that your mother?" Arthur asked once when I was unpacking it.

"No," I said, "that's my Aunt Lou."

"Who's the other one? The fat one."

For a moment I hesitated, on the verge of telling him the truth. "That's my other aunt," I said. "My Aunt Deidre. Aunt Lou was wonderful, but Aunt Deidre was a bitch." (91)

At this point, the only form of mastery open to Joan is to disown herself by naming her image to be someone she is not, an act that brings to the imaginary anatomy a discursive and significatory aspect, concomitant with the fact that ". . . I'd devised an entire spurious past for this shadow on a piece of paper . . ." (91). In Grosz's formulation of the imaginary anatomy, it is "a threshold term" that constitutes the body as signifiable through "an internalization of the corporeal schema of others" (*Jacques Lacan* 46). In the sense that the body image occupies the borderline positions of both Imaginary and Real, self and other, and nature and culture, one may extrapolate by inferring that through the coding of the imaginary anatomy, the body becomes both subject and object to and of itself. In this context, the photograph of Joan-cum-Aunt Deidre may be seen to illustrate the self entangled in a play of otherness, illustrated by the structure of her language, which, as Lacan notes, asserts the subject as an object involved in a relationship, and gives us a clue as to the function of the ego ("Some Reflections" 11).

Having momentarily lost the assumed singularity of the ego, Joan speaks in both the first and third person in what now becomes a dialogue between conflicting parts of herself, as she says to her husband "I didn't like her" (91), pointing to the photograph of herself. In light of this confusion as to whether the ego-identity is the subject or the object of the verb, it is not surprising that some time later Joan's signifying status seems to be in jeopardy, as she says "my voice would sound false, even to myself" (160). The imaginary anatomy, mediated as it is by interaction with the other, is, as Grosz points out, an effect of the particular meanings with which bodies have been endowed within the confines of the nuclear family (*Jacques Lacan* 46). Naturally, the primary caretaker is of prime importance in transmitting gestural and postural positioning; and so it seems logical to expect that Joan's relationship to her own body will be marked by the idiosyncrasies of her relationship with her mother. Kristeva also conceptualizes connections between the body and its surrounding objects through relationships of expenditure that are oriented toward familial structure. In her account, displaced and condensed drive energy is arranged according to the constraints externally imposed upon the body, and the maternal body functions as an ordering principle through which positionality may be inscribed. This inscription of the drives is the articulation of what Kristeva has called "the semiotic chora" (*Revolution* 25–30).

Kristeva makes clear that drives involve pre-oedipal functions and libidinal cathexes that connect and orient the body to the mother. At this point, the infantile body is functioning as the site of cycles of incorporation and expulsion, and "The oral and anal drives, both of which are oriented and structured around the mother's body, dominate this sensorimotor organization" (*Revolution* 27). Freud listed the oral phase as the first in a succession of developmental stages of preliminary organization the infant undergoes ("Anxiety" 131). At this time, energy is channelled in conformity with the way in which the infant is nourished, so that the erotogenic zone of the mouth dominates the libidinal activity of that period of life, which is characterized by the actions of suckling and feeding. Joan's compulsive eating habits are striking in their extremity and their repetitiveness, and if seen to be a displaced form of original oral activity, become evocative not only of pre-oedipal relations with the maternal but of the body as being both choric and driven.

There is little doubt that Joan's compulsive consumption of food re-creates for her a sense of security and containment in the face of change and uncertainty. She readily admits that "I needed something warm in my mouth, to make me feel safe . . ." (25). The sense that, for Joan, orality functions as an act of infantile regression is further heightened when it seems to preclude the formation of her specular identity. She herself tells us that as a baby she had been constantly made to gaze into the lens of a camera. It is significant that on these occasions it is her mother who takes the pictures. It is no less significant that, as Joan notes, ". . . I was never looking at the camera; instead I was trying to get something into my mouth: a toy, a hand, a bottle" (43).

Freud posited the scopophilic instinct as originally being auto-erotic, in that the object is the subject's own body ("Instincts"). Lacan also makes a direct connection between narcissism, the gaze, and the mirror-stage, noting that while the subject actively sees through one line of vision, he or she is simultaneously looked at from all sides, so that there is, in effect, a preexistence to the "seen" of a "given-to-be-seen" (*Four Fundamental* 74). If, then, the gaze is fundamental for the construction of the subject's specular identity, Joan's attempted interruption of it by instead engaging in a simulated act of oral incorporation may be seen to be endangering her own subjective stance. This is a strategy that is successful insofar as the adult Joan manages, as much as possible, to prevent the individualization of her identity through her obesity: ". . . I must've appeared as a huge featureless blur. If I'd ever robbed a bank no witness would have been able to describe me accurately" (82). Her blocking of an adult ego-identity by relying upon food raises the issue of the negative effects of the oral instinct. This reminds us of a point well made by Kristeva, that the " 'drives' are always already ambiguous," and that they are "simultaneously assimilating and destructive" (*Revolution* 27). The potentially disruptive effect of the pre-oedipal oral instinct similarly points to a kind of choric ambiguity, whereby this particular modality both assimilates and destroys subjectivity. As Kristeva states, "the semiotic *chora* is no more than the place where the subject is both generated and negated" (28).

Choric ambiguity in its connection with the oral drive may be conceptualized in a number of ways. In its generative stance, orality is reminiscent of the act of feeding, whereby nutrition becomes the aim through which object relations are organized. Thus, apart from supplying bodily support in answer to biological needs, eating signals the subject's mastery over the object that is incorporated and assimilated by the individual. Furthermore, oral incorporation as a form of infantile regression or return of the repressed works at the level of fantasy. This becomes significant given the work of Laplanche and Pontalis, who redefine the emergence of subjectivity as the first manifestation of desire, and the moment at which fantasy detaches libidinal energy from the fulfilment of need.[11] Lastly, the cycles of union and separation from the maternal body effected through feeding open a kind of space that, while not in itself signifiable, paves the way for the later inscription of signs. Movements of expenditure, of excitation and discharge, and general fluctuations in drive energy mark what Kristeva has termed "discontinuities" in the material supports (voice, gesture, colours) surrounding the infant (*Revolution* 28). Vocal or kinetic rhythms then connect with the rupture and, depending upon similarity or difference, begin to function according to the principles of metaphor or metonymy. While Kristeva emphasizes that the chora is not yet a position that represents something for someone, it is, however, a necessary stage if the subject is to attain a signifying position. For this reason, she says of the chora that it is possible to specify "the *semiotic* as a psychosomatic modality of the signifying process" (28), and "the process by which signifiance is constituted" (26).

If, then, the chora precedes figuration by initiating the process through which libidinal energies may be later directed into representative and signifying practices, by definition it also paves the way for specularization, positionality, and subjectivity. This generative aspect of choric orality may be seen to be illustrated by Joan's attempts at constituting a sense of self through eating. She openly states that food allowed her to try to become "solid, solid as a stone," and that ". . . I also ate from panic. Sometimes I was afraid I wasn't really there . . ." (78). Similarly, when her mother tries to convince her to buy clothes that make her "less conspicuous," Joan's response is to make a spectacle of herself: "Instead I sought out clothes of a peculiar and offensive hideousness, violently coloured, horizontally striped" (87). In this, she may be seen to be consciously constructing herself as object of the gaze: "The brighter the colors, the more rotund the effect, the more certain I was to buy" (88). And it is no surprise to hear that the desired effect is for her to be seen so that she can exist: "I wasn't going to let myself be diminished, neutralized, by a navy-blue polka-dot sack" (88).

The choric space is, however, one that has a distinctly ambivalent relationship with subjectivity. In the words of Kristeva, the subjective stance "moves with and against the chora" (*Revolution* 26) in a simultaneous dependence upon and refusal of it. The most complicated aspect of the negatory chora, and the aspect most ardently illustrated in *Lady Oracle*, is the problematic relationship between the self and the mother, heightened in the case of Joan by its expression through oral fixation. The oral instinct, from its earliest formulation, has been seen to be marked by an incontestable ambivalence. Freud conceived of this as being structured according to two subdivisions within the oral phase. In the first substage, incorporation is the aim, and hence there is no ambivalence toward the object, which in this case is the mother's breast. In the second stage, however, activity is characterized by biting, a behaviour that exhibits for the first time an ambivalence toward the mother, and leads Freud to name this stage as being the "oral-sadistic" one ("Anxiety" 132).

If we accept, as Freud did, that the libidinal activity of little girls in relation to the mother is manifested in oral and sadistic impulses directed toward her ("Female Sexuality" 385), we are led to interpret Joan's behaviour in light of the thoroughly problematic nature of her relationship with Mrs. Foster. For Freud, the confused and contradictory impulses the daughter feels often take the specific form of a fear of being killed by the mother, a fear that, in turn, justifies her own death wish against her mother (385). This blend of fear and aggression is evident in Mrs. Foster's supposed stabbing of Joan: "She looked at me with an expression of rage, which changed quickly to fear. . . . Then she took a paring knife from the kitchen counter

. . . and stuck it into my arm. . . . It went through my sweater, pricked the flesh, then bounced out and fell to the floor" (124). Here, what we suspect to be unconscious animosity on the part of Mrs. Foster is confused with Joan's own reconstruction of the event as being nothing less than a death threat: "'She tried to kill me,' I said. 'Did she tell you that?' I was exaggerating, as the knife hadn't gone in very far. . . .' She stuck a knife in my arm.' I rolled up my sleeve to show him the scratch" (138).

While for Freud the fear of the mother is very often supported by an unconscious hostility on the mother's part that is sensed by the girl ("Female Sexuality" 385), he also stresses that the daughter's libidinal relations to the mother "are completely ambivalent, both affectionate and of a hostile and aggressive nature" ("Femininity" 153). Joan's own unconscious aggression toward her mother may be seen to be imaged in her momentary admission that she is in some indefinable way responsible for the conflict. She places her left hand over the wound "as if I myself had inflicted it" (124); she also proffers a confession that may be seen to foreshadow her guilt when, some years later, her mother dies: "I had left her, walked out on her, even though I was aware that she was unhappy. . . . I had closed the door on her at the very moment of her death. . . . I felt as if I'd killed her myself . . ." (177).

The ambivalence of Joan's relationship with Mrs. Foster, expressed as it is through the desires and realities of death, supports the idea that the ordering of the maternal libido reaches its apotheosis when centred in the theme of death (Kristeva, "Stabat Mater" 175). It further sheds light upon Joan's eventual construction of her own (albeit fictional) death, which, placed in the context of the choric space, may be seen to support Kristeva's contention that "it is ultimately the death drive, most 'instinctual' of the drives, that predominates within the semiotic disposition" (Silverman 103). In considering the nature of the little girl's libidinal relationship with the mother, Freud maintained that the impulses persist through all three phases of infantile sexuality and hence take on the characteristics of anal and phallic as well as oral desires ("Femininity" 153). For Freud, sadistic impulses toward the mother may indeed have their origin in the initial oral phase of development; however, they culminate some time after in the following phase known as the anal-sadistic one ("Anxiety" 132). Eventually, Joan subjects herself to alarming fits of bulimic overeating followed by severe bouts of vomiting. This evocation of the object relationship as being one mediated through processes of expulsion and retention may be seen to function as a direct expression of the anal-aggressive drive. As such, it bespeaks the point that Kristeva makes clearly: that the chora, in its role as physiological and psychosomatic organization of the body, is oriented toward the maternal body through the anal as well as the oral drive (*Revolution* 27).

Mrs. Foster seems to consider her daughter as needing to enter "a laxative phase" (86): "Like most people, she probably thought in images, and her image of me then must have been a one-holed object, like an inner tube, that took things in at one end but didn't let them out at the other: if she could somehow uncork me I would deflate, all at once, like a dirigible" (87). Consequently, she takes drastic measures to push Joan into a dynamic of anal expulsion: "She started to buy patent medicines, disguising her attempts to get me to take them . . . and occasionally slipping them into the food. Once she even iced a chocolate cake with melted Ex-Lax, leaving it on the kitchen counter where I found and devoured it" (87). Freud characterized the anal phase of infantile sexuality as developing with the strengthening of the infant's muscular apparatus ("Anxiety" 131). Implicit, then, is the issue of control, and, given Mrs. Foster's intervention, the conflicting desires of mother and daughter. For Kristeva, anal loss plays an important role in the choric relationship between mother and infant, and in the fixation and sublimation that launches the child into space and subsequent subjectivity ("Place Names" 284). The waste object becomes a "cadaverous" one ("Father" 392), "the fallen and thus the finally possible object" (391) that allows the infant true interaction with the outside world.

If, then, anal expulsion signifies maternal separation as well as a developing mastery over the self, Joan's relations of aggression, be they oral or anal, are really to do with her place in connection with the maternal. It is by now well acknowledged within psychoanalytic thought that there exists a specifically problematic relationship between mother and daughter, due not only to biological needs and anaclitic[12] demands but to the entire matrix of libidinal expenditure, filtered as it is through familial structures. In the context of the oedipal drama, Freud noted the necessity for the daughter's separation from the mother: "The turning-away from her mother is an extremely important step in the course of a little girl's development" ("Female Sexuality" 387). However, even he did not at first suspect how complicated this could become: "We knew, of course, that there had been a preliminary stage of attachment to the mother, but we did not know that it could be so rich in content and so long-lasting, and could leave behind so many opportunities for fixations and dispositions" ("Femininity" 153).

The issue is symbiosis in the face of imminent and necessary separation. Kaja Silverman clearly reiterates the psychoanalytic model when she speaks of the necessity of post-oedipal phallic intervention: "This adhesion of mother to child completely blocks the latter's access to alterity, which now awaits the intervention of the paternal third term" (116). With a greater emphasis upon socialization, Nancy Chodorow claims that the girl never gives up her pre-oedipal relationship with the mother. In her account, while the daughter erotically cathects toward the father, the primary emotional relationship remains always with the mother. In fact, the little girl does not turn away from the mother but merely includes the father in her primary object world.[13] This means that women's subjectivity retains pre-oedipal characteristics, a situation that Irigaray poetically and metaphorically images in her piece "And the One Doesn't Stir without the Other." Here she describes mother and daughter locked in stifling symbiosis, exchanging identities in a play of selves, and reflecting each other in mirrors of specularization. Mutual dependence means that self and other are confused, a dynamic that Mary Anne Doane also describes, saying: "the female subject has more difficulty in freeing herself from the narcissistic dyad. It is thus more strongly true in the case of the woman that she never quite attains the status of subject, never quite leaves the shadow of nondifferentiation associated with the maternal space" (*Desire* 146–47).

It is indisputable that Joan's relationship with Mrs. Foster plagues her continually, as she freely acknowledges that "All this time I carried my mother around my neck like a rotting albatross" (213). Guilt at having left home surfaces repeatedly — "Had I been wrong to take my life in my own hands and walk out the door?" (180) — and this culminates in Joan regarding herself as responsible in some way for her mother's death, because "I had left her, walked out on her" (177). Joan is continually caught between wanting to assert her own needs and fulfilling the desires and demands of her mother. Nowhere is this more evident than in the dream in which Mrs. Foster appears. Having woken up in the middle of the night and heard footsteps outside her window, Joan approaches the terrace only to find her mother is visiting:

"What do you want?" I said, but she didn't answer. She stretched out her arms to me, she wanted me to come with her; she wanted us to be together.

I began to walk towards the door. She was smiling at me now, with her smudged face, could she see I loved her? I loved her but the glass was between us, I would have to go through it. I longed to console her. Together we would go down the corridor into the darkness. I would do what she wanted. (329)

While reunion with the maternal seems inviting and alluring, it is a search for approval that comes perilously close to endangering Joan's own subjective stance. Indeed, Joan seems to hint at danger at the hands of her mother, saying, "She'd come very close that time, she'd almost done it" (329). This sense of peril has previously been implied by Joan's tendency to slide into a trance-like state reminiscent of psychotic loss of self when facing the mirror or the memory of her mother. The entanglement of mother and daughter is brought to the fore when Joan comes to the realization that her mother has in fact been at the base of every image, dream, or fantasy that has haunted her to date: "It had been she standing behind me in the mirror, she was the one who was waiting around each turn, her voice whispered the words. She had been the lady in the boat, the death barge, the tragic lady with flowing hair and stricken eyes, the lady in the tower" (329–30). Finally, the interdependence in their relationship is acknowledged — "She'd never really let go of me because I had never let her go" (329) — as is the dilemma of separation in the face of symbiosis: "How could I renounce her? She needed her freedom also; she had been my reflection too long. What was the charm, what would set her free?" (330).

The subjective stance of the daughter compromised through the demands of the mother is well illustrated in Joan's sentient nature, which attests to an endangered sense of self and is contextualized within a kind of splitting: ". . . I was a sponge, I drank it all in but gave nothing out, despite the temptation to tell everything, all my hatred and jealousy, to reveal myself as the duplicitous monster I knew myself to be" (95). This bespeaks a kind of transitivism through which the boundaries that normally contain the individual become permeable and there is a confusion of self with other. For Lacan, every person undergoes a period of "normal transitivism" usually coincident with the mirror-phase, which has as its base an identification with alterity.[14] Joan's admission that she had made somewhat of a career out of being sensitive to others through "cultivated listening" (42) culminates in the "sloppy" (92) way with which she relates to others. Freely admitting that she felt unable to resist giving money to the Salvation Army at Christmas, to legless men on street corners, to children fibbing about lost bus fare, and to Hare Krishnas on Yonge Street, she considers her sympathetic tendencies: "I empathized with anything in pain; cats hit by cars, old women who fell on icy sidewalks, . . . aldermen who wept on television when they lost an election" (92). While compassion may be a virtue, the lack of containment evident here may signal in Joan what Lacan has posited as being in the transitivistic subject a "state of ambiguity . . . in so far as his ego is actually alienated from itself in the other person" ("Some Reflections" 16). Certainly, a conflict of interests is evident as Joan stifles her own call for recognition: "behind my compassionate smile was a set of tightly clenched teeth, and behind that a legion of voices, crying *What about me? What about my own pain? When is it my turn?*" (92).

This ego displaced and disowned from the self through over-identification with the other is brought to the fore when we realise that Mrs. Foster had named her daughter after Joan Crawford. However, rather than providing an influential role model, the association is little more than baffling: "Did she name me after Joan Crawford because she wanted me to be like the screen characters she played — beautiful, ambitious, ruthless, destructive to men — or because she wanted me to be successful?" (42). The confusion is further heightened by the deferral of the demonstrative evident within a name that has evidently been discursively and consciously constructed: "Come to think of it, Joan Crawford didn't have a name of her own either. Her real name was Lucille LeSueur . . ." (42). The metonymic displacement of identity through naming surfaces some time later when she begins to refer to herself not only through her given name of Foster but as Joan, Elizabeth, Louisa, and Deidre Delacourt. This inability to define herself through singular self-reference is perhaps due to the confusion inherent within her mother's initial choice: "Did she give me someone else's name because she wanted me never to have a name of my own?" (42). If so, it opens the question of Mrs. Foster's responsibility for the formation of her daughter's troubled identity. Certainly, there seem to have been incidents in which Mrs. Foster actively inspired Joan's search for the self through specularization: "she must once have treated me as a child, though I could remember only glimpses, being held up by her to look at myself in the triple mirror when she'd brushed my hair" (180). However, these seem few and far between, and overshadowed by a continual sense of disapproval that repudiates the very person Joan is: "I didn't help my mother. I wasn't allowed to. On the few occasions I'd attempted it, the results had not pleased her. The only way I could have helped her to her satisfaction would have been to change into someone else . . ." (55). It seems, then, that Mrs. Foster is instrumental in Joan's identification of herself — " 'Who do you think you are?' my mother used to ask me" — yet she is also involved in the negation of it — "but she would never wait for an answer" (224).

The contradictory nature of Mrs. Foster's demands may reflect as much upon her own troubled identity as it does upon Joan's. There is no doubt that she feels a sense of frustration at her inability to see herself properly reflected. We are told that it was "as if she saw behind or within the mirror some fleeting image she was unable to capture or duplicate; and when she was finished she was always a little cross" (66). Pictures of Mrs. Foster are associated with the triple mirror in her bedroom (66), which either unhinges her reflection or divides it into a trinity of images. This serves to highlight the artificial nature of her reflection, something further emphasized by her conscious attempts at constructing an image for herself: " 'Sit there quietly, Joan, and watch Mother put on her face,' she'd say on the good days. Then she would tuck a towel around her neck and go to work" (66).

While cosmetic adornment is a fairly standard feminine practice, it functions to construct the imitation of an appearance. As such, it is a mimetic strategy in the representation of the self that involves the displacement of identity, a reproduction that evokes an elsewhere (Irigaray, *This Sex* 76). As Joan later states, "she was not what she seemed" (180). For Lacan, disguise and masquerade are the effects of a mimesis that is, first, connected to the gaze (*Four Fundamental* 73), and second, intended for a sexual aim (100). Both these dynamics are evident in the association of Mrs. Foster's application of a cosmetic self with her photograph album, where "there were snapshots of her in party dresses and bathing suits, with various young men, her looking at the camera, the young men looking at her" (68). The fact that Mrs. Foster feels the war to be an absence of male influence and a time when there was "nobody to take pictures of her" (68) implicates masculine desire within a mimicry that is no less than the inscription of the self in the image. In fact, her behaviour makes her reminiscent of female movie stars who have been almost totally constructed through the gaze of the lens, and for whom acting and identity merge dangerously: "Her lips were thin but she made a larger mouth with lipstick over and around them, like Bette Davis, which gave her a curious double mouth, the real one showing through the false one like a shadow" (68).

For Kristeva, mimesis is a signifying act in that it is the construction of an object at the hands of the drive economy of enunciation.[15] As a representative strategy, mimesis does not disavow signification but goes through its supposed truth to reveal the Real that it is imitating. It is thus noteworthy that Mrs. Foster's lipstick, while positing a second set of lips, does not obliterate her real mouth, but instead reveals and indirectly highlights it. Furthermore, mimesis posits both a signifying and signified object, and it pluralizes denotation by confronting verisimilitude with truth. Both these processes may be seen to be metaphorically represented here by the two mouths, which, functioning as two posited objects of denotation and/or a signifier and signified, serve also to imply displaced, possibly multiple voices of enunciation.

Joan's sacrilegious, albeit unintentional, response to the "privilege" (65) of being allowed to watch her mother at work with makeup is to be totally fascinated as well as thoroughly subversive. She rummages around in her mother's drawers, consumes a lipstick, finds a contraceptive device, and ultimately parodies the whole process when ". . . I couldn't resist covering my entire face with blue eye shadow, to see how I would look blue" (66). Joan is duly punished for what is taken to be a transgression of social decorum. In this, what becomes clear is not only Mrs. Foster's investment in her own methods of disguise and masquerade, but the investment the mimetic construction of self has in the maintenance of the social contract. If makeup is seen to be the response of a femininity dutiful to the demands of society,[16] and mimesis can be seen to posit the very grammaticality of the symbolic order (Kristeva, *Revolution* 57–61), Mrs. Foster is engaged in a dynamic that protects not only her sense of self but the very structure of society. In this sense, Joan's mother is functioning in her role as "structure stabilizer," or what Kristeva has called the "ultimate guarantee of society, without which society will not reproduce and will not maintain a constancy of standardized household" ("Stabat Mater" 183).

Without a doubt, Mrs. Foster had felt impelled to do what was socially expected of her. We are told that she had "done the right thing, she had devoted her life to us, she had made her family her career as she had been told to do" (178). She craves decorum and propriety and above all wants to conform: "My mother didn't want her living rooms to be different from everybody else's, or even very much better. She wanted them to be acceptable, the same as everybody else's . . ." (70). However, try as she might to construct a socially acceptable indistinct home life, her living rooms did end up having "distinct and separate personalities" (176), much like herself. If Miss Fleg's ballet classes are taken as being organized cultural activity representative of social regulation, then Mrs. Foster's "having trouble with the costumes," and the fact that "She'd followed the instructions, but she couldn't get them to look right" (45), become indicative of an underlying inability to completely conform. At this point, we touch upon the paradoxical nature of motherhood: the fact that while the maternal principle reproduces society, it simultaneously functions as a breach in the very order it condones. For Kristeva, this is a consequence of the "nonsymbolic, nonpaternal causality," the corporeal realities of pregnancy, according to which the maternal body has a compulsion to divide and perpetuate in accordance with predetermined biological cycles of life and death ("Motherhood" 239). This aspect of maternity, while emptying the maternal position of any subjective value, also creates a state of distinctly feminine symbiosis, described by Kristeva as being "the homosexual facet of motherhood" (239). Here the mother now comes into contact with her own mother by experiencing a return to her previously repressed body through the corporeal experience of childbirth. As Kristeva explains, "By giving birth, the woman enters into contact with her mother; she becomes, she is her own mother; they are the same continuity differentiating itself" (239).

Joan seems to be aware of this return of the infant to the mother when she points out that "I wanted children, but what if I had a child who would turn out like me?" (213). More threatening still is her own projected return to Mrs. Foster: "Even worse, what if I turned out to be like my mother?" (213). In Kristeva's account, maternity is a locus or function without subjective identity or agency. Pregnancy risks placing the mother into a regressive foreclosure of signifying capacities ("Maternal Body"), resulting in a kind of verbal scarcity through which "The maternal body slips away from the discursive hold . . ." ("Motherhood" 241). Not only has the maternal body a special relationship with the unspoken,[17] but the homosexual facet is the means "through which a woman is simultaneously

97

closer to her instinctual memory, more open to her own psychosis, and consequently, more negatory of the social, symbolic bond" (239). This makes the act of childbirth a form of split symbolization, and places the mother on the threshold between the conscious and the unconscious, and the semiotic and symbolic.

Nowhere are these dynamics of division more evident than in Mrs. Foster's visitations. Three times she appears dressed in a navy blue suit, clutching her purse, her face made up with the two mouths showing through, but "crying soundlessly, horribly, mascara . . . running from her eyes in black tears" (173). These ghostly incarnations may be interpreted as being signifiers that are displaced and condensed so that they have the ubiquitous status of a psychopathological symptom. In this sense, the sightings and visitations may be seen to be the direct expression of a process Kristeva has described: "The Mother and her attributes . . . become representatives of a 'return of the repressed.' . . . They re-establish what is non-verbal and show up as the receptacle of a signifying disposition that is closer to so-called primary processes" ("Stabat Mater" 174).

Mrs. Foster's expression of the maternal principle and Joan's experience of it in this form alludes to the fact that past the oedipal point of entry into the symbolic, the choric configuration of the mother-infant relationship remains beyond conventional modes of representation. As an expression of choric ambiguity, these incidents evidence what Kristeva has called "a 'semiotics' that linguistic communication does not account for" ("Stabat Mater" 174). Seeing these episodes as psychopathological symptoms means placing the maternal principle on the cleavage between the symbolic order of signification and the semiotic realm of the chora. For this reason, we may assert, as Kristeva does, that the maternal body mediates both social figuration and choric nondifferentiation (*Revolution* 27), and is the place of a splitting that remains a constant factor of social reality ("Motherhood" 238).

These symptoms of a divided and discordant subjective existence may be viewed in a number of ways. First, they may be seen as a kind of temporary lapse into psychosis on the part of Joan. In this case, the sightings become the result of a momentary expulsion of the phallic third term from her symbolic ordering with the result that certain signifiers unhinge themselves from their position of primal repression within the unconscious and return, from the outside and located in the Real, in the form of hallucinatory episodes. On the other hand, the supposed manifestations of Mrs. Foster's spiritual aura may be seen to be indicative of her own inability to retain a distinct form and unitary cohesion in the face of symbolic demands and constraints, while located within the matrix of maternity and, as Irigaray puts it, "trapped in a single function — mothering" ("And the One" 66). But deliberating whether these symbolic disturbances are to be seen as Joan's foreclosure in the face of a return of the repressed, or as her mother's transgression of symbolic ordering, is, perhaps, immaterial given the overdetermined nature of semiotic eruptions and the function of the chora as pertaining not solely to the mother or to the infant but as a site, as yet unpositioned, that slides back and forth between the two, generated by anaclitic interdependence and unmediated interaction.

With this formulation of the chora as predetermining of site and position, it becomes not only a realm of need and response but the subject's earliest negotiation and comprehension of space. In this account,[18] the chora is itself a kind of prelinguistic, presubjective space that the mother and child share, as well as being the relationship with the maternal that allows for spatial positioning. In the anaclitic relationship, the mother is able to anchor herself in the child's calls for support. Meanwhile, through the provisional dynamic of the given and withdrawn breast, she provides for the infant an axis or screen for projection. Through the corporeal realities of the maternal body — the breast, the skin, light — the infant can cognitively perceive discontinuity and hence fix an audible or visual point, a place.

Contextualized thus, in the light of the chora as the earliest territorialization of the subject, Mrs. Foster's visitations, otherwise seen as expressions of the maternal-infant connection, may also be seen to simulate a play of spatiality. This aspect first surfaces in Joan's conversations with the spiritualist Leda Sprott. Here she is told of the existence of the astral body that floats around by itself attached to you by way of something like a long rubber band. Danger lay in the fact that one's astral body could defy the corporeal one, and the two could become permanently separated from each other. Then, asks Leda, "where would you be? A vegetable, that's what. . . . Like those cases you read about, in the hospital" (111). Inadequate connection of the psyche with the body seems to run the risk of loss not only of cognitive awareness but of conscious identity. When Mrs. Foster "appears" during a Jordan Chapel ceremony, Leda Sprott implies that for someone not yet dead, astral travel is not a healthy sign: "That happens sometimes, but we don't encourage it; it confuses things, and the reception isn't always good" (111). It seems to be some kind of inability to retain singular form that leads Joan to think of her mother "in the form of some kind of spiritual jello, drifting around after me from place to place, wearing (apparently) her navy-blue suit from 1949" (111).

Mrs. Foster's incapacity to stay within the confines of her own skin may be seen to be evidence of a spatial fragmentation that exists in direct contrast to her conscious desire to be contained and "flint-eyed, distinct, never wavery or moist" (57). If the chora is taken as being an enclosure that figures the unity and nondifferentiation between mother and child,[19] the visitations immediately become the expression of a troubled and symbiotic relationship between Joan and her mother. Eventually, the astral projections are directly placed within the context of their stifling relationship, which is characterized by potential danger to Mrs. Foster, and a sense of frustration on the part of Joan: "How had she found me? . . . It was her astral body. . . . Why couldn't she keep the goddamned thing at home where it belonged? I pictured my mother floating over the Atlantic Ocean, her rubber band getting thinner and thinner the farther it was stretched; she'd better be careful or she'd break that thing and then she'd be with me forever . . ." (173).

Thus, the final visitation openly speaks of the compromised specular identity and an obvious need to separate: "she had been my reflection too long" (330). In light of this, Irigaray's description of the paralysis and potential imprisonment of maternal symbiosis becomes apt. Here the daughter accuses the mother of "Wandering without identity, discharging upon me this endless, and at each step excruciating, wandering of yours" ("And the One" 66), in much the same way as Mrs. Foster haunts Joan across countries and years. Similarly, the visitations characterize choric space in much the same way as Kristeva describes it, when she sees maternal space as being "fascinating, attracting, and puzzling," but something to which we have no direct access because it is "beyond discourse, beyond narrative, beyond psychology, beyond lived experience and biography — in short, beyond figuration" ("Motherhood" 247).

While the dreams and sightings function as psychopathological symptoms illustrative of an enveloping of mother and infant within spatial enclosure, they also shed light upon choric spatial fixation. In the most traumatic of Joan's dreams, she has lost the maternal body as the point around which she can orient herself: "In the worst dream I couldn't see her at all. I would be hiding behind a door, or standing in front of one, it wasn't clear which . . . perhaps a cup-board. I'd been locked in, or out, but on the other side of the door I could hear voices" (214). Her uncertainty as to her location relative to both the objects in the external world and the voices of significa-tion reminds us that subjectivity is a matter only of spatial variation and displacement rather than any actual closure.[20] The role that voices play in her orienting of herself is noteworthy given that choric spatial fixation is what initially allows for vocalization.[21] In this context, Joan's sense of anxiety may be seen to be reminiscent of the infant's anaclitic invocation: "Sometimes there were a lot of voices, sometimes only two; they were talking about me, discussing me, and as I listened I would realize that something very bad was going to happen. I felt helpless, there was nothing I could do" (214).

In the dream, Mrs. Foster is not in sight, nor is she available. This may be seen to represent the positing of maternal absence in response to infantile distress. Further to this, the existence of another's voice effects intervention by a third term into what has previously been a dyadic mother-infant relationship. In the psychoanalytic account, this would enable the holophrastic utterances of anaclitic distress to progress developmentally toward the acquisition of language, which in turn would lead to eventual assumption of an enunciative position. It is fitting, then, that Joan's response to this opening of difference is to fortify her contact with the external world: "In the dream I would back into the farthest corner of the cubicle and wedge myself in, press my arms against the walls, dig my heels against the floor" (214).

This anchoring of herself is an attempt at spatial definition. However, like all else that characterizes the chora, this negotiation of territory is far from simple or straightforward. When Mrs. Foster comes to "visit" her daughter who is now living in England, her function as a point of orientation around which Joan can formulate a perspectival relationship with the world is shown to be rife with ambiguity: "Through her back I could see the dilapidated sofa; it looked as though the stuffing was coming out of her" (173). Mrs. Foster's apparent merging with the furniture points toward a state of interrelation between the self and objects in the external world; and through the blurring of boundaries, they are seen to be mutually constitutive. This lack of demarcation creates an alarming sense of panic in Joan: "The hair on the back of my neck bristled, and I leapt back through the front door, shut it behind me, and leaned against it" (173). She immediately turns to her own external world and, in an attempt to gain control over it, begins frantically to relocate the

furniture. However, this is not enough to repress the spatial indis-
tinctness with which her mother has now threatened her: "I wasn't
sure that rearranging the furniture would keep her out" (174).

With the maternal body as stable support for marking space, the
chora, in its function as the inauguration of spatial positioning,
brings to the infant a new awareness of the body. For now the child's
body, previously polymorphous perverse, is coded, parcelled into
erotogenic zones through drive activity. Drive activity marks an
initial positioning of the infant's body by inscribing energy through
physiological and neurological networks. However, the objects of
this newly regulated body are essentially oral (Kristeva, "Place
Names" 283), so that orality, more than any other channelled
libidinal activity, plays an essential role in the primary fixation of
the subject within the choric space (284). This being the case, it is
significant that eventually Joan feels compelled to lose weight. Her
initial decision to stop eating occurs in the face of a kind of
mirror-awakening: "One day . . . I happened to glance down at my
body. . . . I didn't usually look at my body, in a mirror or in any other
way. . . . It was enormous, it was gross. . . . [A]nd then I thought,
This can't possibly go on" (121). However, what is even more
striking is the fact that she immediately involves her mother: ". . . I
told my mother I was going to reduce" (121). This is sure indication
that at least some of the emotional and psychic energy of her
relationship with her mother has been invested in Joan's relationship
not only with her own body but with food. This, of course, comes
as no great surprise, as some time before, she had named her body
as being the site of a kind of struggle between herself and Mrs. Foster:
". . . I was eating steadily, doggedly, stubbornly, anything I could get.
The war between myself and my mother was on in earnest; the
disputed territory was my body" (69).

Joan's ultimate protection takes the form of obesity: "I ate to defy
her. . . . [S]o she wouldn't be able to get rid of me" (78). A contest
of wills now characterizes their relationship: ". . . I reacted to the
diet booklets she left on my pillow, to the bribes of dresses she would
give me if I would reduce to fit them . . . to her cutting remarks about
my size, to her pleas about my health . . ." (69–70). And on the
surface, Joan appears to be winning: "I swelled visibly, relentlessly,
before her very eyes, I rose like dough, my body advanced inch by
inch toward her across the dining-room table, in this at least I was
undefeated" (70).

It is, of course, only with regard to her mother that Joan derives any sense of satisfaction from overeating; any imaging of herself in the eyes of others makes her feel decidedly uncomfortable: "strangers were different, they saw my obesity as an unfortunate handicap, like a hump or a club foot, rather than the refutation, the victory it was, and watching myself reflected in their eyes shook my confidence. It was only in relation to my mother that I derived a morose pleasure from my weight; in relation to everyone else, including my father, it made me miserable" (74).

Still, despite her own feelings of inadequacy, Joan acknowledges her wilful obesity to be exactly what it is: a show of her own strength. Spoiling her mother's dreams of victory, she arrives home one day in a new lime green outfit chosen to emphasize her one-hundred-and-eighty-two-pound body. At this point, at least, Joan comes out victorious: "She cried hopelessly, passively; she was leaning against the banister, her whole body slack as if she had no bones. My mother had never cried where I could see her and I was dismayed, but elated too at this evidence of my power, my only power. I had defeated her: I wouldn't ever let her make me over in her image, thin and beautiful" (88).

Mrs. Foster's response to Joan's decision to diet is unpredictably contrary. After years of trying to induce weight loss in her daughter, Mrs. Foster now begins to vacillate between irrational denial of her daughter's dieting and fear and anger of it. At first, she is "gratified" in her inimitably begrudging fashion, saying: "Well, it's about time, but it's probably too late" (123). However, eventually she begins to threaten her daughter with the fear of malnutrition, and, obviously alarmed by Joan's anorexic behaviour, goes on baking sprees, leaving pies and cookies lying around the house. She vacillates from fear to fury: "At times she would almost plead with me to stop taking the pills, to take better care of myself; then she would have spasms of rage . . ." (123). Joan admits that she should have been delighted by her mother's distress, but is instead confused by the inconsistency of response. She is able to acknowledge that her mother was grappling with an unnameable anxiety: "I'd really believed that if I became thinner she would be pleased. . . . Instead she was frantic. . . . While I grew thinner, she herself became distraught and uncertain" (123). Finally, all semblance of propriety and social decorum is abandoned when Mrs. Foster deteriorates into a conventional picture of frustrated domesticity. Dressed in a pink dressing gown and furry slippers, sipping scotch early in the morning, her mood swings become unpredictable, and she slides into irrationality.

Joan's explanation for her mother's erratic behaviour is to suspect that having now lost "her last available project" (123), Mrs. Foster is left with nothing to do. However, her rising sense of panic is surely an expression of the melancholy that any mother naturally feels when her child detaches from her and begins to take on a conscious identity of its own.[22] With this, it becomes undeniable that the battle for Joan's body has been a struggle of separation in the face of maternal symbiosis, a dynamic that Grosz alludes to when she writes: "In refusing food, I refuse others, my mother in particular . . ." ("Language" 111). Grosz contextualizes the attempt at detachment from the maternal in Kristeva's concept of abjection. This involves the maternal space in the attempt to define a clearly demarcated and contained body, without which no subjective position may be assumed. In Grosz's formulation,[23] the construction of subjectivity is dependent upon a structuring of the infant's body and a differentiation from the maternal space, both of which are connected to bodily processes, erotogenic zones, and libidinal drives. It is the construction of a controlled and controllable body that is essential, and this is achieved through processes of expulsion. Given that Grosz characterizes abjection as being paradoxical but necessary attempts at self-definition that are inextricably connected with bodily cycles of incorporation, depletion, and loss, Joan's problematic relationship with food may be clearly imaged as an expression of abjection.

Conventional responses to abjection reveal what Grosz has elsewhere called a "body in revolt" ("Body" 89). Certainly, Joan seems to exhibit the recoiling from the flesh that normally characterizes an abjected response. She regards her own thigh with disgust: "it was gross, it was like a diseased limb . . . it spread on forever, like a prairie photographed from a plane, the flesh not green but bluish white, with veins meandering across it like rivers" (121); her reaction also has social implications: "The sight of a fat person on the street . . . I now found revolting" (122). Furthermore, she develops "some spectacular side effects" (122) in the form of fits of weakness, dizzy spells, blinding headaches, stomach cramps, and an accelerated heart rate. And given that "The abject, instead of securing and stabilising the subject, signals its fading, or potential disappearance . . ." (Grosz, "Language" 109), it is noteworthy that in Joan's case there is a literal fading away of the self as she sheds weight and the pounds of flesh disappear.

The abject, then, inhabits the space of the death drive. As such, it is also to do with relations of symbiosis between mother and child, is indisputably on the side of the semiotic chora, and is the space of struggle against the maternal.[24] Given this, it is significant that as a consequence of her dieting, "The world, which I'd seen for so long as a blur, with the huge but ill-defined figure of my mother blocking the foreground, came sharply into focus" (122). Indeed, very much earlier Joan had admitted that her mother's influence had dominated her organization of space: "for years I'd needed to have the main objects in my room arranged in the proper relationship to each other, because of my mother" (18). Now, however, her mother will no longer be able to block her relations with objects in the external world. Even more striking, however, is the fact that Joan's weight loss is directly responsible for her entry into the sexual arena: "Strange men, whose gaze had previously slid over and around me as though I wasn't there, began to look at me from truck-cab windows and construction sites; a speculative look, like a dog eyeing a fire hydrant" (123). She now becomes a potential object of desire, an experience previously unknown to her, in a movement that threatens to take her even further away from the maternal. This is, of course, the ultimate separation: a play of post-oedipal sexual desire.

Within the psychoanalytic account, the normal resolution of the girl's oedipal complex is the turning of her own desire first to her father, and then outward and onward to other men. This effects an interruption of the mother-infant dyad by way of the gaze of desire, and allows the subject to be externalized by becoming the object of the other's look. This desire of and for the other is illustrated in Joan's dance in front of the mirror, which connects the feminine stance, masculine desire, and specularization in an exchange of looks:

> . . . I would close the bedroom door, drape myself in silk or velvet, and get out all the dangly gold earrings and chains and bracelets I could find. I would dab myself with perfume, take off my shoes, and dance in front of the mirror, twirling slowly around, waltzing with an invisible partner. A tall man in evening dress, with an opera cloak and smoldering eyes. As he swept me in circles . . . he would whisper, "Let me take you away. We will dance together always." (23)

While Joan finds this imaginary interlude "a great temptation" (23), we begin to suspect that she finds dealing with masculine desire fraught with difficulty. To begin with, she feels decidedly dislocated from herself: ". . . I wasn't ready yet, I wasn't adjusted. I'd spent all my life learning to be one person and now I was a different one" (144). And she craves the time when she was not caught in the dynamics of desire: ". . . I also longed to be fat again. It would be an insulation, a cocoon. Also it would be a disguise. I could be merely an onlooker again, with nothing too much expected of me. Without my magic cloak of blubber and invisibility I felt naked, pruned, as though some essential covering was missing" (141).

Her fear of exposure echoes the fact that through interaction with men her sense of self will be threatened. In her own words, "I was suffering again from self-doubt" (259), "I was a nervous wreck" (251), "I was . . . hollow, a hoax, a delusion" (251). This insecurity is heightened by the fact that her love affairs actively divide her life into segments. When she is with her husband, her affair with the Royal Porcupine seems nothing more than a dream. But when she is with her lover, it is Arthur who seems unreal: "The difficulty was that I found each of my lives perfectly normal and appropriate, but only at the time" (259). Eventually this sense of unreality infects the rest of her life: "It was true I had two lives, but on off days I felt that neither of them was completely real" (216). It is then that her own identity becomes illusory. In the Chinese restaurant with Arthur and Don and Marlene, the message in Joan's fortune cookie reminds her of the virtues of honesty: "*It is often best to be oneself*, whispered the small, crumby voice, like a conscience" (231). But this is not easy, given her fractured existence: "But which one, which one?" (231). In considering the duplicitous nature of her life, Joan is not naïve about her inability to connect with the men in her life. In a moment of disillusionment, she confesses the counterfeit nature of her feelings: ". . . I was an artist, an escape artist. I'd sometimes talked about love and commitment, but the real romance of my life was that between Houdini and his ropes and locked trunk; entering the embrace of bondage, slithering out again" (334). Consequently, she doubts her ability to really reach out to anyone: "I felt I'd never really loved anyone, not Paul, not Chuck the Royal Porcupine, not even Arthur" (282). Further to this, she immediately acknowledges an overdependence on masculine desire in her formation of her identity by evoking the metaphor of the mirror: "I'd polished them with my love and expected them to shine, brightly enough to return my own reflection, enhanced and sparkling" (282).

Quite apart from the effect the men have on structuring her life, they themselves are subject to divisions of their own. Her father, for instance, is a highly ambiguous figure, who is emotionally abstracted and dislocated from the immediate familial situation. His own identity seems somewhat vacant, and his early absence means that the construction of his personality is almost entirely dependent upon his wife's accounts of him. Is he the resurrectionist who saves lives at the Toronto General Hospital, or the sniper working with the French underground killing in cold blood? Is he the ineffectual suburban man caught in a hapless marriage and home, or the man who yields power in his hands, who had killed people and raised the dead? In Joan's own words, "Was he a bad man or a nice man?" (69). Was he the victim of his wife's demands or the man who had pushed her down the stairs?

If we are to see Mr. Foster as at all figuring in the oedipal drama of Joan's home life, it may be indicative of her continual and problematic relationship with her mother that "Most of the time he was simply an absence" (69). Habitual absence such as his implies a negation of the father, a privileging of the maternal, and the consequent incomplete transference of pre- to post-oedipal desires in the daughter's psyche. This interpretation may be seen to be supported by the fact that it is only with Mrs. Foster's death that the father really takes on any subjective significance, at which time there comes an unprecedented individualization of his countenance: "Previously it had been flat . . . as though the features had been erased, but not completely, they were smudged and indistinct as if viewed through layers of gauze. Now however his face had begun to emerge . . ."(177). In addition, before Mrs. Foster's death, the things Joan and her father had done together had been "wordless things" (76). Now, in the newly acquired absence of the mother, "the need for silence was removed" (181). With this we witness the emergence of a paternal edict. It is one that is, in the final case, a signifying one; a kind of death of the mother that allows for language, or as Kristeva puts it, a "naming" that is "a *replacement* for what the speaker perceives as an archaic mother — a more or less victorious confrontation, never finished with her" ("Place Names" 291).

While the assumption of an enunciative position is directly dependent upon the oedipal transference of desires, in Joan's case discursivity underwrites all her interactions with men who are eventually revealed to live constructed if not counterfeit lives. Joan's first affair is with a man who seems genteel but has a hidden revolver, who calls himself the Polish Count but also lives as Mavis Quilp. Her likening of him to the daffodil man (157) gives him a distinct untrustworthiness that she expresses as her inability to really know him: "I couldn't tell about Paul's identity either, for as time went on he began to change" (157–58). In fact, the manifestations of split personalities and identities become a recurrent feature of her relationships with men. As she herself admits, "Every man I'd ever been involved with, I realized, had two selves: my father, healer and killer; the man in the tweed coat, my rescuer and possibly also a pervert; the Royal Porcupine and his double, Chuck Brewer; even Paul, who I'd always believed had a sinister other life I couldn't penetrate. Why should Arthur be any exception?" (292).

Indeed, Arthur eventually reveals himself to be as duplicitous as Joan is: "Once I'd thought of Arthur as single-minded, single-hearted, single-bodied; I, by contrast, was a sorry assemblage of lies and alibis, each complete in itself but rendering the others worthless. But I soon discovered there were as many of Arthur as there were of me. The difference was that I was simultaneous, whereas Arthur was a sequence" (211). Nevertheless, regardless of how manufactured Arthur's social conscience may be, no one rivals the Royal Porcupine with regard to affected and artificially constructed identity. When the eccentric poet in the flowing robe slowly changes into Chuck Brewer with the chin of a junior accountant (270–71), it becomes clear that he had first created and then killed his own staged personality. The man who had constructed a counterfeit existence had indeed "lived in his own unwritten biography" (267).

While the Royal Porcupine's conscious construction of an identity is both theatrical and pretentious, in connection with his relationship with Joan it raises the issue of representation in the context of sexual desire. This is epitomized by the fact that as the master of the concrete poem, he deals only with "the poetry of things" (241). While he admits that he once "did words" (259), he now desires only to work with "pure acts" of the Real, and create what he calls "art-if-act" (265). If this attempted control over the referent is interpreted as signalling a desire to avert the signifier, it may also be seen as evidence of an inadequate sublimation of incestuous desire, which if properly sublimated would express itself as the overexpenditure of signs normally associated with artistry. Kristeva posits the "baroqueness" ("Stabat Mater" 177) of art as effecting a kind of murder of the mother, and in the context of this, the Royal Porcupine's disavowal of the signifier may be seen to be the expression of a problematic overvaluation of the maternal. Perhaps this is why he displays the tendencies of the fetishist, lusting for Captain Marvel comics,

Mickey Mouse watches, and Coca-Cola bottles in an obsessive quest for cultural objects, and objectifying parts of Joan's body when making love. His irrational reverence for objects turns into the taking of an abnormal object for sexual desire[25] when he turns his artistic endeavours toward a celebration of her arm, first saying, "You've got the sexiest elbows I've ever seen. I'm thinking of doing a show on elbows, it's a very unappreciated part of the body" (241), and then telling her, "I want to make love to your elbow . . ." (242). This desire to segment Joan's body culminates in his planning an exhibit entitled "Joan Foster Kentucky Fried" (255), and her feeling that he is commodifying her: "Each of my gestures was petrified as I performed it, each kiss embalmed, as if he was saving things up. I felt like a collectable" (267). Similarly, his fixation upon the corpses of dead animals intimates a questionable relationship with corporeality. For most people the corpse is prime abject,[26] the realities of which the individual shies away from. However, the Royal Porcupine is fascinated by the mashed and mangled bodies of dead animals, cataloguing their crushed bones and inspecting their internal haemorrhages. His apparent absence of any feelings of repulsion or abjection are indicative of what Grosz has said of fetishism — that it is a turning of the significatory thetic back toward the chora, and the repetition and representation of the choric relationship with the maternal through displacement upon an object.[27] As such, it is a way of gaining an enunciative position while simultaneously retaining the pre-oedipal attachment to the mother. As Grosz states, "the fetishist has one foot in the symbolic, representational order and the other in the pre-oedipal maternal realm" (*Sexual Subversions* 58). Thus, Joan's involvement with the "mortician" (*LO* 257) may be interpreted as being an act of post-oedipal desire enveloped by a cry for the umbilical bond of an earlier time, imaged by their making love amid the not-yet-dry dog's blood (244).

While Joan's relationship with the Royal Porcupine may be seen to be a vacillation between symbolic demands and oedipal desires, her encounter with Fraser Buchanan does nothing more than point to the inevitability of intervention by a masculine, external term. The short man at the book launch, tidily dressed in a tweed jacket and turtleneck sweater, is, in actual fact, a professional blackmailer. As such, he is an agent of exchange and societal positioning, with regard to the circulation of words and the construction of a social persona. His breaking into her apartment, collecting information about her that he will later use in extortion, initiates a circular play of desire centred upon the little black notebook in which he writes his data.

In this context, the notebook functions in much the same way as does the signifier. Both are in themselves empty and nameless and attached to a masculine subject only through visibility and detachability. Neither is actually given in enunciation, but refers outside itself to create a precondition in which other acts of enunciation can be enacted. In addition, Fraser Buchanan's notebook as third term regulates equivalences between exchangeable objects; in Joan's case, the goods are her money and her body in sex, for access to the signs scrawled in his book. Indeed, her entry into the sexual arena underlies the entire episode. Not only does the notebook record her sexual activities with other men but the entire encounter has sexual overtones:

> "What do you want?" I said.
> "Well, that depends," he said crisply, "on what you've got to offer. In exchange, you might say."
> "Let me put on some clothes," I said. . . .
> "I prefer you this way," said Fraser Buchanan. (286)

A little later, he placed "his hand discreetly on my ass" and casually asked, "your place or mine?" (289).

If we accept that the assumption of an enunciative position requires a renunciation of pre-oedipal maternal attachments, and we extend an interpretation of Joan's encounter with Fraser Buchanan as representing the value of the external third term, it is interesting to note that Joan finally finds the notebook. Furthermore, what she loses in order to acquire it is her own writing. Fraser Buchanan steals the manuscript of one of her historical romances and in so doing gains access to her Gothic fantasy world, which, at this point, she has no choice but to relinquish to him. She is furious at the thought of his having invaded her hidden life. Nevertheless, she is willing to accede, saying: "I had the book and I intended to keep it" (291). The negotiation of sexual activity in the face of significatory desire has now surfaced not only in light of Joan's relationships with men but in connection with her secret life as the author of costume romances. With this we are led to consider the subjective stance primarily as a signifying one, and one that is both constitutive and indicative of an enunciative position.

Immediately observable is the fact that the writing of Gothic romances enables Joan to continue in her divided and dislocated ways. Using a pseudonym and manufactured persona, she is able to substantiate an existence that has already become structured by division: "It was the fact that I was two people at once, with two sets of identification papers, two bank accounts, two different groups of people who believed I existed" (213). This undeniably causes anxiety on her part, as she says "I was terrified that sooner or later someone would find out about me, trace down my former self, unearth me" (251). However, she remains addicted to her literary persona, her Gothic world, and her sense of division: "As long as I could spend a certain amount of time each week as Louisa, I was alright.... But if I was cut off, if I couldn't work at my current Costume Gothic, I would become mean and irritable, drink too much and start to cry" (213). Eventually, what becomes clear is that through writing costume romances, Joan is able to create an additional self: "it was as if someone with my name were out there in the real world, impersonating me, saying things I'd never said but which appeared in the newspapers, doing things for which I had to take the consequences" (250–51). On the one hand, this seems to be underwritten by a specular dynamic with a constitutive aspect that allows her to say "I felt very visible" (250). On the other hand, this "funhouse-mirror reflection" (251) images an identity that implies imminent danger through its otherness. The latter becomes clear when Joan speaks of it as being "my dark twin," who was "taller than I was, more beautiful, more threatening," and "wanted to kill me and take my place" (251).

The simultaneously generative and destructive character of authorship now gives Joan's writing of costume Gothics a decidedly textual character. Kristeva has made the point that because the textual process is a way in which the individual can situate him- or herself with regard to the symbolic, the textual experience involves *the subject thus formulated as operating consciousness*" ("From One" 131) and "represents one of the most daring explorations the subject can allow himself, one that delves into his constitutive process" (*Revolution* 67). However, signifying systems and practices simultaneously operate as an unsettling if not outright destructive process that threatens the stability of identity and evokes the "crisis" of the speaking subject ("From One" 125). Within this account, it is the signifying process that Kristeva terms "poetic" that gives rise to this subversive element within representation, and it does so by positing a "heterogeneousness" to meaning and identity ("From One"). This "distinctiveness" is not on the side of the symbolic or of consciousness but is instead the expression of a semiotic activity. This semiotic disposition marks the drives of the desiring body, and hence functions as the expression of the death instinct, orality, and anality. As such it is an "anteriority" that draws upon what symbolic language normally suppresses, the "instinctual drive and continuous relation to the mother" ("From One" 136). For this reason, the artist has a particular relationship with the maternal, and Kristeva formulates this in a number of ways. First, she sees the artist as one who lodges into language his or her own libidinal energies through an identification with the mother ("Motherhood" 242). Second, she sees art as being the function of a particular debt to the maternal body (243). Third, she maintains that the textual process effects the mother's entry into symbolic existence (243). Fourth, perhaps as a consequence of the preceding factors, the artist is seen to renegotiate the choric relationship: "although the symbolic attempts to negate the *chora*, the maternal substratum of subjectivity surfaces in . . . 'poetic' language" (Silverman 106).

   This positioning of the artist in relation to the maternal allows one to interpret Joan's artistic endeavours as an expression of the choric bond by placing them in the context of her relationship with her mother. If this is the case, then Joan's writing is perhaps her own kind of fetishism, as, "poets as individuals fall under the category of fetishism; the very practice of art necessitates reinvesting the maternal *chora* so that it transgresses the symbolic order" (Kristeva, *Revolution* 65). In light of this, it is significant that Joan loses conscious control over much of her artistic activity. The persona who surfaces through her writing is one with whom Joan is cognizant, conversant, and yet has no actual command over (*LO* 250–51). A distinct sense of impotence surfaces in "out-of-control fantasies" of the Fat Lady: "she'd be dancing on a stage . . . she'd start taking off her clothes, while I watched, powerless to stop her" (251). This lack of conscious control is echoed in Joan's experiences with "automatic writing." This is a method inspired by Leda Sprott and adapted by Joan, which entails sitting in front of a mirror with paper and a lighted candle, in order to enter a trancelike state that begins to speak for itself: "There, in a scrawly hand-writing that was certainly not my own, was a single word. . . . I had actually written a word, without being conscious of doing it" (220). The lack of corporeal command here may be seen to be reminiscent of a pre- and early specular stage in which organic prematurity dominates a body subjected only to the primary processes. Here the sense of kinetic inability evokes the choric space and time before pre-oedipal desires were repressed; hence, the marks automatically written may be seen to be the expression of signifiers of the maternal that are usually lodged within the unconscious, but have momentarily become unhinged and have erupted into conscious life.

Such an explanation relies upon a number of theoretical premises. First, there is the acceptance that the daughter's unconscious desire for the mother does not enjoy the same kind of broadly based representational support that sustains her unconscious desire for her father (Silverman 124). With this, any expression of the chora will be ambiguous, subversive, and unintelligible. Second, within any dynamic of libidinal investment through signification, the drive process cannot be released or carried out through narrative, but instead needs the suspension of the "meta-position" (Kristeva, *Revolution* 103). Third, this suspension is structured according to the division of unconscious from conscious discourse, so that the artist bears witness to what the unconscious has to say in an interplay of nonsymbolic with the symbolic effected through the screen of the mother (Kristeva, "Motherhood" 242). Finally, given the unconscious and semiotic underpinning of artistic endeavours, the primary processes of displacement and condensation can and do leave their mark in language, which may then be seen to reflect what Kristeva has called "clearly differentiated subjective experiences" ("Phonetics" 35).

If, then, the text may reflect as well as create an individual's subjective stance in the light of the chora, the automatic writing episodes may be seen to be Joan's investment of the maternal within symbolic practice. It is not surprising, then, that these occasions reveal her alienated subjectivity and are constructed, much like her identity, through the mirror: "I stared at the candle in the mirror, the mirror candle. There was more than one candle, there were three, and I knew that if I moved the two sides of the mirror toward me there would be an infinite number of candles, extending in a line as far as I could see" (220). The chain of infinitely regressing reflections hints at a potentially perpetual series of images totally appropriate for a person who until now has had difficulty retaining a singular self-image. In the context of this being a signifying practice, her inability to reach the end of the corridor may be seen to image the subject's inability ever to grasp the referent once the endless deferral of signification has begun: "if I could only turn the next corner or the next — for these journeys became longer — I would find the thing, the truth or word or person that was mine, that was waiting for me" (221).

On the next occasion, the desire for the unattainable is imaged within the figure of a person — "there had been a figure, standing behind me" (222) — and Joan is driven to "find someone" (220): "I was convinced it was real and someone had a message for me. I wanted to go down that dark, shining corridor again, I wanted to see what was at the other end" (221). However, she remains well aware of the dangers of being overwhelmed, saying: "On the other hand, I didn't want to. It was too frightening" (221). The threat of symbiosis becomes clear, not only with the nature of the words being written that "became increasingly bizarre and even threatening," (222) but with her loss of orientation when "I went into the mirror one evening and I couldn't get out again" (223). Her loss of direction results in immobility: ". . . I was stuck there, in the midst of darkness, unable to move"; a sense of being smothered: "I felt as though I was suffocating"; and a point of no return: "I was afraid to turn around even, in case I ended up going farther in" (223). Finally, although not unexpectedly, the person in the mirror is revealed to be Joan's mother (329–30), and it becomes clear that the entire experience has been underwritten by the maternal presence. This comments harshly upon the dangers inherent within symbiotic desires for union, and so it is significant that Arthur rushes in to save Joan — an external, intervening, and masculine presence for which she was "so thankful" (32).

Joan is initially inspired to embark upon the journey of the mirror and the flame because one of her Gothic heroines has found herself in a similar situation, and, as creator of her plight, Joan feels "I'd have to act it through" (219). Their experiences are shown to be remarkably similar, as we learn that Penelope placed a small table with a mirror on it before her, lit a candle, and set the candle in front of the mirror: *she felt her gaze being drawn to the flame; her mind fluttered, fascinated, helpless as a moth, her own reflection disappeared . . . further into the mirror she went, and further, till she seemed to be walking on the other side of the glass, in a land of indistinct shadows*" (218). The resemblance between Joan and her Gothic heroine deepens until their positions become momentarily interchangeable: "*You are Penelope*, I told myself sternly" (219). Eventually they intertwine to the degree that it is virtually impossible to differentiate one from the other. Worried that the penniless but beautiful Charlotte will never actually capture her man, Joan notes, with some anxiety, that "my own financial future depended on hers" (131).

There are other ways, too, that Joan's fictional world and the real one imitate each other. Her own stay at the Royal York Hotel, "that bogus fairyland of nineteenth-century delights" (136) with its plush carpets and chandeliers, conjures images of beautiful ladies and Victorian gentlemen that then inspire her own choice of setting. Similarly, her fascination with the markets along Portobello Road in which she pores over antique china and silver ornaments is evidence of the merging of both worlds, and "those receding centuries in which, more and more, I was living" (159). However, the resemblance between the real and counterfeit world is most startling when her fictional characters take on a reality all their own. After having tried to kill Felicia, the discarded wife in one of the stories, Joan finds that the character she has created begins to develop outside of her authorial control: ". . . Felicia was still alive, and I couldn't seem to get rid of her. She was losing more and more of her radiant beauty; circles were appearing beneath her eyes, lines between her brows, she had a pimple on her neck, and her complexion was becoming sallow" (316). With a complete failure of authorial intention, Joan tries to warn another character, Charlotte, not to enter the maze, but "She paid no attention to me, she never did; she stood up, put away her embroidery, and prepared to go outside" (332).

These incidents, dependent as they are upon verisimilitude rather than truth, bespeak the mimetic economy that underpins Joan's construction of the Gothic world.[28] In the light of Joan's fractured identity and her problematic relationship with the maternal, this mimetic quality of representation raises a number of important points. The first is that the mimetic strategy pluralizes denotation, and thus, as a textual practice, may be seen to add a certain polysemy to an existence already structured by divisions. The second is that the mimetic economy depends upon a subject who does not suppress the chora but instead raises it to the status of signifier (Kristeva, *Revolution* 57). This may, in fact, be why Joan states: "For a while after my mother's death I couldn't write" (181).

Kristeva has made the point that when the semiotic chora disturbs the thetic, it does so by redistributing the signifying order. Through this "transposition" of the semiotic chora, the denoted object proliferates into a series of fictional, connoted objects that are primarily mimetic in nature (*Revolution* 55–56). With this, we are brought to the connection between poetic language and mimesis[29] — the fact that both posit the symbolic while subverting meaning, and both posit the subject while unsettling identity. In fact, Kristeva has written of the highly subversive nature of both, saying, "poetic language and the mimesis from which it is inseparable, are profoundly a-theological" (61). Speaking of mimesis and poetic language, Kristeva asks "by what specific operations are these corruptions of the symbolic carried out?" (59). She suggests displacement and condensation as an answer (59); and with the highly transgressive nature of both mimesis and textual practice, it becomes appropriate to contextualize Joan's costume romances in light of the primary processes that may be functioning within the text. This means, in effect, looking for the "genotextual" elements operative within the text: the elements that threaten the apparent unity of the work and destabilize it, that give expression to the semiotic energies otherwise contained within the communicational purpose of the text, and that may be seen to stratify the position of enunciation in which Joan as author is positioned.

One example of the psychopathology evident within the Gothic texts is the primary process of displacement. This is definable as the process whereby energy from one idea is cathected along associative pathways to another apparently inconsequential idea, which then accumulates intensity.[30] This dynamic surfaces in the recurrent motif of the maze, the complex labyrinth of paths and hedges that serves as point of mystery in all the stories. The association of the maze with spiritual forces beyond conventional symbolic figuration, and the fact that it is a dangerous place for young girls, ally it with both the earlier mirror experiences in which Joan's specular identity was threatened, and with the potentially overwhelming maternal space of the chora. A displacement of affect onto a seemingly unrelated image means that intensity is transferred from mirror and mother to maze, and the latter is transfigured so that it now carries all the significance of Joan's earlier experiences with automatic writing: *"there's no center to the maze and that's how they get lost, they get into it and can't find their way out. . . . [Charlotte] felt drawn towards the maze, irresistibly, against her will, yet she knew that if she went in, something terrible would happen to her"* (186–87).

Equally significant is the process of condensation whereby energies that have been displaced along associative paths converge upon an image that is located at their intersection.[31] This means that one manifest element may correspond to numerous latent thoughts (Freud, "Revision" 49), and this is precisely what occurs when Felicia finally enters the maze, determined to master its complexities, and comes across the earlier wives who had entered but never returned. With this, the collective figure of Lady Redmond now functions as nodal point[32] for a number of mnemonic traces, the first of which is the memory of Aunt Lou, represented by the middle-aged, eccentric lady wearing the fur around her neck. Joan's recurrent alter-identity as Fat Lady appears in the third wife, who is enormously obese and wearing a short pink skirt covered with spangles. She also carries all the pain and humiliation of the memory of young Joan performing in Miss Fleg's ballet concert. Wearing two antennae and a pair of false wings pinned to her back, this Lady Redmond evokes the time when Joan was to have been a butterfly along with all the other petite seven year olds, but instead became comic relief as the dumpy mothball used to scare them. And, finally, they all carry the sum of those energies cathected onto them through association with the maternal. That is, the fact that one *"could see the dim outline of the bench through their tenuous bodies"* (342) is reminiscent of the fluidity and spatial incongruity expressed so succinctly by Mrs. Foster's visitations. The nearby door, affixed to a frame but nothing else, with a small window at the top through which one could see the outside world, is reminiscent of Joan's earlier dream in which she used the sill of the doorway to negotiate her own position in the external world between the voice of signification and the demands of her mother. Finally, Lady Redmond and Joan directly parallel each other through their talk of fractured identities. One states: *"But every man has more than one wife. Sometimes all at once, sometimes one at a time, sometimes ones he doesn't even know about"* (341); while the other says: *". . . I was more than double, I was triple, multiple, and now I could see that there was more than one life to come, there were many"* (246).

While the similarities are undeniable, what marks these textual experiences as being radically different from Joan's real life is the intervention of an external person and immediate advent of desire. The danger is in staying with the women, there, in the centre of the maze. Salvation lies in swinging the door outward: *"There, standing on the threshold, waiting for her, was Redmond. . . . 'Let me take you away,' he whispered. 'Let me rescue you. We will dance together forever, always'"* (342–43). The entry of a tall, dark, and handsome stranger is, in many ways, expected, as this incident echoes Joan's earlier dance of desire in front of her bedroom mirror. In fact, Joan had always acknowledged that there "would have to be an interruption by a third party" (188). There is little doubt the entrance of a man will effect a movement away from pre-oedipal and feminine attachments. Indeed, Joan's choice of genre and the various titles suggest sexual attraction (*Stalked by Love*; *Love, My Ransom*; *Love, Defied*; *Escape from Love*), and the plots are similarly driven by desire. Felicia, for example, lies in the shrubbery of the maze, her skirt and petticoat hitched to her waist, her fichu disarranged, after having made love with Lord Otterly. Charlotte runs in, blushing crimson at the realization that she is wearing nothing but her nightgown, her breasts moving seductively as she breathes deeply. Further to this, in full accordance with the psychoanalytic model, desire in this Gothic world is both structured by and articulated through the gaze. Hence, Redmond stares at Charlotte with an eye that *"slid like a roving oyster over her blushing countenance . . . appraisingly, lustfully, ruthlessly, causing hot flushes to sweep over her"* (317). Tom, the coachman, watches Felicia's sexual encounter through a hole in the shrubbery. Redmond raises his left eyebrow at a reflection of himself he glimpses in the windowpane, while Felicia sits in front of her vanity table, brushing her extravagant, red, waist-length hair, beholding herself with a narcissistic eye: *"gazing up at herself from beneath the surface of a river"* (319).

The Gothic texts are, then, marked by desire, and one could well contemplate what wishes are being satisfied through Joan's manipulation of the text in this way. Both automatic writing and costume romances allow for the emergence of the choric space and satisfy the demand of the maternal for expression. Consequently, they give rise to the anality, orality, and death instinct that have previously structured her real life.[33] Condensation and displacement are expressions of the unconscious, and, as Freud points out, the psychopathological symptom, while a momentary transgression, is never an arbitrary one for the symptom represents something fulfilled ("Paths" 413). What demands, then, are the condensed and displaced images trying to fulfil? And what are these to do with the fact that the texts are dominated by desire?

The answer must surely be that through the act of writing, Joan is able to create for herself, through fantasy and textual process, a new enunciative position dominated by desire. If desire is defined as the introduction of the other to the subject and the condition that this demand now pass through the signifier,[34] Joan's investment in writing may well be seen to effect a separation from the maternal through the expression of post-oedipal longing expressed in signification and sexual attraction. Through her writing, then, Joan is able to create for herself a new enunciative position with regard to symbolic discourse and articulate a new subjective position with regard to desire. This signals a new intentionality behind the textual practice, tantamount to a resolution upon which the novel may end. In the final chapter, Joan no longer feels compelled to write, saying: "I won't write any more Costume Gothics, though; I think they were bad for me" (345). This accompanies her decision to return to Canada, resolve her marriage, and resume her life. But all this is possible because, some two chapters earlier, she finally discovered the full significance of her relationship with her mother. Admitting that her mother had been "waiting around each turn" (330), she is free now to acknowledge the insatiable demands that had been placed upon her: "My mother was a vortex, a dark vacuum, I would never be able to make her happy" (330). This new awareness means she can now protect herself, recognizing that "Maybe it was time for me to stop trying" (330). With this we suspect she will now be able to confront fears and dangers and renounce all that had previously been a threat to her.

Lady Oracle ends with a resolution of Joan's relationship with her mother, a relationship that has been expressed as a preoccupation with death, a divided sense of self, a number of fractured identities, and a problematic relationship with food and with the body. It is a relationship that has been imaged in familial networks, bodily drives, sexual relations, and textual practices. But if Joan's story has been the story of a relationship with the maternal, it has equally been the story of an individual self and the struggle for subjectivity in the context of such a relationship. With this, subjective identity has been shown to be a function of various forms of division: the split between the symbolic and the semiotic, the rift between conscious and unconscious discourse, and the difference between corporeal existence and imaging of the body.

[1] "If it is true that . . . life once proceeded out of inorganic matter, then . . . an instinct must have arisen which sought to do away with life once more and to reestablish the inorganic state" (Freud, "Anxiety" 140).

[2] In his algorithmic formulation of the dynamic of signification, Lacan makes clear the positions of the signifier and signified as being of different orders separated by a bar. This "cut in discourse" is what allows signification to take place, as this cut in the signifying chain alone verifies the structure of the subject as discontinuity in the Real ("Subversion" 299).

[3] This refers to the mythical murder and ritual devouring of the primal Father that commemorates the beginning of society as it is explicated in Freud's *Totem and Taboo*.

[4] The Fort-Da is a term coined by Freud to describe a game he found his eighteen-month-old grandson playing. The child made a cotton reel disappear and reappear while making sounds similar to the German words "fort" (away) and "da" (here it is). The game has significance for a number of reasons. First, it may be seen to be the earliest example of representation, where signifiers replace the referent. Second, as the symbolic expression of presence and absence, it may be seen to reflect upon the child's coming to terms with the absence of the mother and/or the breast. Third, it may be seen to be a functional and active expression of control, whereby the child is mastering the dynamics of representation.

[5] The following account is drawn from Kristeva's *Revolution in Poetic Language*.

[6] This is a Freudian term used to describe the libidinal impulses of the pre-oedipal child that are not yet hierarchically organized under the drives of the oral, anal, or phallic stages, or focused around erotogenic zones.

[7] I refer here to D.W. Winnicott's ideas on the transitional object as they are outlined in "Transitional Objects." Here a material object (thumb, teddy bear, etc.) is designated by the child and used to make the transition from the first suckling relationship with the mother to an object relationship with an other external to the mother-child dyad.

[8] It is from this myth that Freud coins the term "narcissism" to describe the process whereby the ego takes itself as a love-object ("Anxiety" 135). However, his most comprehensive account features in "On Narcissism: An Introduction" and "The Libido Theory and Narcissism."

[9] Freud does not completely renege upon the idea of narcissism being of potential danger. Eventually, he identifies two types of narcissism: one that is "secondary" and is in accordance with the normal development of the ego because it is based upon identification with others (explicated in "The Ego and

the Id"), and one that is a "primary" psychotic libidinal recathection of the ego characterized by a complete lack of any relationship to the outside world.

[10] Lacan states: "[the] imaginary Anatomy which has typical forms of its own . . . varies with the ideas (clear or confused) about bodily functions which are prevalent in a given culture" ("Some Reflections" 13).

[11] This is explained by Jacobus (178–79).

[12] Anaclisis is a term Kristeva uses to describe the distress the infant experiences and expresses due to its biological insufficiency. Anaclisis is an appeal or invocation for support, warmth, and nourishment in the absence of intra-uterine life ("Place Names" 281–83).

[13] The reasons why the father fails to break the maternal connection are to do with the fact that in our particular form of social organization, the father is not the primary caretaker, and remains less emotionally available.

[14] This is exemplified by the phenomenon whereby the child who strikes another will say that he or she has been struck, and the child who sees another fall will cry (Lacan, "Aggressivity" 19).

[15] The following account is taken from Kristeva's *Revolution in Poetic Language* (57–61).

[16] Irigaray speaks of "a few garments, a little jewelry, some makeup, a disguise" as a way of being the "good" and "nearly perfect" girl who does what is expected of her ("And the One" 62).

[17] "The unspoken doubtless weighs first on the maternal body . . . the signifier is always meaning, communication or structure, whereas a woman as mother would be, instead, a strange fold that changes culture into nature, the speaking into biology" (Kristeva, "Stabat Mater" 182).

[18] Drawn from Kristeva's "Place Names."

[19] Silverman makes the point that this is one of the most familiar formulations of Kristeva's chora (102).

[20] This is a point Kristeva makes in "Place Names" (281).

[21] This is because voice is the vehicle for the distressed cry of anaclisis (Kristeva, "Place Names" 280–86).

[22] Kristeva speaks of feelings that turn into melancholy "as soon as the child becomes an object, a gift to others, neither self nor part of the self, an object destined to be a subject, an other" ("Motherhood" 239).

[23] The following account is taken from "Language and the Limits of the Body: Kristeva and Abjection."

[24] I draw here upon Grosz's formulation of abjection as it features in *Sexual Subversions*.

[25] Freud defines fetishism as a dynamic by which the normal sexual object is replaced by another that bears some relation to it, but is entirely unsuited to serve the normal sexual aim. What is substituted for the sexual object is some

part of the body (such as the foot or hair) that is in general very inappropriate for sexual purposes, or some inanimate object that bears an assignable relation to the person whom it replaces and preferably to that person's sexuality ("Three Essays" 65–66).

26 The corpse renders the body indistinct through decay and is undeniable proof of predestined biological cycles.

27 Grosz defines fetishism as a disavowal of maternal castration, the substitution of an object in what is normally perceived to be the mother's lack (*Sexual Subversions* 57–59).

28 Kristeva defines mimesis as the positing or construction of an object not according to truth but to verisimilitude (*Revolution* 57).

29 Kristeva discusses this in *Revolution in Poetic Language* (57–61).

30 This definition of the Freudian term is taken from Laplanche and Pontalis (121–24).

31 This is also a Freudian term explained by Laplanche and Pontalis (82–83).

32 A nodal point is a point or connection where associative chains (relations of contiguity and similarity) overlap.

33 While these have surfaced in other areas of Joan's life, Kristeva's point that within the text there is always the predominance of the negative, of aggression, of anality, and of death is relevant ("Four Types" 71).

34 This is Lacan's definition of desire in "The Direction" (64).

CHAPTER THREE

Life before Man:

The SPLIT SUBJECT, *the* IMAGINATION, *and the* IMAGINARY

Life before Man (LBM) appears to be a novel concerned only with the fine detail of domestic and social realism. There is a kind of stillness informed by inactivity in terms of plot, annotation, time scheme, and narrative structure, which faithfully reproduces the ordinary life of an ordinary person. However, within this literary construction of the conventional there is a recurrent motif that is striking and distinctive — the fantasy life of one of the major characters. Beginning with the belief that Lesje's paleontological dreamland is more than an ornamental device, my approach is inspired by the fact that while *Life before Man* is a novel of actuality, it is at the same time illustrating the play of fantasy with reality. Thus, my account takes as its starting point the interface between the imagination and the Real, aiming to examine how it is that an individual negotiates the complex interplay and demands of both.

My account assumes two of the more conventional notions regarding the imagination. First, the idea that to imagine is to form a mental image or concept of an object that is not immediately present to the senses. Second, the idea that to imagine is to draw upon a creative faculty of the mind. This means that the act of imagination is qualifiably a type of production, which is functional primarily through the dynamic of the visual, auditory, or emotional image. As such, imagination is a kind of representation, simulation, and construction. However, while the act of imagination may indeed implicate people, places, times, and events that are in real life external to the person involved, ultimately what is being hallucinated is the individual's self. That is, regardless of the form or content of the phantasm, what is always being conjured is, in fact, an image of the self; the mirage, as it were, is the apparition of the I.

Precisely because it is the very self that is located on the threshold of image and reality, my approach turns toward psychoanalytic and phenomenological accounts of the formation of identity. With this, there is a shift away from the more conventional use of the word "imagination" toward the more technical and theoretically precise term "Imaginary." Lacan's seminal formulation of the term provides the philosophical underpinning of my argument; however, the works of other theorists are drawn upon to enhance and explicate where necessary.

The result is a textual analysis of Lesje's daydreaming as signifying the Imaginary captation of the subject. As such, it is seen to function as a psychopathological symptom and form of regression. In this context, by creating a fictional world of her own, Lesje is in fact stepping into another place — the space of the unconscious. This raises the issue of positionality — an issue bespoken by the negotiation of spatial dynamics as evidenced in the character of Elizabeth Schoenhoff.

While my approach is inspired by, and begins with, interest in the subjective life of Lesje, it broadens to include analysis of the other characters, in keeping with the belief that the fictional world of all three protagonists in *Life before Man* illustrates the realm of the Imaginary. This is a necessity because in this novel, like no other, there is, in a sense, no single protagonist who may claim precedence. Unlike the other novels I discuss, in *Life before Man,* narrative voice and focalization, as well as the events that structure the plot, are shared among Lesje, Elizabeth, and Nate. Thus, there is no difficulty in turning from analysis of Lesje's character to Elizabeth's, as this parallels the direction the text itself takes in its construction of a fictional world.

Close textual analysis of Elizabeth's relationship with her physical surroundings revolves around her negotiation of personal, domestic, and universal space. What is striking, however, is that this involves the dynamics of disconnection. Just as the psychopathological symptom was seen as a kind of overlaying of discursive systems that bespoke a certain rupture between the realm of the conscious and the place of the unconscious, Elizabeth's sequestered existence raises the issue of dislocation between the self and the space in which the self acts. At this point, drawing upon Gaston Bachelard's work on the poetics of space, my account draws together spatial positioning and otherness in an interwoven theoretical stance that gives spatiality an Imaginary aspect. This is then implicated in the very construction of the self, and Elizabeth's subjective status is examined in light of her eroding identity and place within the world.

Through analysis of Elizabeth's negotiation of herself in the context of her home and the world around her, the emphasis upon domesticity in the novel is brought to the point where it is implicated in the threshold between the unconscious and consciousness, and that of presubjective experience as opposed to subjective positioning. However, the dynamics of individualization and domestication of space never lose their Imaginary significance. Consequently, at this point in my argument, the image, the unconscious, and space are brought together in the notion of the personal prehistory of the individual in a theoretical move that draws upon the work of Maurice Merleau-Ponty for its justification.

Settling upon notions of the preexistent self as an angle of approach in discussing *Life before Man* paves the way for discussion of the novel's dominant metaphor of prehistory in both personal and mythical psychic structures. Freudian notions that conflate the organization of an individual psyche with collective unconscious history allow Lesje's recalcitrant fantasy life to be seen as being prehistoric in form as well as in name. In terms of its structuring Lesje's subjectivity, this means contextualizing her fantastical regression in light of the pre-oedipal — a move that brings the analysis to the formulation of the Imaginary as being a phenomenon that predates oedipal resolution.

The notion that Lesje's fantasies are Imaginary in form and function, in combination with the idea that the Imaginary may be pre-oedipal, justifies a close reading of the paleontological apparitions in light of the sexual difference with which they are marked. Thus, the maternal connotations of the fantasies are discussed in relation to the potentially alienating yet very necessary intervention of paternal desire represented by the men in Lesje's life.

At this point, different dynamics of division are evoked: dynamics of estrangement based upon intersubjective relations between the sexes. This raises the issue of the intrusion of the other, an aspect in keeping with a formulation of the Imaginary register as being based upon a relationship with the counterpart and located firmly within the realm of duality. The dichotomous Imaginary relationship is operative in a number of ways. The first is a type of intrasubjective Imaginary association of the self with the self, whereby through narcissistic appraisal, the individual collates images into a representation of the self that may then function as an ego-identity for the subject. At this point, drawing upon Lacanian notions of mirror-stage specularization, my account interprets Lesje's characterization in the context of it being an attempt at self-imaging. What makes these formulations of character noteworthy is the impingement of the views of those external to her. With this we are brought to the narcissistic formation of a self-image in light of identification, introjection, and projection with and of the other. The Imaginary thus taken into the realm of the other now becomes a distinctly intersubjective relation, which is further manifested in the forms of erotic and sexual encounter, and aggressivity. Psychoanalytic formulations of these provide a perfect framework through which to analyse the elements often mentioned in critical appraisals of *Life before Man*: Elizabeth's ruthless and intimidating nature, Nate's indecision and malleability, Lesje's struggle for status, and, in general, the dynamics of power play contextualized as they are within a network of romantic intrigues between bedfellows. What differentiates my account from those previous to it is that in my analysis the perspective through which these oft-mentioned elements are viewed focuses upon their claims upon and relation to identity, contextualizing the dynamics of division specific to the novel in light of the construction and maintenance of subjectivity.

* * *

The Lacanian Imaginary is one of the three orders in which the subject is constituted through Borromean entanglement.[1] Opposed to the symbolic, which is the register of signification and cultural production, or the Real, which is the natural state foreclosed on assumption of an enunciative position, the Imaginary is characterized by a relationship with the image. From the moment of mirror-phase specularization, the subject is immersed in a play of images upon which a subsequent reality is constituted. From this moment also, the misrecognition Lacan terms *méconnaissance* becomes specific to subjective identity and initiates in the subject an everlasting interaction of unreality with appearance.

Within Lacan's formulation, the Imaginary process that is initiated by specular identification is a kind of threshold entity. In his words:

"I am led . . . to regard the function of the mirror-stage as a particular case of the function of the *imago*, which is to establish a relation between the organism and its reality — or, as they say, between the *Innenwelt and the Umwelt*" ("Mirror Stage" 4). Further to this, Imaginary captation is made manifest in the form of the psycho-pathological symptom because both lie at the threshold of inner and outer psychic worlds: "Here speech is driven out of the concrete discourse that orders the subject's consciousness, but it finds its support either in the natural functions of the subject . . . or in the images that organize at the limit of the *Umwelt* and of the *Innenwelt* their relational structuring" ("Function" 69).

Both aspects of the Lacanian Imaginary — its position on the borderline between psychic agencies and its expression in the form of unconscious regression — are well illustrated in *Life before Man*, a novel in which one of the characters, Lesje Green, constructs a life of fantasy by daydreaming of a prehistoric world. The sudden interruption of images that are almost hallucinatory into her ordinary life positions Lesje's subjective identity as being on the Imaginary threshold between image and reality. During a game of cribbage, Lesje "permits herself a walk by moonlight, along a path trampled by the giant but herbivorous iguanodons" (*LBM* 45). On another occasion, when she is walking hand in hand with William along a city street, in the middle of a conversation a dinosaur suddenly bursts in on the scene: "a Gorgosaurus pushes through the north wall of the Colonnade and stands there uncertainly, sniffing the unfamiliar smell of human flesh, balancing on its powerful hind legs" (30). This is no less startling than a quiet Saturday morning in her own home, which is no longer in suburban Canada but in a prehistoric world: "Lesje is in the living room, in the Upper Jurassic, where she runs along the path worn by the iguanodons. She's wearing her Adidas and a navy-blue sweatshirt" (264).

This is an interfacing of two separate worlds by way of semicon-scious dream work. It illustrates a type of overlaying of signifying systems in which signifiers lying dormant in the unconscious are condensed and displaced to re-form and appear in the manifest content of fantasy. With this interpretation, the figments of Lesje's imagination function as the signifiers of signifieds repressed from consciousness. This in turn bespeaks a kind of division within the subject according to traditional notions of the psychopathological symptom: "for a symptom . . . to be admitted in psychoanalytic psychopathology, Freud insists on the minimum of overdetermination constituted by a double meaning (symbol of a conflict long dead over and above its function in a *no less symbolic* present conflict)" (Lacan, "Function" 59).

This definition emphasizes the fact that the intertwining of past with present through the intersection of unconscious with conscious gives the symptom a heightened symbolic or discursive aspect, so that "the symptom is itself structured like a language" (Lacan, "Function" 59). With this, the symptom bespeaks a particular relation of the symbolic to the Imaginary, and in this context, by creating a private Mesozoic world through dream work, Lesje may be seen to be connecting the submerged contents of her unconscious with the signifying material of consciousness in the type of production a number of theorists have termed "suture."

Jean-Pierre Oudart has characterized suture in the context of cinematic discourse by drawing upon the conventional definition of it as being the surgical uniting of edges of a wound by stitching. The focus of this, as Stephen Heath points out, is upon symbolic operation: "Suture names the relation of the subject to the chain of its discourse . . ." ("Notes" 55). However, Heath is equally adamant that the process "cannot be a concept merely for the symbolic" (55), because within this division of the subject is the "*encroachment* of the unconscious" at the expense of the subject who is "thenceforth held in the ceaselessly displacing joining of symbolic and imaginary" (54). The result of this specific joining of symbolic with Imaginary is that "an image comes to the position of bearing all the cost of desire: projection, function of the imaginary" (54).

In this context, the figments of Lesje's imagination — the visions of gorgosauruses, pterodactyls, and iguanodons — function at the point of suture as the seamlike line of junction between her Imaginary existence and a symbolic one. As such they position her identity on the threshold of division and fracture it according to a number of oppositions: the discursively constructed and the unspoken, the visible and the hidden, fantasy and the constraints of reality, and the conscious and unconscious. As Lacan points out, the psychopathological symptom is indeed a function of divided subjectivity: "it is in the disintegration of the imaginary unity constituted by the ego that the subject finds the signifying material of his symptoms" ("Freudian Thing" 137).

Lacan has said of the unconscious that "what happens there is inaccessible to contradiction, to spatio-temporal location and also to the function of time" (*Four Fundamental* 31). Within the play of symbolic with Imaginary that characterizes Lesje's fantasy world there is, time and time again, a sense that she is deliberately placing herself in a different time and place:

> There's nothing behind her, nothing in front of her but the muddy path. To either side the undergrowth is unbroken; moisture drips from the fronds, it's hot as a steambath, her flesh simmers. The lake is miles away. She slows to a walk. In the distance ahead, where she knows there will be open space, scrub and hot sunlight, she can hear the raucous cries of the circling pterodactyls, intent on carrion. (264)

The detail with which her surroundings are described, the specific mention of her orientation, and the focus upon her own physical stature and the sensuous qualities of this other world, make the experience, above all, one of spatial relocation. In this sense, Lesje's compulsive daydreaming implies a certain spatial discontinuity. Furthermore, in its function as psychopathological symptom, the daydreaming implies that the other place into which Lesje steps is, in fact, the space of the unconscious. Indeed, J. Laplanche and J.B. Pontalis, in defining regression, maintain that it "can be understood as readily in a logical or spatial sense as in a temporal one" (386); and Lacan explicitly makes the point that symptoms of unconscious regression are to do with a discontinuity within the subject that may be seen to be spatial in nature: "The primary process . . . in the form of the unconscious — must, once again, be apprehended in its experience of rupture, between perception and consciousness, in that non-temporal locus . . . which forces us to posit what Freud calls . . . the idea of another locality, another space, another scene, *the between perception and consciousness*" (*Four Fundamental* 56).

At this point, Imaginary captation lends itself to analysis in terms of spatial configuration. The characterization of Elizabeth Schoenhoff lends itself well to such an analysis, for, unlike Lesje, whose Imaginary projections take the form of the daydream, Elizabeth's Imaginary existence is expressed by way of the positioning and repositioning of herself relative to her physical surroundings. Reminiscing about her childhood, she herself admits that being deserted by her father initiated within her a specific dynamic of disconnection, because "It was after this that space became discontinuous" (150). Now in adult life, this segmentation seems to take the form of a contrast between domestic space and the cosmos that lies beyond it. Descriptions of Elizabeth very often position her within her home:

lying in her bed with the Indian bedspread pulled up around her chin (212), sitting at the antique desk in her bedroom (135), or even in Aunt Muriel's parlour (119) in the house in which she lived as a child. Contemplating her reasons for having married Nate, Elizabeth recognizes that in doing so she had sought security with the promise to herself that "She would become a homemaker, she would make a home" (263). Her problem now was to "make it solid" (263); and when the desolation of Nate having left her finally makes her lose control, it is the sensation that "she's locked in this house" (251) that culminates in her walking to his new home in the middle of the night. Standing outside Nate's new bedroom, her overriding sensation is that "they've locked her out" (251), and she craves to leave her mark on this new place by throwing a brick through the window or kicking over the garbage can.

Similarly, Elizabeth seems to manoeuvre interpersonal relationships through a negotiation of space. Arguing with Auntie Muriel, she "feels the ground sliding from beneath her feet" (216), and tries to "dominate her through height" (215). When confronting Lesje, Elizabeth "seems to fill all the available space" (210) and forces her opponent back against the wall. However, even more pointed is the fact that Elizabeth expresses territoriality in the context of marital and sexual experience through the dynamics of domestic space. Addressing her lover, she says: "There was your room and there was everything else outside, and that barrier between the two. You carried that room around with you like a smell, it was a smell like formaldehyde and the insides of old cupboards, mousy, secretive, like musk, dusky and rich. Whenever I was with you I was in that room, even when we were outside, even when we were here" (25). However, even domestic spaces are able to contain nothing, as do the three Kayo bowls that sit on her sideboard and are testimony to Elizabeth's good taste and style: "Right now they hold their own space, their own beautifully shaped absence" (25). Eventually, space loses its reference to the domestic objects that contain it and are contained by it, so that what used to protect Elizabeth from emptiness now opens her to the void of the unsegmented universe:

She's staked to this chair, she can't move, a chill moves up her back. Her eyes flicker, sweep the room for something that will save her. Familiar. The stove, pot on it, frying pan unwashed, the cutting board by the sink. . . . The refrigerator. Nancy's drawing from Grade One stuck to it. . . .

Behind the blue sky is not white enamel but the dark of outer space, blackness shot with fiery bubbles. Somewhere out there the collapsed body floats, no bigger than a fist, tugging at her with immense gravity. Irresistible. She falls towards it, space filling her ears. (205)

This characterization of the domestic sphere as being the threshold between the subjective and the infinity of the external world seems to illustrate Bachelard's point that inside the house things are differentiated, and intimacy arises from what is then the diminished entity of the outside world (40–41). He extends his point that the house and outside space are not merely juxtaposed but interact dialectically (43) by maintaining that the cosmos outside the house is "a non-house in the same way that metaphysicians speak of a non-I" (40). This raises the issue of spatial configuration in connection with subjectivity and otherness that opposes it, and gives spatiality an Imaginary quality that is fundamental to the constitution of subjectivity: "the real beginnings of images, if we study them phenomenologically, will give concrete evidence of the values of inhabited space, of the non-I that protects the I" (5).

Indeed, the fact that, for Elizabeth, spatiality is either a threat to her subjective identity or its relative safety is acknowledged when she awakes one night and feels the need to reassure herself that the walls are in their rightful place, "the floor is there," and "the ceiling has healed over": "Space is a cube around her, she is the center. There is something to be defended" (162). The threat of alterity impinging upon the subject by encroaching space is well illustrated by Elizabeth's fainting spell at her aunt's funeral: "The cloudy green of the trees stretches into the distance, spongy, soft as gauze, there's nothing to push against it, hold on to. A black vacuum sucks at her, there's a wind, a slow roar. Still clutching Janet's hand Elizabeth falls through space" (300). Her inability to position herself in a world that contains "dissolving trees" and "chasms that open at her feet" (302), and is nothing more than "a transparent veil or a whirlwind" (302), becomes overtly connected to her own subjective identity at the mention of her lover's suicide. Asking herself how often and how close she has come to doing what Chris did, she thinks of the competing death wishes of those teenagers she once knew who raced their cars to the edge of a cliff, and "she feels the horrified relief of someone who has stopped just in time to watch an opponent topple in slow motion over the edge" (301). Implicating Chris's death in the undifferentiated and infinite space of the universe by speaking of his power as being "that piece of outer space he'd carried" (301), Elizabeth calms herself once more by reverting to the relative safety of a compartmentalized, domestic life. In fact, the incident ends with her acknowledging its necessity:

> She thinks with anticipation of her house, her quiet living room with its empty bowls, pure grace, her kitchen table. Her house is not perfect; parts of it are in fact crumbling, most noticeably the front porch. But it's a wonder that she has a house at all, that she's managed to accomplish a house. Despite the wreckage. She's built a dwelling over the abyss, but where else was there to build it? So far, it stands. (302)

In his poetics of space, Bachelard characterizes the motif of the house as signifying the realm of matter that is the world into which we are thrust (5–8). However, given that inhabited space becomes a home, or the subject's first world, the house metaphorically functions as cradle or womb (5–8). Furthermore, when we return to such spaces through dreams, we are returning to the "pre-human" (10), which implies a return to a presubjective existence. Regression to the natural state of nondifferentiation that exists before the intervention of the phallic third term is regression to existence before the repression of oedipal desires has constituted an unconscious. This raises the issue of the unconscious and its position within the negotiation of subjective and domestic space; the fact that, as Bachelard points out, "the unconscious is housed" (10).

For Elizabeth, all that is conscious and necessary for maintenance of her identity seems to be contained within the domestic sphere, which is, after all, marked by human intention. By contrast, nothingness is connected with the universe outside, and its oblivion may well be seen metaphorically to represent and be represented by the unconscious. Her experience in the Laserium, for example, is decidedly uncomfortable: "She's cold. She knows it's warm in the room . . . but the Northern Lights are making her cold. She wants to get up and leave the auditorium" (77). And when the black hole is described in a manner in which it comes to resemble the unconscious, her discomfort becomes explicable: "No one can see a black hole . . . but because of their effects on objects around them they are known to exist. . . . Nobody quite understands black holes yet. . . . They suck energy in instead of giving it out. If you fell into a black hole, you would disappear forever . . ." (77).

The idea of a free-floating bottomless chasm into which the subject may fall may be seen to image the unconscious energies that underpin subjective identity and threaten its stability. This description of the black hole, then, if taken as symbolizing the forces of the unconscious, becomes reminiscent of the concept of the unconscious as being preontological (Lacan, *Four Fundamental* 29), or based upon the withdrawal of cathectic energy and passage of elements between and within two systems (Laplanche and Leclaire). However, like the very nature of the contents of the unconscious, the Laserium is merely a play of images that constitutes a simulated reality: "Elizabeth, shivering, stares up at the sky, which isn't really a sky but a complicated machine with tiny lights projected by slides and push-buttons" (78).

Bachelard believes that any domicile must integrate an element of unreality within its construction (59). This "unreality of reality" is linked to memory and imagination and the dream world of the unconscious, and has a decidedly Imaginary nature: "The image is created through co-operation between real and unreal, with the help of the functions of the real and the unreal" (59). Further to this, Bachelard links the unreality of reality not only to "the threshold of our space" but to "the borderline between our own personal history and an indefinite pre-history" (58). Merleau-Ponty also connects anchorage and particularization in space to prehistory.[2] He states that personal existence is a "resumption of a prepersonal tradition" (254), so that the primordial level, which is the subject's first hold upon the world, must be in accordance with an earlier agreement between x and the world in general. In this account, each subject has a prehistory, so that beneath each "momentary body," which is the instrument of personal choices located in a specific time or place and based upon concrete movements, there is another "natural" body that marks a place in the world through a system of anonymous functions with a generalized focus: "There is, therefore, another subject beneath me, for whom a world exists before I am here, and who marks out my place in it" (254). This, in effect, makes space a form of communication with the world that is more ancient than thought.

This concept of a loosely defined yet preexistent self is one psychoanalysts as well as phenomenologists recognize. For Lacan, the traditions and legends that "in a heroicized form, bear my history," as well as "archival documents" ("Function" 50) in the form of childhood memories, are places in which we find the unconscious inscribed. Thus, we may begin to interpret Lesje's daydreaming not only in light of it being a symptom of the unconscious in the form of fantasy but as a form of regression that takes the subject back to an earlier, rudimentary phase of existence. Laplanche and Pontalis define regression as having a specifically temporal aspect by which it is connected to an ordered succession of systems, particularly Freud's stages of infantile psychosexual development that follow each other in a predetermined order (386). They explain regression as "a harking back to older psychical structures" (387), and a reversion to earlier forms in the development of thought, object relationships, or behaviour (386). However, they stress the fact that Freud identified this reversion to an earlier point as touching upon collective psychology, such as "the history of civilisations" (387), as well as a subject's individual psychopathology or dream work: "Freud often laid stress on the fact that the infantile past — of the individual or even of humanity as a whole — remains forever within us: '. . . the primitive stages can always be re-established; the primitive mind is, in the fullest meaning of the word, imperishable' " (387).

Richard Klein addresses the issue of an anteriority synchronic with a point of origin by also placing it at the gap between the conscious and the unconscious. He argues that the way in which one can metaphorically conceptualize a "non-originary origin" (68), which is a continuity between two regions while at the same time being a radical disjunction, is to see it in terms of the pre-oedipal feminine phase that Freud posited but left largely unexplored. Indeed, Freud himself admitted that this phase of prehistory remains difficult to determine: "Everything in the sphere of this first attachment to the mother seemed to me so difficult to grasp in analysis — so grey with age and shadowy and almost impossible to revivify — that it was as if it had succumbed to an especially inexorable repression" ("Female Sexuality" 373). However, based upon anatomical difference and aspects of castration and the oedipal complex that are specific to the little girl, he was able to image the pre-oedipal prehistory of subjective identity as having a special relationship with the feminine: "We see, then, that the phase of exclusive attachment to the mother, which may be called the *pre-Oedipus* phase, possesses a far greater importance in women than it can have in men" (377). Further to this, Freud uses archaeological metaphors to characterize it: "Our insight into this early, pre-Oedipus, phase in girls comes to us as a surprise, like the discovery, in another field, of the Minoan-Mycenaean civilization behind the civilization of Greece" (372).

Freud's metaphorical description of the pre-oedipal phase in terms of ancient history is particularly relevant for an analysis of *Life before Man* that sees Lesje's recalcitrant fantasy life as being a type of prehistorical existence in form as well as in name. To begin with, Lesje is characterized as being "compulsive" (183) about paleontology, and the way in which she seems compelled to create her Imaginary existence bespeaks a repetition compulsion that signals the reemergence of the past in the present.[3] Also, her particular type of dream work is a blatant disregard of the dictates of conscious, shared reality: "she allows herself to violate shamelessly whatever official version of paleontological reality she chooses" (18).

This is, perhaps, reminiscent of the fact that the pre-oedipal phase of psychosexual development is one dominated by the polymorphous perverse drives of the pleasure principle, rather than one dictated by the confines of the reality principle. However, most significant is the fact that her fantasy life seems to be constructed in light of issues of sexual difference; and this may be seen to connect the manifestations of Imaginary existence surfacing in adult life through fantasy to an earlier absence or point of emergence of the oedipal triangle. This brings to the fore two important points. The first is the fact that the Imaginary, while inclusive of illusion and image, should not be solely defined by the mechanics of visual or hallucinatory identification. As Heath explains, "the imaginary and the specular are not, as is too commonly thought, a simple equivalence; the latter — reflections, mirrorings, imaginings — is part of the former but does not exhaust it" ("Difference" 77). Secondly, the Imaginary may involve identifications that predate actual subjective positioning, notably those that are antecedent to oedipal resolution. The Imaginary is, as Heath points out, "a site of reference of the pre-Oedipal bond of daughter-mother" (75); or as Jacqueline Rose explains, "The imaginary also contains the realm of pre-Oedipality to which the sexuality of the woman is bound. . . . a repressed reference to the pre-Oedipal relation between the mother and the girl-child" (155–56).

Lesje's stepping back into a time and place that is other than her own present-day reality is characterized in the novel as her reentering "The Lost World" (45). It is, however, a world that is particularly maternal in nature and thus may be seen to touch upon Freud's own emphasis upon the specificity and significance of the primary relationship between mother and daughter. Lesje's secret belief that her grandmother should have been placed in the museum on her death

(95) connects her matrilineal ancestry to her imagined prehistoric one, as does the caricaturing of both her grandmothers in a way that they come to resemble dinosaurs: "they're fixed, mounted specimens in her head, cut from their own wrecked and shadowy backgrounds and pasted here. Anachronisms, the last of their kind" (268).

Her own later acknowledgement that "someday they [she and Elizabeth] may be grandmothers" (309) is a kind of recognition of the fact that the evolutionary process that she chooses to image in the form of the demise of the Mesozoic period may in fact metaphorically represent her own individual and subjective development. On a number of occasions, this "tree of evolution" (308) is contextualized in terms of sexual difference and marital or sexual economies. William, for instance, is seen to have "frightened everything away" (141) as he momentarily wanders through Lesje's fantasy world. And Nate's back problem is seen in terms that make his masculine form "an evolutionary mistake" (48). This disruptive presence of men within her imagined world implies that, in terms of psychosexual stages of development, the pre-oedipal must at some point be interrupted by the oedipal triangle of paternal and phallic desire. Nate, for instance, introduces the dynamics of sexual desire into the world of paleontology when he imagines "sweeping Lesje up from the carpeted floor of the Vertebrate Evolution Gallery and running up the stairs with her to the seclusion of Mammals and Insects" (84). Indeed, Lesje admits that her fantasy life is subject to the same intervention by men that has shaped history: "Men replaced dinosaurs . . . in her head as in geological time . . ." (19). However, her contention that "in prehistory there are no men" (19) broadens the issue of sexual encounter between the sexes into one of alterity and a general emergence of the other, because in this prehistorical life there are also "no other human beings" (19). Thus, the eventual replacement of feminine and unconscious libidinal energies with masculine desire is a dynamic that is destined to introduce the presence of others, and in doing so inaugurate a positioning that is subjective.

The fact that prehistoric existence is presubjective and does not in itself allow for the assumption of an enunciative position may be seen to be illustrated by the fact that this phase is both unnamed — "But does the Mesozoic exist? When it did it was called nothing" (290) — and foreclosed, much like the presignifying natural state of the referential order: *The Mesozoic isn't real. It's only a word for a place you can't go to any more because it isn't there*" (290). Lesje had longed for a new kind of dinosaur that, by naming it "Aliceo-saurus" (194) after herself, she could have used to bolster her identity. Her never having the opportunity to do this implies that prehistoric existence is incompatible with the enunciative position associated with a name. This foretells of the eventual relinquishing of an antiquated, pre-oedipal state: "For a moment Lesje glimpses warm tranquil seas, gentle winds, the immense fur-covered pteranodons soaring like wisps of white cotton high overhead. Such visions are still possible, but they don't last long. Inevitably she sees a later phase: the stench of dying seas, dead fish on the mud-covered shores, the huge flocks dwindling, stranded, their time done" (238).

In terms of the narrative, this pessimism is a consequence of her unfulfilling relationship with Nate, who by now has moved out of his marital home and has supposedly established a new life with Lesje. Given that the demise of the prehistoric world is connected in this way with the dynamics of sexual interaction, the intervention of paternal desire, while necessary, may not represent an altogether positive experience for women. Juliet Mitchell maintains that a dichotomy between pre- and post-oedipal existence is inevitable in the case of women: "In all types of women, the two-tiered structure — the civilization of Minos-Mycenae and that of the superimposed Greeks makes itself felt in one way or another" (119). This is because the pre-oedipal period that Mitchell also names as being "pre-historic" is, for the girl, never fully replaced by an oedipal figuration, and never becomes a temporally distinct phase. Mary Anne Doane explains this in another way, saying "the female never fully resolves her Oedipal complex and is thus linked more strongly to the realm of the pre-Oedipal than the male" (*Desire* 144). Her explanation echoes Freud's belief that, owing to anatomical differences between the sexes, girls lack the fear of castration necessary for surmounting the oedipal complex: "Girls remain in it for an indeterminate length of time; they demolish it late and, even so, incompletely" ("Feminin-ity" 163). For Mitchell, this results in a particularly problematic situation for female identity, because "in the case of the boy the two are far more compatible. The distinction between them could avoid perception because here the Greeks just took over and built on the strength of their Minoan-Mycenean predecessors. But for women Greek history represented a massive defeat, and it will be at their peril that their prehistory, though it will always be in evidence, will continue to dominate in their lives" (110).

The conflicting nature of Imaginary existence as a function of pre-

and post-oedipal dynamics is emphasized when Lesje and Nate argue about their marital status, and the hostility is expressed in terms of the prehistoric metaphor. Lesje has been staying late at the Museum or bringing home books on fossilized teeth in an attempt to avoid conversation:

> "Dinosaurs are dead," he said to her one day, trying to lighten things up. "But I'm still alive."
> "Are you sure?" she said, with one of those ball-shriveling looks. As if he was a teeny little dog turd. (258)

Indeed, in considering her life with William, Lesje had admitted that while the mechanics of sexual desire had indeed replaced much of her energy for paleontology, "thinking about men has become too unrewarding" (19). Similarly, faced by an inability to retain signifi-cance in Nate's life in the face of his commitment to his children and former wife, Lesje flushes her contraceptive pills down the toilet in an act of anger and defiance, while we are told: "It's long been her theoretical opinion that Man is a danger to the universe, a mis-chievous ape, spiteful, destructive, malevolent" (293). This is height-ened by the kind of world William presents to her when they are still living together, supposedly in domestic bliss: "He's bombarding her with gloom: pollutants are pouring into the air, over three hundred of them, more than have yet been identified. Sulphuric acid and mercury are falling, metallic mist, acid rain, into the pure lakes of Muskoka and points north. Queasy fish rise, roll over, exposing bellies soon to bloat. If ten times more control is not implemented at once (at once!) the Great Lakes will die" (142).

This seems in firm opposition to the fact that her imagined prehistoric existence is decidedly soothing (224, 307), and "a pre-serve" (67) to which she repeatedly escapes when life with the men with whom she is involved becomes too difficult (143, 264, 208–09). In fact, she is decidedly alienated from her present reality, as "She herself does not feel that the time through which she's presently living is particularly hers" (237). By contrast, access to the ancient lost world is seen to be "privileged" (45), and the sanctity of this past is hinted at when the museum is described as being "like a church or shrine": "It was quiet and smelled mysterious, and was full of sacred objects: quartz, amethyst, basalt" (95). The hallowed halls of the museum are seen to contain the wisdom of past civilizations: "Some-times she thinks of the Museum as a repository of knowledge, the resort of scholars, a palace built in the pursuit of truth, . . . other times it's a bandits' cave: the past has been vandalized and this is where the loot is stored" (308). Lesje likes to see herself as the "guardian" (308) of this treasure, and there is a sense of urgency in her commitment to preserving the legacy: "Surely these things are important, surely her knowledge should not perish with her. She must be allowed to continue her investigations. . . . [T]he bones have to be named, you have to know what to call them, otherwise what are they, they're lost, cut adrift from their own meanings, they may as well not have been saved for you" (157).

Compared to contemporary existence, the lost world appears to be much more significant. The chart in Lesje's office illustrates the relativity: "On her office wall the tree of evolution branches like coral towards the ceiling: Fishes, Amphibians, Therapsids, Thecodonts, Archosaurs, Pterosaurs, Birds, Mammals, and Man, a mere dot" (308); "Dinosaurs, a hundred and twenty million years of tawny yellow; man, a speck of red" (210). And this bygone era seems to hold the promise of a new life. One is reminded of Lesje's fantasy of reclaiming a world that is sensuous and rudimentary: "the place Lesje intended to discover would be tropical, rich and crawling with wondrous life forms, all of them either archaic and thought extinct, or totally unknown even in fossil records" (92). Similarly, the day she found the Albertosaurus thigh, Lesje responded with the joy of having found the promised land: "*Live again!* she'd wanted to cry, like some Old Testament prophet, like God, throwing up her arms, willing thunderbolts; and the strange flesh would grow again, cover the bones, the badlands would moisten and flower" (80–81). Perhaps it is this potential for rejuvenation that keeps alive in Lesje the desire for the past. She herself finds it difficult to explain: "They're merely bones, bones and wire in a scenery of dusty plastic, and she's an adult; why does she continue to think of them as alive?" (310). Equally as difficult to rationalize is her secret desire that one day "her old acquaintances" in the museum could be magically brought to life: "the things were silent and unmoving, true, but somewhere there existed an implement or force (a secret ray, atomic energy) that would bring them back to life" (310).

If the Mesozoic space is imaged, even momentarily, as being a pre-oedipal one, then Lesje's construction of a fantasy life may be seen to be a symptom of regression not only to the unconscious but to a maternal and therefore feminine state. In this sense, Lesje's desire to bring back to life an existence that lies beyond symbolic discourse and the metonymy of paternal desire may then be interpreted as being the creation of what Luce Irigaray has called the "feminine imaginary" (*This Sex*). For Irigaray, conventional notions of the Imaginary characterize it as being a masculine one, isomorphic with the male body and reliant upon production, property, singularity, and unity ("Is the Subject" 77). A feminine Imaginary, on the other hand, would function according to the dynamics of the female form, be characterized by fluidity and plurality, and be innately admitting of alterity and feminine specificity. Given free expression, this Imaginary, normally repressed, would allow for new forms of thought and models of signification in an act of liberation for both men and women. Viewed in terms of the Irigarayan model, Lesje may be seen to be creating a form of Imaginary existence in reaction to and from the position of her feminine role in a post-oedipal libidinal economy. And in this way, Lesje may be seen to be doing exactly what Irigaray puts forward as being her own theoretical manifesto: to "(re)discover a possible space for the feminine imaginary" (*This Sex* 164).

Interpreting Lesje's fantasy world in terms of issues of sexual difference bespeaks the issue of the Imaginary as a pre-oedipal economy, while it also explains the highly emotive nature of her reactions. Much as she would like to bring the prehistoric world of the museum into existence, Lesje acknowledges that "that can't happen, so the next best thing is these displays" (81). Admittedly, even the freedom of her private Imaginary existence is destined to be interrupted by the necessary constraints of a shared, subjective reality. Contemplating her inability to remain indefinitely in her own personal fantasy world, she recognizes that "she can't do it" because "In the foreground, pushing in whether she wants it to or not, is . . . life" (311). While Lesje acknowledges the importance of her personal and collective prehistory, realizing that "without the past she would not exist" (308), there is the undeniable necessity for introjecting images from the external world in order to maintain an intersubjective existence. In her own words, "the fragments of new images intrude" (311); and while this makes the daydreaming a phenomenon that is individual and intrasubjective, it concludes by reminding us that subjectivity is by necessity a symbolic identity tempered by Imaginary reflections.

The intrusion of an external world into the psyche suggests an impingement upon the self by others that brings to the fore the fact that the Imaginary, apart from being the dimension of images immersed in the pre-oedipal realm, is based upon a relationship with the counterpart. As such, it is irrevocably dichotomous in nature. Laplanche and Pontalis define the intrasubjective duality of the Imaginary as being the narcissistic relation of the subject to his or her own ego (210). In doing so they draw upon Lacan's formulation of the mirror-stage as initiating the earliest form of Imaginary captation by way of its providing a specular image with which the infant may identify. For Lacan, the moment of jubilant recognition at the sight of the reflected imago signals an active narcissism typified as being "an essential libidinal relationship with the body image" ("Some Reflections" 14). It is this narcissistic relation with an image of the self that will subsequently allow for the formation of a subjective identity: "It is in this erotic relation, in which the human individual fixes upon himself an image that alienates him from himself, that are to be found the energy and the form on which this organization of the passions that he will call his ego is based" (Lacan, "Aggressivity" 19).

The amorous entrancement of the subject by his or her own image is clearly evident when Lesje admits the attraction of her eyes and the lure of the veil, and shows that the ego may present itself to the self as love-object: "Sometimes when she's alone she holds one of her flowered pillowcases across the lower half of her face. . . . Her eyes, dark, almost black, look back at her in the bathroom mirror, enigmatic above the blue and purple flowers" (22). This appraisal of the self in terms of the body and its image widens onto an ego-identity by which Lesje is able to classify herself as being "timorous" (19) and unassuming: "she isn't wheedling or devious, she doesn't wear negligées or paint her toenails. William may think she's exotic, but she isn't really; she's straightforward, narrow and unadorned, a scientist; not a web-spinner . . ." (127). However, mention of her lover's opinion as opposed to her own characterization of herself shows that the relation of the subject to his or her own ego-identity is as much a matter of introjecting an image provided by others as it is a function of identification with a self-constructed imago. Indeed, much is made of other people's images of Lesje. Elizabeth, we are told, sees her as being a "clown" or "giraffe," with a certain "gawkiness and lack of poise" (161). William, by contrast, finds her "impossibly exotic" and admires her mind, tantalized by her ability to use technical language (29). Yet by far the most prominent is Nate's characterization of her as having stepped out of a Byzantine icon: "He takes a dime from his pocket, holds it. His token, his talisman, his one hope of salvation. At the other end of the line a thin woman waits, her pale face framed by dark hair, her hand lifted, fingers upraised in blessing" (35).

Nate sees involvement with Lesje as his chance to be transported to "somewhere he's never been before" (71), and he is thoroughly entranced by her: "Holding Lesje would be like holding some strange plant, smooth, thin, with sudden orange flowers. *Exotics*, the florists called them" (71). For him, she holds all the promise of an enchanted desert paradise: "He thinks of her waiting for him, somewhere else, an island, subtropical, not muggy, her long hair waving in the sea breeze, a red hibiscus tucked behind one ear" (246). Not only is she unknown but she is as mysterious and intriguing as a baroque heroine playing a harpsichord: "He's in love with her, with that cool thin body, the face turned in upon itself in statue-like contemplation. She sits behind a lighted window, draped in soft white, playing the spinet, her moving fingers luminous against the keys" (134). And she herself participates in this creation of her identity. When Nate telephones her at work, nasal and forlorn, she wilfully takes on the role of Florence Nightingale: "Lesje walks to the rescue in her gum-soled snowboots, a nurse hurrying over frozen Siberia, driven on by love. She will put her hand on his forehead and miraculously he will revive" (167). Eventually, she acknowledges the seductive quality of such imagery: "The fact is that she's addicted to Nate's version of her. . . . She's realized with something close to panic that the picture he's devised of her is untrue. . . . [S]he isn't like this at all. Nevertheless she wants to be; she wants to be this beautiful phantom, this boneless wraith he's conjured up" (267).

The misrecognition and subsequent alienation that Lacan postulates as being a function of specular and Imaginary identity formation is clearly evident here in the discrepancy between Lesje's self-constructed images and those projected upon her. The illusory quality of an identity provided by others gives her sense of self a distinctly Imaginary nature: "Sometimes, when he [Nate] touches her, she feels not naked but clothed, in some long unspecified garment that spreads around her like a shimmering cloud" (267). While appearing as a kind of cocoon in which Lesje can wrap herself, this identity projected by others on to the self, described as it is in its libidinal aspect, is also a function of intercourse with the other. At this point, the narcissistic relation becomes one of interaction with otherness. As Laplanche and Pontalis explain, "with the ego taking form by virtue of an identification with the other, narcissism . . . is no longer seen as a state independent of any intersubjective relationship, but rather as the internalisation of a relationship" (256). In this sense, Lacanian narcissism, structured by mirror-stage specularization, equates with what Freud termed "secondary narcissism." In Freud's account, "primary narcissism"[4] is a rudimentary state that is objectless, egoless, and totally devoid of any relationship to the outside world. By contrast, the secondary form of narcissism that eventually replaces this primitive state is permitting of object relations, and is "contemporaneous with the formation of the ego through identification with the other person" (Laplanche and Pontalis 256).

The identification with an image that is of the self yet also of the other is also well illustrated through the characterization of Elizabeth. More than any other character in the novel, she tries to insulate herself from those around her. Walking along the street, "She doesn't glance into the store windows; she knows what she looks like and she doesn't indulge in fantasies of looking any other way. She doesn't need her own reflection or the reflections of other people's ideas of her or of themselves" (57). However, even she is unable to completely detach from the perceptions of others. Some time later, she admits that "Living with Nate has been like living with a huge mirror in which her flaws are magnified and distorted," and that "She's been forced to see herself measured constantly . . ." (206) next to his suburban middle-class values. Like Lesje, she confronts a number of perceptions that do not coincide with her idea of herself. Nate feels constantly manipulated by "that dying swan look of hers" (16), and "that nymph-on-a-lilypad pose" (105). For him, she had played the role of "earthmother" (162), protecting him in the darkness of the night; and, through years of marriage, she changes from being his "Madonna in a shrine, shedding a quiet light" (49) to being "the lady with the axe" (49) toward whom he is propelled.

Of course, Elizabeth does much to propagate images of herself that portray her as being detached and in control. After the death of her lover, she is careful to present a respectable front to her family, carrying her grief "like some bereft queen out of a Shakespearean play" (64). At her own birthday party, she is nothing if not refined, even though other emotions lurk beneath the genteel surface: "she tightened the corners of her mouth, widened her eyes, and negotiated the stairs, holding on to the banister. Nude descending the staircase, in cunning fragments. Stewed, descending the staircase" (248). Lesje seems unfooled by the well-bred and polished persona, choosing instead to see her as being ruthless and manipulative: "Today she classifies Elizabeth as a shark; on other days it's a huge Jurassic toad, primitive, squat, venomous; on other days a cephalopod, a giant squid, soft and tentacled, with a hidden beak" (265). Indeed, it is only toward the end of the novel, after years of being intimidated by her, that Lesje is able to see her as "ordinary" and "mortal" (309). By contrast, the "real" Elizabeth is neither urbane nor in control. By her own admission, she has lost the shell with which she once protected herself and is now living "like a peeled snail" (11). Although no one except Chris ever realized it, "she's a refugee, with a refugee's desperate habits" (150). In fact, behind her cultivated, elegant appearance, "there's nothing in her that will compel her to behave decently" (150).

Elizabeth's ruthlessly determined nature, the fact that "If pushed she'll stop at nothing" (150), illustrates the theory that Imaginary narcissism, based as it is upon the intervention and image of the other, is structurally responsible for forms of aggression. This is because the subject needs recognition and is placed in a situation of rivalry with others. Elizabeth's aggressive intention toward the other, motivated by self-preservation, demonstrates that aggressivity is a composite of both the Imaginary narcissism and specular identity formation that underlies the constitution of subjectivity. Thus we witness the dynamic that allows Lacan to speak of "the notion of an aggressivity linked to the narcissistic relation and to the structures of systematic *méconnaissance* and objectification that characterize the formation of the ego" ("Aggressivity" 21).

For Laplanche and Pontalis, aggressive tension is one of two expressions of the intersubjective dual relationship with the image of a counterpart that defines the Imaginary. The other is erotic attraction (210). For Elizabeth and Lesje, who inadvertently become involved in a battle for possession of Nate, sexual attraction for an other becomes inextricably connected to a power struggle that echoes the fact that "the ego is a function of mastery, a play of presence, of bearing . . . and of constituted rivalry" (Lacan, "Subversion" 307). Standing outside Nate and Lesje's new house in the middle of the night, Elizabeth feels rejected and alone and longs to make her presence felt (251–52). For her, Nate is territory to be protected, and her strategy is to control or, as Martha puts it, to "supervise" (147) his affairs with other women. Eventually, she begins to oversee the affair with Lesje as well, so that at any given moment Lesje half expects Elizabeth and her children to move right into her house (241), having already moved into her life. Lesje even considers that her right to have a child is denied through Elizabeth's behaviour (266). In general, Lesje struggles under the weight of Elizabeth's strategies of intimidation, realizing that "People like Elizabeth could . . . blot you out . . ." (293).

Indeed, until the moment when Lesje takes a decisive step to protect herself by fighting the battle on the grounds of pregnancy, the strength of her rival's convictions are seen to endanger her very identity by placing her in an "ambiguous position in the universe" (223). As she herself admits, without the legitimate status of being a wife she is unsure of who and where she is: "Marriage is an event, a fact. . . . So is divorce. They create a framework, a beginning, an ending. Without them everything is amorphous, an endless middle ground . . ." (192). Elizabeth and Lesje's feud over Nate, then, demonstrates that aggressive rivalry underpins object relations mediated by the intervention and desire of the other. After all, as Lacan points out, "It is, in fact, the earliest jealousy that sets the stage on which the triangular relationship between the ego, the object and 'someone else' comes into being" ("Some Reflections" 12).

Lesje, too, struggles for proprietary rights in the face of what becomes a triangular contest of wills: "Lesje knows that when Nate moved completely in, or as completely as he's going to, Elizabeth should have felt deserted and betrayed and she herself should have felt, if not victorious, at least conventionally smug. Instead it seems to be the other way around" (238). But it is Elizabeth who pushes the boundaries of the contest further by entering Lesje's sexual terrain: "Either she will seduce William, to create some balance in the universe, a tit for a tat, or she'll tell him about Lesje and Nate; or perhaps both" (177). When she finally does seduce her enemy's ex-lover, the man with whom sex is like sleeping with a large albeit fairly active slab of Philadelphia cream cheese (213), what becomes evident is the fact that the object fought for is essentially interchangeable with other objects, provided they have similar properties. This is indicative of Lacan's contention that "The object of man's desire . . . is essentially an object desired by someone else," and that "One object can become equivalent to another, owing to the effect produced by this intermediary, in making it possible for objects to be exchanged and compared" ("Some Reflections" 12). Further to this, "This process tends to diminish the special significance of any one particular object . . ." (12), a point that becomes important when considering the characterization of Nate.

Nate's loss of specificity means that he increasingly comes to resemble a pawn in a game in which the women with whom he is involved are the active combatants. As Lesje acknowledges, in whatever message is transmitted, ". . . Elizabeth [is] the sender, Nate merely the unwitting deliverer" (185). Elizabeth, too, recognizes Nate's passivity and his status as innocent victim: "She isn't trying to torture Nate: torture is a by-product. She's merely trying to win, . . . she knows she will win, there's no way she can help winning. She'll win, and she hopes it will make her feel better" (263). Nate himself is not naive in understanding the part he plays. By his own admission, he appraises the situation by stating, "It was part of her campaign, part of the squeeze to get him into this corner where he now crouches" (256). Indeed, for Elizabeth, this connection between love, sex, and power is not unfamiliar. Her recollection of her very first sexual experience shows it to have been characterized by anger and violence, and motivated by a desire to defeat Auntie Muriel and the memory of her mother — the two women who had, up until this point, dominated her life. But she is also aware of the potential for mastery over men: "There's danger . . . but she knows she can control it. She enjoys the latent power of her own hands . . ." (178). Of course, later in life, she rules not only her husband but even men as strong as Chris, whom she characterizes as dark, dangerous, and unpredictable, and the only one who ever seriously posed any threat to her: "She hates it when anyone has power over her. Nate doesn't have that kind of power, he never had" (23). Yet, invincible as he seemed, Chris's encounter with Elizabeth leaves him looking "bludgeoned" and "beaten," with "dark horizontal welts under his eyes, as if he's been slugged across the face with a belt" (234). Eventually, he is left looking "like a straggler from a defeated army" (236), and blows his head off with a shotgun.

While Chris's injuries are imaged in terms of a deteriorating physique and stature, Nate is as much a casualty. His body is described as sagging from his spine, "the flesh drooping like warm taffy on a sucker stick" (32). Martha characterizes him as being food for Elizabeth to consume (33), although he broadens the comparison to include all the women in his life, even his mother: ". . . Nate thinks of himself as a lump of putty, helplessly molded by the relentless demands and flinty disapprovals of the women he can't help being involved with" (41). Trapped between his ex-wife and his lover, "He's caught in a vise, the handle is turning, slowly, inexorably" (259). He feels himself slowly becoming fossilized (82), and fears that he is obsolete, even in the procreation of his own children (83).

Yet even more dangerous is the fact that the dislocation from his duties as father and husband within the domestic and marital economy is causing him to lead a "divided life" (200), which in turn leads to a loss of specular identity: "Already his reflection in the mirror was fading, the house was forgetting him, he was negligible" (198). His endangered subjectivity becomes clear when we learn that "He should have two sets of clothes, two identities, one for each house . . . ," and that he sees the dissolution as being "literal": "He has been separated; he is separate. Dismembered" (244). Realization of this dislocation makes him think of himself as being nothing more than a vacant effigy, "a tin man" who is mere "patchwork" (246) who can no longer connect acts with consequences. Consequently, his world becomes disconnected to the point where houses in the street "look segmented, a collection of units, not really attached. The leaves aren't attached to the trees, the roofs aren't attached to the houses . . ." (244). He is losing his ability to order or territorialize space, and in this land of make-believe, Nate too has become subdivided, a "segmented man" like the toy man built of wooden rings slipped over a central post: "This is his body, stiff fragments held together by his spine and his screwtop head" (244).

At this point, Nate becomes an example of the individual suffering at the hands of both the aggressivity and erotic entanglement that are, in this context, expressions of the intersubjective relationship that defines the Imaginary. Thus, while Lesje and Elizabeth have been the protagonists in the play of the Imaginary, Nate has been a kind of ancillary figure to their dynamics, with the result that his own subjective stance has been endangered through this kind of involvement. This interpretation is in full accordance with a psychoanalytic model that specifies that the subject who is to retain a functional subjectivity needs to control the Imaginary through symbolic demands so that the subjective stance becomes a negotiation of both realms. It is also in accordance with the conclusion of the novel, which leaves Nate's position unresolved and William's role distinctly peripheral, but ends with a sense that Elizabeth's identity will remain firm, while Lesje will positively assert a new sense of self through the conception of a new life.

¹ Lacan uses the metaphor of the Borromean knot to describe how it is that the symbolic, Real, and Imaginary are connected. Ragland-Sullivan explains that if one ring of the Borromean knot is broken, the other two are loosened as well, and "Any shift of equilibrium among Lacan's three orders has the same effect on the psychic system" (*Jacques Lacan* 131).

² The following account is drawn from Merleau-Ponty (254).

³ Laplanche and Pontalis maintain that the repetition compulsion points to the reemergence of the past in the present (387).

⁴ The following account is taken from Laplanche and Pontalis (255–57).

CHAPTER FOUR

Bodily Harm:

The SPLIT SUBJECT *as a* FUNCTION *of* SPATIAL *and* SIGNIFICATORY POSITIONING

My account begins with that which differentiates *Bodily Harm* (*BH*) from the other novels studied: its overt investigative focus. The protagonist's unwitting involvement in local politics and international espionage makes her a kind of detective figure who attempts to unravel the deceit and intrigue surrounding her situation. However, in focusing upon a number of factors, including the concatenated network through which people on the island inform each other, shifting points of view and conflicting versions of the same event, and Rennie's own journalistic ability to construct an account and the responsibility of having that privilege, my interpretation sees Rennie's search for knowledge as bespeaking a wider issue: the discursivity of truth.

With the plot revolving around the construction and disclosure of truth, my account assumes signification to be a primary issue. However, signification demands not only a sign but a speaker and a position from which it may be spoken; and this, in turn, brings to the fore the issue of subjectivity. Lacanian theory well explains the relationship between the signifier and the subject as one that effects a fading or dislocation of subjective identity. This, in addition to Kristevan theories of enunciation, which reveal that the assumption of an enunciative position requires reinvestment of libidinal and hence bodily energies, justifies a new interpretation of Rennie's cancer. Such an interpretation takes into account the subject as signifiable, as corporeal, and, because of both of these, as endangered.

In general, the cancer now becomes a motif of the threat to subjective identity conditional upon the assumption of an enunciative position. It is my contention that this danger is also imaged by the threat of actual bodily harm as a direct consequence of the protagonist's pursuit of knowledge. However, at this point, reliant upon the work of a number of psychoanalytic theorists, the cancer is interpreted in terms of its representing the misrecognition that marks the earliest moment of specular identity formation, the moment of castration through which the signifier effects a discontinuity with the Real, and the positing of the subject as signifiable through bodily loss.

These dynamics are seen to image not only the connections between the corporeal and the enunciative and hence the subjective, but to contextualize the cancer as a function of abjection. Drawing upon Kristeva's formulation of the abject, the cancer is seen to be functional in two important ways. First, on an intrasubjective level, it marks both the constitution of Rennie's subjective identity and its potential dissolution, in this way expressing the psychic ambivalence of the subjective position. Second, on a communal level, abjection is held responsible for the particular social dynamics that feature in the novel, and in doing so bespeaks the broader, intersubjective connotations of the corporeal nature of identity.

With this in mind, my account turns to the episodes of Rennie's imprisonment, implicated as they are in corruption and political hypocrisy, in an analysis that sees them as social formations underwritten by abjection. As such, they are also a kind of malignancy, functional between rather than within individuals. With this, we are brought to the relations of danger between self and other, a point from which it becomes most appropriate to analyse the protagonist's relationships with men.

Focusing upon the circulatory relations of power and passivity between Rennie and Jake, and the contractual obligations of incision inflicted by Daniel, the protagonist's involvement with men is seen, within my account, to illustrate the fact that sexual relations are symbolic relations, and are inscribed, as it were, in corporeality. These dynamics further imply the necessity for intervention by and of the other, and bring to the amorous encounter an aspect that makes it a type of support for subjectivity. With this, Kristeva's concept of love is best suited to explaining Rennie's need for affirmation through sexual contact with Paul. Allowing her a potential for narcissistic self-imaging, through her encounter with men Rennie is able to come to terms not only with her self but her body and her illness.

In this negotiation and resolution of the corporeal aspects of the self, Rennie is brought to confront and to accept her own mortality. However, the potential fading of the self glimpsed throughout her experience with illness and her interaction with men now becomes characteristic of the kind of aphanisis that, by definition, marks all subjectivity. Since the subjective stance is an enunciative one and signification bespeaks the assumption of a position, at this point my account turns to analysis of the protagonist and her fictional world not only in significatory but in spatial terms. This approach is well justified in terms of *Bodily Harm*, for while all the other novels are set firmly in suburban Canada, the story of Rennie Wilford is notable in its wider international context. I take this point of departure as an invitation to explore issues of location, positionality, and the negotiation of space.

Drawing mostly upon Kristeva's work to clarify the connection between signification and spatiality, I interpret bodily experience as a matter of difference and symbolic exchange. The introduction of Irigaray's model of spatial dynamics, which function according to sexual difference, allows for continuing analysis of Rennie's relationship with her lover in a way that accounts perfectly for the spatial metaphors that characterize their liaison. With this, sexual encounter becomes a play of absence and presence in space, and a kind of structure upon which subjectivity and objectivity can be anchored. This theoretical shift toward the way in which phenomena are perceived motivates the introduction of the work of Maurice Merleau-Ponty and Gaston Bachelard in exploring the function of space in structuring subjectivity.

Inspired by phenomenological theory, my account then proceeds to focus upon a number of issues: namely, the positing of self and the determination of objects, the function of the surface in delineating boundaries between self and other, and the power plays evident within the domestication of space. Thus, I am able to shed new light on incidents within the novel that do not seem immediately relevant to the present in which Rennie is situated. For example, Rennie's dreams and her relationship with her grandmother are analysed in light of Bachelard's notion of how it is that one's immediate space is inhabited, and the ways in which it becomes a territory of the mind as well as of the body. In this way, the incidents are interpreted as being dynamics of domestication of the external world on the part of the subject. Furthermore, these early childhood experiences are contextualized within the psychic compulsion for them to be repeated and to reemerge in adult forms. This connects them to the protagonist's current predicament on St. Antoine, so that her incarceration on the Caribbean island harks back to the traumatic incidents of her early life. The association has a number of consequences. First, it brings an immediacy to what are otherwise little more than reminiscences. Second, it allows for a new interpretation of the aggressivity and estrangement that mark the memories, and the conflict that drives the plot in its present tense. Third, it opens the question of intersubjectivity within the localization of one's surroundings.

This last point means that enclosure and spatial captation take on new meaning in terms of a social dimension. As a result, those elements within the novel that are otherwise seen only as images of a society in crisis now reflect the potential danger in intersubjective relations. Thus, the incidents of corruption, incarceration, and cruelty are now indicative of the difference between self and other, the sado-aggressive intention, and the potential for objectification of the individual within a social system.

With this, the inner world of the individual consciousness is made to confront the external world that is shared, so that domestication of that space becomes not only a personal issue but a collective one. In addition, the construction of shared space becomes a matter of its representation, a theoretical point that justifies an emphasis upon the symbolic or discursive aspects of space.

Motivated by a focus upon the way in which social relations are forged and maintained in and through the negotiation of territory, my account proceeds to draw upon the phenomenological theories of Henri Lefebvre in order to explore the use and production of space within the fictional world of the novel. Lefebvre's underlying reliance upon dynamics of internationalization, ideological and political operations, and dialectical structures involves assumptions well suited to analysing a situation in which the protagonist, above all, is engaged in a practical interaction between the self and external surroundings. Through this analysis, Rennie's incarceration is contextualized in terms of collectivization and social practice, while the cell, the island, and its society become examples of social infra- and superstructure.

While Lefebvre's work provides the most appropriate theoretical framework for examining the incidents in light of the intentional production of a social being, psychoanalytic theories are able to explain the consistently corporeal nature of Rennie's experiences in prison. Bearing in mind the fact that the social being is reliant upon bodily function, those aspects that make the incidents so very dramatic — the beatings, the sense of decay and of flesh — all become part of the corporeal reality of the societal construction of space. At this point, drawing upon Kristeva's formulation of the chora as being a mode of spatial positioning through which the subject regresses to a presocial existence, Rennie's interaction with Lora is now characterized as being intuitive, presubjective, and pretopological. This makes Rennie's interaction with Lora semiotic in nature and fragmentary in function. However, since the focus of the narrative remains consistently upon the protagonist, and the focus of analysis upon the construction of subjectivity, the choric cell becomes the place where Rennie's sense of self is both threatened and posited. Since this revolves around the function of the chora as that which predetermines the subject's ability to signify, analysis of the novel is, at this point, brought back to the very issue that opened the interpretation: discourse and signification.

At this point, however, the dialectic is one of enunciation with pure unspoken materiality, and it is seen to be imaged through Rennie's final interaction with Lora's half-conscious body. In a moment that otherwise remains fairly obscure, Rennie's connection with the other woman's body is interpreted as being a mediation between silenced choric existence and symbolic law. By preempting Lora's return to an enunciative and hence symbolic stance, the incident is seen to bespeak the issue of subjective positioning. This is then further explored by interpreting it to be a form of abstract and imaginary movement, and contrasting it with the concrete movement of Rennie's flight back to Canada. By raising the issues of intentionality of consciousness, projection and orientation of the body, and the perception of the external world, Rennie's final flight home resolves not only the events of the plot but the issue of her subjective status, so that she is able to reexperience her self in light of spatial variation. Her return home thus becomes not only an act of protecting herself against bodily harm but an intentional projection of consciousness, a negotiation of spatial relativity, and an appropriation of territory.

The conclusion of both the novel and my account of it is one in which consciousness of the body and its position is paramount. This is in perfect accordance with the tone of optimism on which the novel ends, for in more ways than one, Rennie Wilford takes her self back to Canada.

* * *

Rennie Wilford's sojourn in the Caribbean was intended to be an escape from a reality in which disintegration had begun to affect all aspects of her life. Landing in St. Antoine, however, she unwittingly becomes involved with local personalities and embroiled in a web of domestic politics and, possibly, international espionage. Her journey, apart from being one that crosses countries, takes her from a state of detachment to a level of involvement, an involvement so intense that it brings her face to face with death.

In *Bodily Harm*, the displaced and endangered subjectivity of the protagonist is a function of exile, both in spatial and significatory terms. Analysis of Rennie's subjective identity in the light of psycho-analytical and phenomenological theories illustrates that the assumption of a speaking position requires a material foundation that is, in fact, corporeality positioned in space. Meanwhile, the dynamics that take Rennie from one country to another, outline her relationships with men, and ultimately attack her own body are the very dynamics through which positionality becomes a structuring principle of her psyche.

Bodily Harm is a novel preoccupied with signification and the construction of discursive knowledge. The protagonist finds herself enmeshed within a tangled web of deceit and intrigue in which she must somehow ascertain who knows what, and what it is they know. Rennie is introduced as a journalist who traffics in words and creates her own truths. In college, she had "believed there was a real story, not several and not almost real" (*BH* 64); but now, in St. Antoine, she is confronted by a concatenated web of half-truths dependent upon who is speaking and from what position they speak.

On arriving in the Caribbean island, she is shocked by the fact that everyone seems to know about her already:

"You write for the magazines, eh?" the woman says.
"How did you know that?" Rennie asks, a little annoyed. This is the third time today.

"Everyone knows everything around here," the woman says. "Word of mouth, the grapevine you might say. Everyone knows what's happening." (88–89)

Similarly, it does not take long for most of the island to find out that she is staying with Paul:

"You are enjoying yourself at the home of your American friend?" he says slyly.
Rennie, who believes in personal privacy, is annoyed.
"How did you know I'm staying there?" she says. . . .
Dr Minnow smiles, showing his skewed teeth. "Everyone knows," he says. (227)

Meanwhile, her own attempts at informing herself are continually frustrated. Over and over again, she senses that her "real question hasn't been answered and she can see it won't be" (97), until it gets to the point where "Rennie doesn't understand anything" (260). Every scrap of information she manages to learn is revealed to be constructed by someone for some reason. Lora initially denies that Paul works for the CIA, saying instead that he sells drugs. However, later Rennie learns that Paul is a gunrunner, and when he is suspected of killing Minnow, Lora hints at his involvement with the American government after all. Prime ministerial candidates accuse each other of being corrupt, politicians are shot dead, the police are unethical, a state of emergency is proclaimed — all of which revolve around the deliberate and conscious construction of truths. As Lora herself admits, "there's a lot of stories," and it is difficult to tell the difference between them (277).

Rennie's inadvertent involvement in the situation also revolves around what appears to be her privileged position of having access to representational discourse. No one seems to believe that she intends to write nothing more than a travel piece; indeed, Minnow directly asks her to inform the rest of the world because she has access to the media. While she denies her own ability to do so, eventually her social conscience is drawn upon when the imprisoned Lora asks her to let the world know of her plight:

"Tell someone I'm here," says Lora. "Tell someone what happened. . . ."
"Who should I tell?" says Rennie.

155

"I don't know," says Lora. "Someone." (282)

Her own release, however, is conditional upon her silence, and the representative of the Canadian government, while proclaiming himself a believer in the freedom of the press, warns her about becoming involved in the internal affairs of other countries, and requests that she not write about her experiences (295–96).

While much of the narrative development of the novel revolves around the construction and disclosure of knowledge, the thematic content may be seen to be connected to the issues of signification through its concern with the subjective status of the protagonist. Kristeva makes the point that "It is impossible to treat the problems of signification seriously, in linguistics or semiology, without including in these considerations the *subject thus formulated as operating consciousness*" ("From One" 131). This raises the issue of subjective identity in the context of an enunciative position. For Lacan, the signifier determines the subject, and not the reverse: "This passion of the signifier now becomes a new dimension of the human condition in that it is not only man who speaks, but that in man and through man *it* speaks . . . that his nature is woven by effects in which is to be found the structure of language, of which he becomes the material . . ." ("Signification" 284).

This "subjection of the subject to the signifier" (Lacan, "Subversion" 304) has far-reaching consequences for the ego-identity of the individual. In Lacan's account, the signifying chain that governs the constitution of the subject is situated in the locus of the other (*Four Fundamental* 203). While the signifier, produced in the field of the other, makes manifest the subject of its signification, it does so by reducing the subject to being no more than another signifier in the concatenated chain (207). This results in a kind of exile through which the subject is decentred and displaced from a secure position of knowledge: "If he is apprehended at his birth in the field of the Other, the characteristic of the subject of the unconscious is that of being, beneath the signifier that develops its networks, its chains and its history, at an indeterminate place" (208). Lacan names this dynamic as inducing a "feeling of alienation" (217) that has, as its effect, the "aphanisis" of the subject. This is an actual division whereby the subject appears in one position as meaning, but is manifested elsewhere as "fading" (208), or "disappearance" (218). Such splitting is, in fact, the structural and founding principle of subjective identity and the assumption of a speaking position: "There is no subject without, somewhere, *aphanisis* of the subject, and it is in this alienation, in this fundamental division, that the dialectic of the subject is established" (221).

In *Bodily Harm*, the subjective status of the protagonist, the potential fading and alienation conditional upon the assumption of an enunciative position, is explored in light of the corporeal nature of identity. Indeed, signification, like all forms of symbolic discourse, is reliant upon the body and its sublimation. In this sense, language may be seen to be the connection of the corporeal being to signifiers through a redirection of libidinal and drive energy. Kristeva specifies the phonatory capacity of the infant as being due to an impulsional activity in the form of an exploration of the vocal apparatus and of the fragmented body.[1] The prelinguistic babble is not yet tied to the referent and signifier/signified dichotomy, and exists prior to holophrastic utterances or phrastic intonations. Eventually, vocalism in its prelinguistic function is limited, and the impulsivity becomes disciplined and organized into a system of phonic differences regulated by processes of condensation and displacement. This system is, of course, language; and it now exists for the newly emerged subject as a way to represent experiences of the Real and of objects in the external world.

For Kristeva, signification is a realm of positions. This positionality is structured as a rupture through which the identity of the subject and its objects may be established. This break is what she terms "a thetic phase" and it occurs initially at two points: the mirror-stage and castration. It is these thetic moments that allow the infant to emit holophrastic utterances that separate subject from object and attribute to this difference a signifier.[2]

The first thetic moment — the mirror-stage — and the issue of rupture so crucial to the assumption of a signifying position feature in the account of Rennie's identity when, sometime before her scheduled mastectomy, she glances in the mirror. "Her body was in the mirror, looking the same as ever" (20), and she has difficulty accepting that within a few days some part of her will have been amputated. In some ways, this scene is reminiscent of Lacan's account of specularization that is marred by a certain misrecognition — the "systematic refusal to acknowledge reality" ("Some Reflections" 12) — in which the image reflected to the child is a unified one that belies the actual organic insufficiency and bodily experience of fragmentation that the infant is subject to. At precisely the moment in which Rennie looks into the mirror and perceives a unified image, her actual (albeit unrepresented) corporeal experience is one of fragmentation and dissolution: "She lies down on the bed again, hearing the blood running through her body, which is still alive. She thinks of the cells, whispering, dividing in darkness, replacing each other one at a time; and of the other cells, the evil ones which may or may not be there, working away in her with furious energy, like yeast" (100).

Rennie places herself in very real danger through her pursuit of knowledge, which graphically culminates in scenes of imprisonment and actual bodily threat. Her cancer, while not of any conscious doing, may be seen to underwrite the threat to her subjective identity that is conditional upon her exercising her position within symbolic discourse. In this sense, the dynamics of fading and disappearance that endanger any subject caught in the net of the signifier are played out, within Rennie's life, on an overtly corporeal plane.

The constitution of subjective identity and the individual's access to representational discourse are conditional upon the unmediated unity of the body being broken. In light of this, Rennie's fragmenting body may be seen to be a return to the original traumatic moment when the body split and separated, thereby effecting a discontinuity between it and the Real. For Lacan, it is a "cut" in the signifying chain, taking the form of a bar between signifier and signified, which verifies the structure of the subject as being that of disconnection with the Real ("Agency"). In his account, the structure of the signifier is based upon "the topological function of the rim," and "a process of gap" (*Four Fundamental* 206) through which otherness is encountered. For Kristeva, it is the second thetic moment of castration, the perception of anatomical difference, that posits the subject as signifiable through separation (*Revolution* 47). While Freud's formulation of the castration complex is inherently connected to the phallic stage of infantile development, his account allows for the possibility of the threatened object being displaced or replaced by other types of dismemberment (Laplanche and Pontalis 56).

That Rennie is threatened by the possibility of being dissected is obvious: "She had a horror of someone, anyone, putting a knife into her and cutting some of her off. . . . She disliked the idea of being buried one piece at a time instead of all at once" (*BH* 23). In the psychoanalytic context, however, Rennie's mastectomy may be seen to be reminiscent of the decisive moment through which lack and separation from the maternal propels the subject toward the symbolic function. J. Laplanche and J.B. Pontalis, placing castration in the context of a series of traumatic experiences of detachment, name the breast as being one of the various part-objects that must inevitably be lost.[3] Indeed, weaning and loss of the breast holds a privileged place within psychoanalytic theories of castration anxiety: "This *primary castration*, which is repeated at every feed and culminates with the weaning of the child, is considered to be the only real experience capable of accounting for the universal presence of the castration complex: the withdrawal of the mother's nipple, it is argued, is the ultimate unconscious meaning to be found behind the thoughts, fears and wishes which go to make up this complex" (58).

It seems significant, then, that what is an attack upon the wholeness of Rennie's body takes the particular form of an excision or amputation of a breast. In fact, the mastectomy may be seen to function as a graphic illustration, through a corporeal metaphor, of the first piece of bodily substance the infant must lose in its move toward subjectivity. As such, the amputated breast now becomes a detachable part of the body, inducing a loss that allows for the libidinal energies to be redirected through representation.

Lacan names the perceptually detachable object of the body the *"objet a."* It is something from which the subject has separated itself off in order to constitute itself as such (*Four Fundamental* 103). For this reason, the *objet a* is structurally responsible for the alienation that forms the basis of the ego (258). Furthermore, it retains algorithmic status as that which symbolizes lack and desire (105), and becomes the object caught in the net of the signifier.

The detachability of the body is made clear through the comment that "we're not all that well glued together, any minute we'll vaporize. These bodies are only provisional" (*BH* 143). Further to this, the novel features a recurrent motif of corporeal dismemberment that takes on new significance if interpreted in light of the Lacanian *objet a*. It is the symbol of the loss of the hands: "Her hands are cold, she lifts them up to look at them, but they elude her. Something's missing" (274). Rennie's experience of the missing hands evokes the alienation particular to specular identity formation, in that she gazes upon herself in an attempt to grasp a unified image of herself, but is instead confronted by a picture of fragmentation. This raises the issue that Laplanche and Pontalis see as being a theoretical consideration when discussing the castration complex: its impact upon narcissism (57). The subject's self-image must inevitably be endangered through the loss of any narcissistically invested object. Thus, the momentary loss of Rennie's hands may be seen to parallel the permanent loss of her breast, in its effect upon the way she has seen herself in the past, its effect upon her ego-identity, and the way in which she will now see herself in the future.

Noteworthy also in the loss-of-hands episode is Rennie's sense that there is something fundamental missing in her relationship with the corporeal. This may be seen to touch upon the role the *objet a* plays in linking corporeality with the symbolic; that is, in initiating, through loss, a desire which from that point on will only ever be expressed through the metonymy of signification. What is always missing, in the acquisition of subjectivity, is the Real. The referent may in itself and in its own realm be complete and fully present; however, the subject's representation of it, whether through signification or through specular identification, is by necessity partial and illusory. Thus, the detachable hands, in their role as *objet a*, are representing the point at which the Real accedes to symbolic representation of it. The hands appear to be there but in fact they are eclipsed, just as the referent eludes the sign. They provide an image but one that is, in some ways, empty. In this respect, this episode resembles another one in which Rennie's grandmother expresses her senility:

My hands, she said. I've left them somewhere and now I can't find them. She was holding her hands in the air, helplessly, as if she couldn't move them.

They're right there, I said. On the ends of your arms.

No, no, she said impatiently. Not those, those are no good any more. My other hands, the ones I had before, the ones I touch things with. (57)

Here the image as duplicitous and distinct from the referent is highlighted as the grandmother searches in vain for something she once possessed but has since lost. If the hands for which the grandmother searches are the hands with which she once touched the Real, she is, in fact, searching for the corporeal existence in which she moved as an infant, before she gained access to representational discourse. This was, however, foreclosed to her once she acquired a subjective identity, and was no longer able to draw upon unmediated experience. The hands that are there for her to use now are a mere reflection of those she once had; but, as an *objet a*, they connect her corporeal nature to signification by becoming objects of desire. As objects made of her own flesh, they attest to the corporeal terms through which she, as subject, enters the signifying realm of the symbolic. They also function now in their symbolic capacity as the standard that regulates exchange, as it is through them that she is forced to swap the Real for the imaged. It is through these hands, also, that she encounters a concrete representation of alterity, through a part of her body that is clearly her own and yet seems to be other.

The *objet a*, as loss of an object once experienced as the self, functions as the prephallic and pre-oedipal agent of separation, and its relationship to the subject involves a rupture or an edge. Nowhere is this more evident than in Rennie's own response to her mastectomy: "Her real fear, irrational but a fear, is that the scar will come undone in the water, split open like a faulty zipper, and she will turn inside out" (80). Within her distress at her body being torn apart, time and time again Rennie expresses a fascination with the surface, which articulates the opposition between internal and external. However, as Ellie Ragland-Sullivan points out, distinctions between inside and outside are "only imaginary monuments based on confusing the bodily organism with the imaginary image it spawns" ("Seeking" 59). The representational self-image upon which Rennie has relied until now has been based on a specular identification of unity. However, this now seems little more than an external facade, able to deceive her conscious mind and misrepresent a corporeal reality that seems to have its own intentions: "Maybe it would turn out to be benign; on the other hand, maybe they would open her up and find that she was permeated, riddled, rotting away from the inside" (19).

For this reason "she no longer trusts surfaces" (48); and her preoccupation with their defying boundaries and marking the body as being indistinct and ambiguous testifies to what Kristeva has termed "abjection."[4] This is the horror felt by the subject when faced by that which defies subjective delineation; it is the denial and rejection of the object that is able to transgress the border between inside and out, self and other.

The abject is primarily manifested in the form of bodily fluids and particles that are severed after having been part of the self, and this is evident in Rennie's case when it becomes obvious that "she's afraid she'll see blood, leakage, her stuffing coming out" (22). Like other forms of disease, Rennie's cancer functions as abject in that it constitutes her body as being both dead and alive, and questions its posited solidity. It is abject, also, in that it threatens the border between the inside of Rennie's existence and what is usually posi-

tioned as being outside her and other: "she's been having bad dreams
. . . [where] the scar on her breast splits open like a diseased fruit
and something like this [centipede] crawls out" (60).

The cancer, in its role as abject, places Rennie on the border of life
and death; and while it endangers her at a basic physiological level,
it is also indicative of the danger in which she is placed psychically.
Abjection marks the threshold of an enunciative position by working
to define the delimited, appropriate body necessary for access to
representational discourse. However, it simultaneously expresses the
potential fading of the subject, the threat that the difference upon
which subjective identity is based will dissolve. Thus, Rennie's
disgust at the kind of dissolution and disintegration the cancer
represents is, on the one hand, part of the way in which she
constitutes her subjectivity by maintaining an imaged projection of
her self; on the other hand, however, it robs her of her ability to feel
like a conventional social being, attesting to what amounts to a threat
to her subjective identity: "I don't feel human any more, she said. I
feel infested. I have bad dreams, I dream I'm full of white maggots
eating away at me from the inside" (83).

E.A. Grosz makes the point that the ways in which the inside and
the outside of the body are structured answers the question of how
it is that signifying systems are able to latch onto bodily and
experiential processes. She goes on to say that it is in the spaces from
which the abject has been expelled that regulated vocal exchange
may insert itself, and the speaking subject may be constituted
("Language"). This connection between signification and the abject
may be used to interpret a specific kind of abjection that features in
Bodily Harm.

Rennie is particularly disgusted by Lora's undeniably material
nature: " 'You smoke?' says the woman. The fingers holding the
cigarette are bitten to the quick, stub-tipped, slightly grubby, the raw
skin around the nails nibbled as if mice have been at them, and this
both surprises Rennie and repels her slightly. She wouldn't want to
touch this gnawed hand, or have it touch her. She doesn't like the
sight of ravage, damage, the edge between inside and outside blurred
like that" (86). Her disgust at the sight of this permeation of
corporeal boundaries is even further heightened when Rennie witnesses Lora being beaten in prison by the guards. Rennie's response
may be seen to illustrate what Kristeva names as being the most
extreme abject: the corpse. In this sense, she may be displaying horror
at being faced by mortality and the inevitable finiteness of each

subject. However, Rennie's repulsion, placed in the context of the imprisonment, evokes the backdrop of political intrigue and misuse of power, which in turn implicates Rennie's status as journalist who occupies a privileged position from which to speak. Her disgust, now placed in the light of her own access to representational discourse and its role in social formations, may thus be understood in the context of Kristeva's assertion that abjection may take the secondary forms of corruption and political hypocrisy: "The traitor, the liar, the criminal with a good conscience, the shameless rapist, the killer who claims he is a saviour. . . . Any crime, because it draws attention to the fragility of the law, is abject, but premeditated crime, cunning murder, hypocritical revenge are even more so because they heighten the display of such fragility" (*Powers* 4).

Rennie's experience with the rope man, her loathing at witnessing the old mute man being beaten by police, the execution of prisoners, and her knowledge of Lora's sexual abuse now take on a significance that places them in light of their functioning as social manifestations of abjection. In this sense, the novel, through its portrayal of a society in which democracy is failing, represents the threatening elements upon which sociality rests, which civilization tries to exclude, but which intrude when a culture finds itself at a point of vulnerability. In these forms, described as being as "malignant" (289) as Rennie's cancer, abjection poses a threat to subjectivity along a wider collective plane, and represents, in a larger social context, the kinds of disintegration that may endanger each individual.

Dissolution at the hands of social relations is an issue that also features in Rennie's relationships with men. For her, being in love is "foolhardy," much like "running barefoot along a street covered with broken bottles" (102). While it is not unusual to consider loving another a threat to the ego of the individual, which changes to include the love-object in its grasp, Rennie seems to be in jeopardy of becoming "visible, soft, penetrable" (102). The implication that being with a man will in some way perforate her is heightened by the hints of violence and bondage that characterize her sexual relationship with Jake: "Jake liked to pin her hands down, he liked to hold her so she couldn't move. He liked that, he liked thinking of sex as something he could win at. Sometimes he really hurt her, once he put his arm across her throat and she really did stop breathing" (207). The threat that such a relationship poses to her subjective identity revolves around her being used as a kind of inanimate body upon which Jake may play out his desires:

For a couple of weeks after that she had a hard time making love with Jake. She didn't want him grabbing her from behind when she wasn't expecting it, she didn't like being thrown onto the bed or held so she couldn't move. She had trouble dismissing it as a game. She now felt that in some way that had never been spelled out between them he thought of her as the enemy. Please don't do that any more, she said. At least not for a while. She didn't want to be afraid of men, she wanted Jake to tell her why she didn't have to be.

I thought you said it's okay if you trust me, he said. Don't you trust me?

It's not you, she said. It's not you I don't trust.

Then what is it? he said.

I don't know, she said. Lately I feel I'm being used; though not by you exactly.

Used for what? said Jake.

Rennie thought about it. Raw material, she said. (211–12)

Through the relationship, she seems to be in danger of regressing to a materiality in which her sense of self is in peril. The anonymity with which she addresses Jake, and with which Jake undresses her, gives them both a kind of namelessness and lack of identity that is reflected in the fact that Rennie is "designed" by him in much the same way as he designs rooms or magazines: "Sometimes I feel like a blank sheet of paper, she said. For you to doodle on" (105). This comparison of Rennie to an empty surface upon which almost anything can be written by an other places her fear of being penetrated in the context of a castration that touches upon the loss of the referent in the rupture of the Real induced by language, and the various splittings through which subjectivity is constituted:

You're so closed, Jake said once. I like that. I want to be the one you open up for.

But she could never remember afterwards what he had actually said. Perhaps he'd said, I want to be the one who opens you up. (106)

Since her entry into sexual relations is, as it were, inscribed in her own flesh, the dynamic attests to the fact that sociality, symbolic relations, and post-oedipal interaction between the sexes need a material underpinning and subsequent rupture of it. Indeed, Daniel, who epitomizes social conformity and places sexual relations in the context of conventional contractual obligations, is marked by the fact that he makes his living "cutting parts off other people's bodies" (197). For Rennie, he holds a privileged place as the only man who has literally cut her open, and it is at this point that the necessity of some form of castration becomes evident. Thus, Daniel, the man whose "soul was in his hands" (198), provides the possibility of salvation: "she wanted to lie down beside him and touch him and be touched by him; at the moment she believed in it, the touch of the hand that could transform you, change everything, magic" (195).

The issue of being "opened up" by a man, of being dislocated and yet possibly developed, is one of potential constitution through rupture. What is at stake is, as Kristeva points out, the fact that the amorous state is the support of all possible subjectivity ("Histoires d'amour"). For Rennie, sexual relationships with men involve a narcissistic investment in a relationship through which she images herself. She herself admits that "I imprinted on him . . . like a duckling, like a baby chick" (33). In the last stages of her relationship with Jake, their inability to continue having sex is directly related, in her mind, to her own appearance and takes the form of a test of her self-worth: "So they were going to try. She'd stood in front of her open closet, wondering what you should wear to try, to a trial. . . . She wanted to wear something and knew she had to; these days she always wore something to bed. She didn't want to be seen, the way she was, damaged, amputated" (198). Meanwhile, the comfort she finds in Daniel depends upon a vicarious sense of being ordinary, of indulging in "a fantasy of the normal" (237). In her attempt at becoming the object of desire for Daniel, she may also be seen to be attempting to compensate for her own amputation/castration. Perhaps it is for these reasons that she begins to desire corporeal affirmation through sex: "She wants somebody to be with her, she wants somebody to be with. A warm body, she doesn't much care whose" (159). When she finally sleeps with Paul, the man who is, above all, "tangible" (217), she experiences a kind of grounding of her sense of self. She herself characterizes Paul as "the one who gave her back her body" (248), illustrating Kristeva's belief that in the amorous state, the individual is affected by someone outside his or her own identity, with whom there is little actual contact, but who nevertheless "poses" the subject. This constitutes a kind of opening of subjectivity rather than its centring or splitting, and allows for a fresh combination of the ego with the other (Kristeva, "Histoires d'amour").

Corporeal affirmation as necessary for the positing of a subjective identity is evident in her interaction with Paul: "He reaches out his hands and Rennie can't remember ever having been touched before. . . . She's open now, she's been opened, she's being drawn back down, she enters her body again . . . she's solid after all, she's still here on the earth, she's grateful, he's touching her, she can still be touched" (204). Within this encounter, juxtaposed with the reaffirmation of her corporeal self, is a kind of awakening through which she finally comes to terms with her illness. Finally, she is able to see it as a kind of risk from which no one is exempt: "Nobody lives forever, who said you could? This much will have to do, this much is enough" (204). This foreshadows the ending of the novel in which she resolves her attitude toward the cancer, and accepts her own finiteness and mortality, without submitting to its dangers: "Zero is waiting somewhere, whoever said there was life everlasting; so why feel grateful? She doesn't have much time left, for anything. But neither does anyone else. She's paying attention, that's all" (301).

What has been Rennie's momentary loss of body is presented as a kind of fading of corporeal reality: "already she feels light, insubstantial, as if she's died and gone to heaven and come back minus a body" (203). However, another kind of fading may be associated with this negation: Lacanian aphanisis of the subject — the fading of the subject as he or she is apprenticed to speech. As Kristeva maintains, "Signification exists precisely because there is no subject in signification" (*Revolution* 48). In Rennie's case, what may be interpreted as subjectivity placed "elsewhere" through signification may be seen to be imaged through a kind of spatiotemporal vacancy. This raises the issue that the sensory and libidinal experiences of difference inscribed in the unconscious as signifiers rely upon visual, auditory, or tactile sensations that are positioned upon a body located within space. Kristeva has made the point that it is precisely because he or she speaks that the subject is spatially bound ("Place Names"); and indeed, there are a number of ways in which an enunciative position is dependent upon spatial dynamics.

To begin with, specular identity formation in the mirror-stage is reliant upon the infant being able to foreground him- or herself by drawing upon a sense of distance, breadth, and depth. It is the synthesis of visual identification with a negotiation of territory that brings Lacan to speak of the formation of the ego in this phase as being "the spatial captation manifested in the mirror-stage" ("Mirror Stage" 4). Furthermore, signification, as an act of predication that asserts something about a subject, posits an object or what Kristeva, drawing upon Gottlob Frege's work, terms "a denotation." Within this account, the naming of objects reflects upon "the subject's ability to separate himself from the ecosystem into which he was fused, so that, as a result of this separation, he may designate it" (Kristeva, *Revolution* 52). Apart from the denotation of an object or object-ness, signification also involves the "enunciation . . . of a displaced subject" and divides one from the other through the opposition and juxtaposition of syntagms. The positing and posited are reflected through the two modalities known as "subject" ("noun") and "predicate" ("verb"), and this predicative function is the element in which "the spatio-temporal and communicational positing of the speaking subject is marked" (54).

If the sign is material projected from the eroticized body onto an object, it is clear that signification, as "a system of finite positions" (Kristeva, *Revolution* 48), requires a detachment from surrounding continuity in the Real. It requires, in other words, that both subjectivity and objectivity be located in space in a way that allows for identification and symbolic exchange. For Irigaray, this becomes a matter of sexual difference.[5] Using the model of the proton and electron to designate the kind of encounter that occurs between the sexes, Irigaray believes that the masculine inhabits the positive pole of the atom, and the female inhabits the negative. Until the subject is made of both poles, no genuine and equitable exchange will be possible.

In *Bodily Harm*, intimate exchange in a situation of close proximity is also sexualized. Thinking of Jake's new lover, Rennie hypothesizes: "The new lady stretched out before her, a future, a space, a blank, into which Jake would now throw himself night after night the way he had thrown himself into her, each time extreme and final, as if he was pitching himself headlong over a cliff" (235). Rennie also compares having an affair with Daniel with going over Niagara Falls in a spin dryer (142), and so it is interesting to note the use of spatial metaphors to describe sexual relations. Sexual encounters are undoubtedly situations in which the usual spatial boundaries between people are negated; and on the part of the men with whom Rennie is involved, the nullification of these limits is indeed drastic. Looking once more at Irigaray's account of the dynamic by which the sexes interact, the positive particle always attracts, while the other remains in movement and without a place of its own. This leads to the possibility of disintegration and decomposition in the place of separation that permits the encounter.

In Rennie's experience, the repositioning of male subjectivity through sex is indeed marked by a particular inequality: "She wondered what it was like to be able to throw yourself into another person, another body, a darkness like that. Women could not do it. Instead they had darkness thrown into them" (235–36). Furthermore, the inequilibrium freezes her within her surrounds: "Rennie couldn't put the two things together, the urgency and blindness of the act, which had been urgent and blind for her too, and [so] this result, her well-lit visible frozen pose at the kitchen table" (236). This lack of reciprocity by which her sexual relations are marked is further illustrated by the fact that her encounters with men seem to function as a structural anchorage upon which she hinges her own position. When Jake leaves, her world is described as being vacuous and entirely devoid of any matter that occupies space or weight. It is definitely a male, albeit anonymous, presence that is drawn in through the consequent shrinkage of space that marks an overwhelmingly close proximity of object to self: "When Jake moved out, naturally there was a vacuum. Something had to come in to fill it. Maybe the man with the rope hadn't so much broken into her apartment as been sucked in, by force of gravity" (39).

This collapse of spatial boundaries so that objects enter and no longer keep their rightful distance touches upon the structure of space in the constitution of subjectivity. Merleau-Ponty sees space as being not the setting in which things are arranged but the means whereby the position of these things is made possible. In his phenomenological account of perception, the mind needs a type of starting point or absolute "here" from which it can confer spatial determinations upon objects (98–147). In light of this, it is pertinent that Rennie's memories of growing up with her grandmother reveal a kind of insecurity and inability to position herself as her own anchoring point:

One of the first things I can remember, says Rennie, is standing in my grandmother's bedroom. . . . I know I've done something wrong, but I can't remember what. I'm crying, I'm holding my grandmother around both legs, but I didn't think of them as legs, I thought of her as one solid piece from the neck down to the bottom of her skirt. I feel as if I'm holding on to the edge of something, safety, if I let go I'll fall. . . . (53)

Bachelard maintains that the house in which one was born is psychically inscribed in each individual, and engraves in the subject the dynamics of inhabiting that he or she takes to other houses for the rest of his or her life (14–15). In light of this, it is interesting to note the overriding anxiety with which Rennie negotiated her domestic space, and the fact that it was almost entirely dominated by another person to whom she was acquiescent. It is also interesting to note the importance placed upon the rim in her account of her fear; the fact that the grandmother's body is unbroken and without margin, but functions as the verge between Rennie and the rest of the world. In his analysis of the poetics of images, Bachelard draws attention to the fact that "the being of man" may be considered "the being of a surface," and this notion of boundaries and corporeal limits takes the form of "the surface that separates the region of the same from the region of the other" (222). Bachelard's project is a phenomenology of "the image as an excess of the imagination" (112) in order to give it psychoanalytical efficacy. The dream is exactly the kind of image that warrants investigation, and it is just such an imaginary formation that draws attention to the notion of the surface or rim, illustrates the dynamic of confused boundaries that haunts Rennie's relationship with her grandmother, and implies a confused relationship between self and other. She describes a dream in which the spatial and corporeal limits usually bounded by skin become permeable: "She's standing in her grandmother's garden, around at the side of the house. . . . [H]er grandmother is there. . . . Rennie puts out her hands but she can't touch her grandmother, her hands go right in, through, it's like touching water or new snow" (115). For Bachelard, the notion of the surface, of "this side" and "beyond," is related to "the dialectics of outside and inside" (212), which are, in fact, "a dialectic of division" (211). This division, which is after all a necessary one for the constitution of the self, is in Rennie's case ambiguously drawn. Furthermore, Bachelard sees outside and inside as "tinged with aggressivity" (212) and the terms upon which alienation is founded. Both aggression and estrangement are evident in Rennie's memory of her grandmother, and within the dialectics that were played out on a spatial plane, through enclosure:

I know I will be shut in the cellar by myself. I'm afraid of that, I know what's down there, a single light bulb which at least they leave on, a cement floor which is always cold, cobwebs, the winter coats hanging on hooks beside the wooden stairs, the furnace. It's the only place in the house that isn't clean. When I was shut in the cellar I always sat on the top stair. Sometimes there were things down there, I could hear them moving around, small things that might get on you and run up your legs. I'm crying because I'm afraid, I can't stop, and even if I hadn't done anything wrong I'd still be put down there, for making a noise, for crying. (53)

In Bachelard's "topoanalysis," or study of the sites of the individual's intimate life and localization of intimacy and memory (10), verticality within the childhood house, expressed through the polarity of the cellar and attic, is an imaginary response to the function of constructing. It functions by way of a tension between the aerial and terrestrial, whereby the attic becomes the realm of sublimated social activity, while the cellar comes to epitomize all that is on the side of irrationality and the unconscious: "The dreamer constructs and reconstructs the upper stories and the attic until they are well constructed. And . . . when we dream of the heights we are in the rational zone of intellectualized projects. But for the cellar, the impassioned inhabitant digs and re-digs, making its very depth active" (18).

What is striking in Bachelard's account is the implication that the processes of identity construction externalized through the dynamics of spatial positioning are subject to a kind of repetition compulsion. In this, the individual replays experiences from the past that have been formative. Concerning the compulsion on the part of the subject to repeat significant experiences, Lacan makes the point that "What is repeated, in fact, is always something that occurs . . . *as if by chance*" (*Four Fundamental* 54). In Rennie's case, the chance occurrence through which she once again experiences childhood dynamics of incarceration within a subterranean world is her imprisonment in St. Antoine: "The room they're in is about five feet by seven feet, with a high ceiling. The walls are damp and cool, the stone slick to the touch as if something's growing on it, some form of mildew. The back of Rennie's shirt is damp, from the wall. This is the first time she's been cold since coming down here" (*BH* 268–69).

However, unlike her early experiences of confinement, which were implicated in the dynamics of blurred boundaries and ill-defined identity, the adult experience of imprisonment is marked by difference. The difference between being inside the jail and outside it, the difference between her jailers and herself that is characterized by an aggressivity second only to sadism, and the fact that a literal opening of the cell is needed for her self-preservation, illustrate the dynamics of separation and intervention that are being abused. For Bachelard, the house and the rest of the cosmos outside are not merely juxtaposed but interact dialectically (38–73). In fact, he maintains that the universe outside the house is "a non-house in the same way that metaphysicians speak of a non-I" (40). Broadening this definition and applying it to any building that is collectively constructed, the prison cell in which Rennie is held captive becomes a striking illustration of the dynamics of division that are a structuring principle not only of her subjectivity but of her life. Space will mean either the life or death of Rennie, and there is a necessity for her enclosure to be opened in much the same way as the subject needs to open onto an outside in a discovery of difference and an act of externalization. Such projection from the inner world of consciousness onto the external world that is shared raises the issue of social construction and the role space plays in structuring symbolic discourse.

For Lefebvre, social relations are concrete abstractions that only exist in and through space (404). His method of "spatio-analysis" aims not to construct a model of space but to expose its production and use (404). His thesis is that space consists of the political use of knowledge, implies an ideology, and is operational in forms of production (8–11). While Lefebvre's analysis goes on to focus upon capitalism, the state, world markets, and industrialization at the level of local, regional, national, and international levels, what is relevant is his attempt to identify spatial codes and emphasize their dialectical character, so that these codes may be seen in the context of being a practical interaction between subjects and their surroundings.

Rennie is placed within a space that is alien to her and that she is forced to negotiate. It is a space that serves the purpose of collectivization, and is defined only by the part it plays in organizing society. Her prison cell in a St. Antoine jail may thus be seen as a spatial moment structured according to what Lefebvre calls "social space." This is the space of social practice and is the result of a dialectical relationship between three factors.[6] The first is "the perceived" or "spatial practice" that is the projection onto a spatial field of all aspects of social practice. This encompasses production, guarantees a level of competence and performance, and takes the form of infrastructure — roads, buildings, et cetera — that make the necessary routines possible. The second is "the conceived" or "representations of space" and takes the form of a specific kind of knowledge that conceptualizes urban realities through architecture. The third is what Lefebvre calls "the lived" or "representational space." This is the space of action and lived situations — the bedroom, the house, the graveyard — and may be directional, situational, or relational. The prison cell is consciously constructed to preserve society from elements that would otherwise threaten it. As such, it is overdetermined by all three factors: it is an infrastructural installation, anonymous authors have designed and orchestrated it, and Rennie is living the reality of it as it impinges upon an individual's experience.

There are other ways in which the jail may be seen to function in accordance with Lefebvre's notion of social space. It is both a precondition and a result of social superstructures (Lefebvre 85), its form is encounter, assembly, and simultaneity, implying the possibility of accumulation (101), and it is not merely an empty container distinct from its contents (87) but is instead determined by whoever inhabits it. Although it appears to have visible boundaries and separate space because of walls and locks, in reality there exists an ambiguous continuity between inside and out (87). In short, it is the materialization of a social being (102).

Moments of social space, however, need a material underpinning, and so "The whole of (social) space proceeds from the body, even though it so metamorphoses the body that it may forget it altogether — even though it may separate itself so radically from the body as to kill it" (405). Lefebvre speaks of the practical and fleshy body that has spatial qualities of both symmetry and asymmetry, and energetic properties, namely discharges, economies, and waste (61). It is precisely this body of corporeal reality that begins to degenerate while Rennie is imprisoned and both she and Lora are deprived of fresh water, food, and the chance to sleep soundly and maintain personal hygiene: "Neither of them is saying anything. Rennie can smell their bodies, unwashed flesh, and the putrid smell from the bucket, Lora is out of cigarettes for the time being, she's picking at her fingers, Rennie can see her out of the corners of her eyes, it's an irritating habit, they've both run out, run down" (280).

The prison cell, in its capacity as a moment of social space, is destroying the very body upon which it depends. While Rennie feels her Canadian citizenship will effectively protect her from any ultimate danger, she holds fears for Lora's well-being. The day Lora is beaten, Rennie is called upon to salvage what is left of Lora's sense of self:

> She's holding Lora's left hand, between both of her own, perfectly still, nothing is moving, and yet she knows she is pulling on the hand, as hard as she can, there's an invisible hole in the air, Lora is on the other side of it and she has to pull her through, she's gritting her teeth with the effort, she can hear herself, a moaning, it must be her own voice, this is a gift, this is the hardest thing she's ever done. (299)

The maternal qualities of this interaction, the fact that Rennie is investing the bodily contact with the intention that "something will get born" (299), and the fact that there is a kind of instinctual and inexpressible spatial manoeuvring, makes the scene reminiscent of what Kristeva has called the "chora."

As Kaja Silverman points out, the concept of the chora is an extensive one, not necessarily limited to one definitive explanation (102). She posits three primary definitions, all of which see the choric fantasy as shifting the subject away from the structuring and regimenting thesis of the symbolic. One of Kristeva's formulations of the chora is dependent upon conceptualizing subjectivity as being "a spatial series" (Silverman 104). While Kristeva herself sees the chora as being different from the "*disposition* which falls already within the domain of representation (of the sign, of language) and which lends itself to spatial phenomenological intuition giving rise to a geometry" ("Subject" 22), she nevertheless sees the chora as being a "rhythmic space, which has no thesis and no position" (*Revolution* 26). Rennie and Lora are momentarily locked into a space and a positioning that is beyond that of conventional subjective interaction. Furthermore, since the entire experience is initiated by Lora being beaten, it is a space reached through bodily modulations, abrasions, and intonations. It is also a space recalled by the basic relations of corporeal division and spatial ordering that Kristeva names as the processes responsible for making the semiotic a psychosomatic modality: "the relations (eventually representable as topological spaces) that connect the zones of the fragmented body to each other and also to "external 'objects' and 'subjects' " (*Revolution* 28).

Silverman names another characteristic of the chora as being "perceptual immaturity and discursive incapacity" (103). Lora is marked by a temporary cognitive incapacity, which is due to her body being beaten and mutilated. This may be seen to be a striking illustration of the fact that the chora is semiotic in disposition, and draws upon the socialized body thrust into a state of corporeal fragmentation: "The semiotic is articulated by flow and marks: facilitation, energy transfers, the cutting up of the corporeal and social continuum as well as that of signifying material, the establishment of a distinctiveness and its ordering in a pulsating *chora*, in a rhythmic but nonexpressive totality" (Kristeva, *Revolution* 40). Kristeva also makes the point that the semiotic is dominated by the most instinctual of the drives (28), and it is precisely this death drive that is vividly represented through Lora's dying body. However, paradoxically, the semiotic chora is the place where the subject is generated as well as negated. In the words of Silverman, it is "the site where it both assumes a pulsional or rhythmic consistency and is dissolved as a psychic or social coherence" (103). Its formative role in structuring subjectivity revolves around its initiation of a signifying position for the subject, of being "the process by which signifiance is constituted" (Kristeva, *Revolution* 26). Although the chora is antecedent and subjacent to actual symbolic representation, it does foreshadow the subject's signifying ability through its ordering of vocal and kinetic rhythms and vowellic and gestural organization: "The *chora* is not a position which represents something for someone, that is, a sign, nor yet is it a position which represents someone for another position, that is, a *signifiant*, though it functions (or is generated) towards such a signifying position" (Kristeva, "Subject" 22).

When Rennie first finds Lora's beaten body, it is described as being one that has lost its symbolic identity and is nameless: "Rennie wants to throw up, it's no one she recognizes . . . it's the face of a stranger, someone without a name, the word *Lora* has come unhooked and is hovering in the air, apart from this ruin" (298). This is a body without an enunciative position; words are detached from its existence, which has regressed into the purely material. However, once Rennie intervenes and takes on the choric maternal role of mediator between the silenced body and the social law, bringing Lora's inert body back once more to its symbolic position, Lora is not only named but assumes her speaking position: "She holds the hand, perfectly still, with all her strength . . . 'Lora,' she says. The name descends and enters the body, there's something, a movement; isn't there? 'Oh God,' says Lora" (299).

The incident has depicted the intersection of space with significa-tion through the positioning of a body overdetermined by both. Merleau-Ponty makes the point that relations of externality are brought into existence only by the body, through which "objective" and "oriented" space can be perceived.[7] But the spatiality of the body itself comes into being only through movement, which, whether actual or potential, creates intention. In this account, consciousness is a network of intentions, without which the mind would relapse into "existence-in-itself" and remain ignorant of the outside world.

Rennie's experience with Lora's beaten body in prison makes use of a kind of imaginary movement, which, drawing upon Merleau-Ponty's work, resembles what he calls "abstract movement." Abstract movement is a movement in and of itself that is not triggered by any already existing object.[8] It outlines in space a gratuitous intention that has reference to one's own body, thus making the body an object of itself rather than reaching out to something other. Abstract movement breaks with the given world and thus allows for the emergence of an imaginary situation. Superimposing upon an abso-lute physical universe a "virtual" or "human" space, it carves out in that world, where actual concrete movement takes place, a zone of "reflection and subjectivity" (111). It does so by "projecting," whereby the subject keeps in front of him- or herself an area of free space in which what does not naturally exist may take on a sem-blance of existence. Rennie is tracing Lora's body, which at this stage is in jeopardy, within a space that is equally ambiguous. The dynamic is illusory and not of the real; like abstract movement in general, it is of the realm of the nonexistent. In this sense, it contrasts directly with the actual movement, described immediately after, in which she leaves St. Antoine and travels back to Canada: "Then the plane will take off. It will be a 707. Rennie will sit halfway down, it will not be full, at this time of year the traffic is north to south. She will be heading into winter. In seven hours she'll be at the airport, the terminal, the end of the line, where you get off. Also where you can get on, to go somewhere else" (299).

"Concrete movement" in Merleau-Ponty's account occurs in the realm of the actual. It adheres to a given background externally established, and in this instance, where Rennie is wilfully relocating herself by movement through space and time, it expresses the kind of intentionality that determines consciousness and establishes her subjective position in the world. Indeed, up until this point, the gradual collapse in her mind of her own constructed world has paralleled the other ways in which her subjective identity and enunciative position had been threatened. When arrested, Rennie asks herself "does Toronto exist?" (262); and it seems incongruous that any space other than the one she is currently caught up in can exist: "From here it's hard to believe that Daniel really exists: surely the world cannot contain both places" (284). This touches upon the fact that space cannot exist for the individual without a consciousness and subjective position through which to perceive it, the fact that the body is "necessarily 'here'" (Merleau-Ponty 140).

Merleau-Ponty makes the point that motility is never merely transporting the body to a point in space of which the individual already has a formed representation. Thus, Rennie constructs Canada as she approaches it. At the same time, however, she is renegotiating her own subjectivity. As Bachelard notes, "by changing space, by leaving the space of one's usual sensibilities, one enters into communication with a space that is psychically innovating. . . . This change of *concrete* space can no longer be a mere mental operation that could be compared with consciousness of geometrical relativity. For we do not change place, we change our nature" (206). While imprisoned, Rennie had come to the realization that, by physically placing herself in another country, her entire sense of self had been threatened. In fact, spatial variation, apart from threatening her actual bodily existence, had affected the structure of her spatial limits and organization of her ego and its objects, because, as she admits, "She has been turned inside out, there's no longer a *here* and a *there*" (290). Now, by travelling back to her own country, she will relinquish spatiotemporal relativity, and position herself once more in a familiar setting with which she can identify and anchor herself. In Merleau-Ponty's account, motility is basic intentionality; to move the body is to project the body toward things that exist as objects in the real world. In this sense, motility provides the subject with access to the world, and an intentionality that defines consciousness as "being-towards-the-thing through the intermediary of the body" (138–39): "Our bodily experience of movement is not a particular case of knowledge; it provides us with a way of access to the world and the object . . . which has to be recognized as original and perhaps as primary" (140). In taking herself back to Canada, then, Rennie is reconstituting her own subjectivity by renegotiating the spatial dimensions of the subject-object relationship, reaffirming intentionality through movement, while also protecting her own corporeal existence.

For Kristeva, the history of the speaking being is one of spatial variation ("Place Names"). For Rennie, throughout the course of *Bodily Harm*, it has depended upon the appropriation of territory, and spatial relativity. After having placed herself in a situation of temporary exile in which "she's truly no longer *at home*. She is away, she is *out* . . ." (39), Rennie crosses the world to place herself in a position in which her ego-identity will be safe. She does this by negotiating what Merleau-Ponty calls a "spatial level," which is the gearing of the body to the world: "She looks out the window of the plane, it's so bright, the sea is below and there are some islands, she doesn't know which ones. The shadow of the plane is down there, crossing over sea, now land, like a cloud, like magic" (301).

The spatial level of the individual is a means of constituting an integrated world. It comes into existence when "motor intentions," or the body as the potential for movements, connect with the "perceptual field" or the spectacle perceived as invitation to move. The combination of these, of Rennie as a subject able to transport herself from one country in the world to another, with a universe in which a horizon separates land from air and sea, leads to what Merleau-Ponty has called a "perceptual ground." This is the general setting in which the subject's body can exist in the universe, an experience of the "body-in-the-world" (Merleau-Ponty 141). This interpretation of the conclusion of the novel depends upon seeing the body "not only as a system of present positions, but besides, and thereby, as an open system of an infinite number of equivalent positions directed to other ends" (141). This system of equivalents, in this account, constitutes the body image; and in light of this, it is interesting to see that in negotiating the absolute space of the world, Rennie is inadvertently brought back to her own individual bodily experience: "There's too much air conditioning, wind from outer space blowing in through the small nozzles, Rennie's cold. She crosses her arms, right thumb against the scar under her dress. The scar prods at her, a reminder, a silent voice counting, a countdown" (301). She is brought also to face her own individual body as being the "general medium for having a world" (Merleau-Ponty 146), and the acceptance of her illness signals a safe return to her home and to her self: "She will never be rescued. She has already been rescued. She is not exempt. Instead she is lucky, suddenly, finally, she's overflowing with luck, it's this luck holding her up" (*BH* 301).

With this, the novel concludes on a positive note whereby a return to familiar territory accompanies a reclamation of the self, a self that is no longer subject to the same threat of bodily harm because now a new position has been found in which to exist. This is consistent with the protagonist's acceptance of her illness and her acknowledgement of the mortality of the body. It is also consistent with a theoretical interpretation that has seen her negotiate space, signification, position, and subjectivity.

[1] This account is drawn from Kristeva's "Phonetics, Phonology and Impulsional Bases."

[2] This account is drawn from Kristeva's *Revolution in Poetic Language* (43–51).

[3] The other part-objects named are penis, faeces, and infant in childbirth (57).

[4] The following account of abjection is drawn from Kristeva's *Powers of Horror*.

[5] The following draws upon Grosz's account of Irigaray's *L'Ethique de la différence sexuelle* in *Sexual Subversions* (175).

[6] The following account is drawn from *The Production of Space* (36–46).

[7] The following account is drawn from *Phenomenology of Perception* (98–147).

[8] Merleau-Ponty gives the example of the act of pointing a finger but at no one in particular.

CHAPTER FIVE

Cat's Eye:

The SPLIT SUBJECT, MIMESIS, *and the* CONSTRUCTION *of* REALITY

What differentiates *Cat's Eye* (*CE*) from the other novels is the sense, in terms of narrative development and characterization, of time passing. As readers, we witness the effect the years have upon the fictional world of Elaine Risley, and it is with this focus upon the temporal phases and cycles of life that my account begins. Drawing upon phenomenological accounts of the role time plays in perception of and by the subject, my account begins with the supposition that while the self is necessarily located in the present, each instant in which the subject exists is an accumulation of past moments. This means the future endlessly becomes present, which in turn becomes past. With this, subjective experience constantly shifts along lines of metonymic displacement and chronology, and the history of the subject bespeaks a specific kind of displacement of the self along lines of temporal succession.

The subject dislocated by time is the subject who dislocates time, and both draw the self away from the self. This becomes evident in textual examples of the way in which Elaine becomes barely recognizable to herself, culminating in various images of the self that are fractured and dissimilar. The notion of the self as an effigy effected through the passage of time is the notion of an external form endlessly constructed, and it characterizes subjective identity as being of the order of semblance and imitation. With this, we are brought theoretically to the role that mimesis plays in the constitution of subjectivity, and the significance of discourse and representation in its continued maintenance.

Drawing upon the work of Kristeva for theoretical justification, mimesis is first explored as a symbolic phenomenon, reflected in the division between the constructed facade and the unattainable reality of social formations. In their role as the grammar of the social order, dynamics of imitation are seen to be imaged in the various social monuments that now become representative of symbolism, signification, and representation. By definition, the spoken demands a speaker, and enunciation a position from which to speak, and so we are brought to the issue of subjective identity, both in terms of mimesis as theoretical slant for analysis and *Cat's Eye* as material for analysis. Drawing upon the work of Lacan, mimesis is seen as being at the base of specular identification insofar as the subject imprints with a reflected image of the self that is, to all intents and purposes, a misnomer. In the light of this earliest mimetic inscription, characterization is seen as a kind of self-imaging. Thus, descriptions of Elaine's personality, the differing personae who play a role in the narrative, and certain incidents in her life are viewed in the context of a sense of detachment through which she is taken away from herself, the superimposition of one identity upon the other, and the disguises she has consciously assumed. With this we are brought once more to the dynamics of division and dislocation earlier introduced in the context of the effects of time upon the subject, and they now gain new significance as being indicative of the way in which a self is mimetically constructed.

What becomes paramount at this point is the issue of truth and fiction. Drawing upon Kristeva's work concerning the convergence of truth and verisimilitude, the discursive denotation of objects, and their status as false in opposition to the referent, Elaine's account of her childhood experiences with Cordelia is analysed in a way that sheds new light on the deception that marks their teenage friendship. Through this analysis, it is shown that while the girls construct events and people around them, they simultaneously act to construct themselves. In light of this, Cordelia, easily the most important character in the narrative aside from the protagonist herself, is analysed with the kind of significance that befits her role within the novel. This means a kind of critical "coming to terms" with the many Cordelias, by understanding them as a function of the invention and reinvention of the self.

Cordelia is, however, constructed not only through her own actions but by those around her. Hence, Elaine's role in the construction of Cordelia's identity is brought to the fore. This bespeaks the issue of intersubjectivity, which in turn is used to explain Elaine's reliance upon Cordelia's opinion, influence, even her existence. The reciprocity of self and other expressed within the relationship between the two women culminates in specific incidents of specular identification, which are marked by overt references to mirrors and reflected images of the self. However, the mirror is instrument not only of identity and simulation but of rivalry; and just as specularization is, in Lacanian theory, tinged with aggressivity, so too is Elaine's relationship with Cordelia characterized by competition and domination. The concept of an aggressive relativity that originates in the earliest moment of specular identification is perfectly suited for explaining an element of the novel that is striking in its intensity: the power struggle between Elaine and Cordelia. Contextualizing this in light of the emergence of subjective identity well explains why the relations of aggressivity become, for Elaine, a matter of her own identity. Thus, in a move that momentarily preempts the conclusion of the novel, Elaine's resolution of the problematic relationship that has plagued her throughout the years is seen to signal a newly resolute subjective stance.

While relations between subjects are of the order of rivalry and struggle, they are at the same time an attraction of a sexual kind. Drawing upon the work of Lacan, mimetic activity is shown to have a sexual intent, orchestrated through disguise and masquerade. At this point, incidents in which Elaine is glimpsed trying to manufacture an image for herself, involving cosmetics and camouflaging, bespeak an economy that is inherently a feminine one. With this, mimetic discourse becomes a matter of sexual difference, a theoretical platform perfectly suited to examining Elaine's relation to other women, now implicated in a kind of role-modelling through which she negotiates an image for herself.

However, the sexual aim is by definition an intersubjective one, and with this, mimesis becomes a kind of invitation to the other. Hence, feminine artifice and masquerade are now examined in the light of paternal desire and the gaze of men. Not only does the textual evidence of pantomime point toward this connection between mimesis and desire, but so too does Lacanian theory, which situates the mimetic dynamic as being a post-oedipal one. Supported by the theory of exactly how it is that mimesis allows for the relinquishing of incestuous demands and the construction of new objects of desire, my account then proceeds to interpret Elaine's relationship with her parents and her brother in light of the role they will play in terms of a mimetically induced metonymy of post-oedipal desire. The progression is then, as expected, toward other men, and so the protagonist's relationships with Jon and Josef are then analysed. Elaine's relationships with men are shown to have the quality of a facade, with a kind of posturing that is echoed in descriptions of her marriage to Jon, and a tendency toward manipulation that is imaged in Josef's treatment of her. In both cases, representation is a key issue, and it culminates in the realization that through her participation in the adult world of desire, the effigy being constructed is, in fact, Elaine herself. Analysis of incidents in which she is moulded and shaped into an image by the men in her life reveals that the construction of feminine identity as a function of the paternal gaze of desire is one in which Elaine is endlessly reproduced. With this, her self-image becomes both a sexual and a symbolic phenomenon, a point that introduces a new aspect of mimesis: mimicry as pictorial creation.

Elaine is an artist, and as such she trades in artifice and illusion. Thus, her feelings about painting and her responses to her creations are interpreted in the light of a number of issues to do with mimetic creation. These include the simulation of reality, hidden processes of construction, the phenomenological and ontological status of the represented object, and the schism between referential reality and its representation evident within the artistic economy.

At this point, the analysis, while detailed in its own right, is geared toward the issues of consciousness and intentionality and Elaine's role as subject and creator of her own reality. This is, in fact, the issue of the subjective stance in relation to a lived and mimed reality, and by way of Lacanian theory and relevant textual examples, this is shown also to be an issue of the gaze.

The satisfaction of the gaze is linked to specular misrecognition and the illusory nature of the painted image. Furthermore, the enraptured subject is a captured one. With this, the counterfeit quality of the painted portrait is shown to be indicative of the assembling and dissembling of subjective identity at the hands of the mimetic economy. The self-portrait raises the issue of Elaine's image of herself and contextualizes the displacement of her identity, hitherto discussed in terms of temporal succession, sexual relations, and the like, in light of the specular alienation that underlies mimetic self-representation. Thus, Elaine's constitution of the self becomes a function of herself as both subject and object of the gaze. By introducing Maurice Merleau-Ponty's work into an account that has largely been Lacanian, the scopic drive becomes at this point a subjective entity: the emergence of the "I" at the hands of the eye. The symbolic function of the gaze and those aspects that make it constitutive of subjectivity now become the theoretical framework through which to analyse both childhood memories and incidents in Elaine's adult life. The emphasis in this interpretation is upon the way in which the protagonist's subjective identity is determined and structured by way of the look. Thus, intentionality, aggressivity, projection and reversal of the gaze, interaction with alterity, and inter- as well as intrasubjectivity all serve to explain the ways in which Elaine sees herself and is seen by others. The motif of the cat's eye to which the novel owes its title is now awarded the significance it deserves — as symbol of the subjective significance of the gaze — and it is with this, and mimesis as the inscription of the subject, that my account ends.

* * *

Cat's Eye is a novel in which the protagonist ages and the world around her changes. Meeting Elaine as a young child, we watch her mature into adolescence, then marry and have children of her own. We watch her parents grow old, her brother die, her friends fade, and her husbands leave. However, in witnessing these events, we witness also the fact that the body's structure is a temporal one that, as Merleau-Ponty points out, is permeated with gaps (98–147). While the body is necessarily "now," the present consists of drawing together a succession of previous positions so that every change that reaches consciousness does so already loaded with its relations to what has preceded it (98–147). This means that subjective identity is not one that is ever complete or fully centred. As Merleau-Ponty states, "the subject of perception never being an absolute subjectivity . . . [is] destined to become an object for an ulterior *I*" (240). The future then consists of endless repositionings and constructions that are new but quickly become familiar and add to the sum total of a singular subjective existence. This state of continual change in which a present immediately becomes a past and becomes lost to a new present that once was a future is what leads Merleau-Ponty to conclude that "nowhere do I enjoy absolute possession of myself by myself" (240). Indeed, temporal ordering depends upon a break in subjective identity: "The past, therefore, *is* not past, nor the future future. It exists only when a subjectivity is there to disrupt the plenitude of being in itself, to adumbrate a perspective, and introduce non-being into it" (421). In this, Merleau-Ponty is in agreement with Wolfgang Iser, who similarly describes a subject dislocated by time: "all experience . . . will constantly be in a state of flux, so that what has been experienced can never be fully understood, and what has been understood can never coincide totally with what constitutes the self" (144).

Time as experienced by a subject is the structuration of the self. Conversely, the self becomes more than the passive object of time but actually determines it: "it is only through subjectivity itself that time takes on its form of past, present, and future" (Iser 144). On preparing to go to high school, a young Elaine clears her cupboard of old toys and finds treasures once important to her but now hardly remembered. She finds photographs that she herself took but now "I can't recall taking"; and her own signature: "It's my writing, but I don't remember printing this" (203). Time passing has meant that her own existence has become layered, and the self she once was has been replaced by someone else. In fact, placing herself momentarily in her brother's position, she feels she is almost barely recognizable: "He no longer knows who he's writing to, because I have surely changed beyond all recognition" (291). There is a sense here that the self is a form, much like the fossils that are "fragments of the past" (332). Similarly, the self is imagistic, made of etchings that, like the photographs of old lovers in which the sharp contours fade, are subject to time, "bleaching out gradually . . . until nothing remains but the general outlines" (266).

Furthermore, the self is marked by similarity through difference. As a young Stephen explains, with the passing of time apparent resemblance splinters into disparity: "if you put one identical twin in a high-speed rocket for a week, he'd come back to find his brother ten years older than he is himself" (219). Here the self is an effigy and interconnected with the other, aspects that hint at the fact that the self is never singular, but a collection of different frames that surface according to precipitating circumstances. At one point, Elaine predicts that she will fall prey to a disease in which time will no longer hold to its usual boundaries, and she will lose whole chunks of her life: "you can lose your entire past; you start afresh. . . . [W]ith another form, you keep the distant past but lose the present" (263). Here the self is a kind of mould with the potential to change form, and an arrangement of parts that has an almost tangible aspect. In fact, the novel opens with a formulation of time as "having a shape, something you could see, like a series of liquid transparencies, one laid on top of another. You don't look back along time but down through it, like water. Sometimes this comes to the surface, sometimes that, sometimes nothing" (3).

Subject to time, then, the self becomes a composition, an effigy of an external form that varies and that is constructed. Subject to time, the self becomes collected and collective imagery, through which identity takes the form of semblance and imitation. With this, we are brought to the concept of mimesis, and a definition of the subject as the function of an economy that is a matter of discourse and representation. For Kristeva, "mimesis partakes of the symbolic order" (*Revolution* 57). By this, one may assume that mimesis explores the social contract, based on the fact that all signification is mimetic in that the sign stands in for absence in the Real. Mimesis in its role of reproducing the "grammaticality" or "constitutive rules" (57) of social interaction may be seen to be imaged in Elaine's reaction to the various social monuments that structure her life and hold a place in her memory. The major cities in which she lives, for example, may be seen to function as the epitome of sublimated cultural activity. In this role, they reveal the mimetic nature of society:

I live in a house, with window curtains and a lawn, in British Columbia. . . . The unreality of the landscape there encourages me: the greeting-card mountains, of the sunset-and-sloppy-message variety, the cottagey houses that look as if they were built by the Seven Dwarfs in the thirties, the giant slugs, so much larger than a slug needs to be. Even the rain is overdone, I can't take it seriously. . . . [O]n good days it feels like a vacation, an evasion. (14–15)

Other social structures seem just as parodic. The Woolworths, where "Just about everything . . . is imitation something else" (210), implies that society not only produces artificiality but consumes it. The annual Christmas parade, in which people are dressed as snowflakes, elves, rabbits, and sugar plum fairies, is, even to a young child, obviously fake: "I know he isn't the real Santa Claus, just someone dressed up like him" (37). However, the spectacle serves the purpose of restating social myths and continuing tradition, in much the same way as the monarchy persists as a figurehead. Elaine's childhood memories of schoolteachers loyal to the British Empire trying to instil a sense of pride in being part of the Commonwealth are tied up with an image of the Queen that is unchanging, even if constructed: "I've never got used to the Queen being grown up. Whenever I see her cut-off head on the money, I think of her as fourteen years old, in her Girl Guide uniform . . ." (399). Her conviction that there are dual, perhaps multiple, queens hints at the fact that social constructions are, in fact, effigies: "The Queen has had grandchildren since, discarded thousands of hats, grown a bosom and (heresy to think it) the beginning of a double chin. None of this fools me. She's in there somewhere, that other one" (399).

However, more than anything else, her fascination with monuments, with "Statues of saints, and of crusaders on their biers, or those pretending to be crusaders; effigies of all kinds" (197), illustrates the structural divisions that lie at the base of symbolic and mimetic discourse. In a church in Mexico, Elaine is mesmerized by a statue of the Virgin Mary that is unlike the usual representation in that it is not dressed in the conventional blue or white gown but is cloaked in black. Even more significant is the fact that to her dress is pinned a variety of brass or tin objects: arms, legs, hands, sheep, donkeys, chickens, and hearts. This may be seen to be indicative of the fact that as representative discourse, mimesis posits what Kristeva terms the "connoted" object (*Revolution* 57). This connoted object is fictional in that it stands in opposition to the denoted object of the Real. It is imitative in that it replaces the phenomenally real object that is foreclosed to the subject upon assumption of a speaking position. In this incident, the Virgin Mary may be seen to be symbolic of the trajectory whereby signification is induced through loss of the referent, and the real objects now absent must be represented through brass and tin effigies. Kristeva's point that "mimetic discourse takes on the structure of language and, through narrative sentences, posits a signified and signifying object" (58) may be seen to be illustrated here in light of the fact that "she was a Virgin of lost things, one who restored what was lost" (*CE* 198).

With this, the Madonna reigns over the principle of loss and substitution that underlies all representative discourse. Further to this, the Virgin Mary, as myth and ultimate representation of maternity, may be seen to represent the fact that beneath all metonymic displacements lies the loss of the maternal that founds symbolic discourse. Indeed, Kristeva sees the representation of virgin motherhood as an effort to reconcile the unconscious needs of primary narcissism and matrilinearism with a social necessity for exchange and production that rely upon the symbolic paternal agency ("Stabat Mater" 181–82). And Mary Jacobus makes the point that "the Mother is a necessary pendant to the Word in Christian theology — just as the fantasized preverbal mother is a means of attempting to heal the split in language, providing an image of undivided signs, plenitude, and imaginary fullness to compensate for the actual poverty of language" (169).

In a momentary state of amnesia and bodily collapse that is akin to a moment of unconscious regression, Elaine seems to glimpse the fact that this statue expresses the reality of her existence: "She was the only one of these wood or marble or plaster Virgins who had ever seemed at all real to me. There could be some point in praying to her, kneeling down, lighting a candle" (198). However, the only truth evident in constructed discourse is the fact that it is marked by untruth and absence, and Elaine is unable even to touch upon that which has been foreclosed to her: "But I didn't do it, because I didn't know what to pray for. What was lost, what I could pin on her dress" (198). This blind spot hints at a kind of resistance within Elaine when faced with her own enunciative position, and a desire to not speak at all. In this sense, her fascination with the statue may be connected with it functioning as symbol of preverbal abundance and completeness. She herself admits that "My dreams are brightly coloured and without sound" (145); and, safe from the cruel bullying of her friends, "I go for long periods without saying anything at all. I can be free of words now, I can lapse back into wordlessness" (143). At this point, mimesis, in exploring the social contract, is questioning not only the denotation of objects but the very positioning and identity of the subject upon whom it is dependent. The position of enunciation is, by definition, held by a subject, but in *Cat's Eye* it is this very subjective identity that is posited, questioned, then ultimately displaced.

At the base of specular identification lies mimesis. In the formative mirror-phase, the "systematic refusal to acknowledge reality" (Lacan, "Some Reflections" 12) that is constitutive of the ego is an imprinting based upon a mirrored image taken to be real. This "essential libidinal relationship with the body-image" (14), which Lacan sees as crucial for the formation of subjective identity, is thus misrecognition anchored within a mimetic construction of reality. Little wonder, then, that elsewhere Lacan defines "the origin of mimicry" as "the inscription of the subject in the picture" (*Four Fundamental* 99), seeing mimesis as "the function in which the subject has to map himself as such" (100).

However, while "grasping" (100) the subject, the mimetic process also dislocates his or her identity. For Lacan, what is involved is "the libidinal tension that shackles the subject to the constant pursuit of an illusory unity which is always luring him away from himself" ("Some Reflections" 16). Thus, while Elaine, like any other subject, is positioned by the mimetic function, she is also distanced from herself and placed "elsewhere." Nowhere is this more evident than in the fainting spells in which she consciously cultivates a state of detachment: ". . . I can see my own body lying on the ground, just lying there. I can see the girls pointing and gathering. I can see Miss Lumley stalking over, bending with difficulty to look at me. But I'm seeing all this from above, as if I'm in the air, somewhere near the girls sign over the door, looking down like a bird" (172). This bodily experience, through which Elaine admits ". . . I slip sideways, out of my body, and I'm somewhere else" (173), is an expression of the self being foreign to the self, which is, perhaps, reminiscent of the *méconnaissance* of the earlier specular identification. However, it also raises the issue of a duality of the self, as she says, "At these times I feel blurred, as if there are two of me, one superimposed on the other, but imperfectly" (173). Lacan sees splintering of the self as fundamental to mimicry, saying, ". . . I set out from the fact that there is something that establishes a fracture, a bi-partition, a splitting of the being to which the being accommodates itself, even in the natural world" (*Four Fundamental* 106). Being more precise, he names this division as involving a play of masks and spectacle: "the being gives of himself, or receives from the other, something that is like a mask, a double, an envelope, a thrown-off skin, thrown off in order to cover the frame of a shield" (107).

Indeed, Elaine's "doubling of the other, or of oneself" (Lacan, *Four Fundamental* 107) seems structured by a number of surface layers that may be discarded at appropriate times. In the opening pages of the novel, we are introduced to a middle-aged Elaine whose life is dominated by pretence: ". . . I do of course have a real life. I sometimes have trouble believing in it, because it doesn't seem like the kind of life I could ever get away with, or deserve. This goes along with another belief of mine: that everyone else my age is an adult, whereas I am merely in disguise" (14). Eventually, we learn that she has, at all times in her life, adopted whatever guise was most appropriate, even to the point of deception. Speaking of the teenage years in which she too eats doughnuts covered in powdered sugar, gazes upon glossy photos of movie stars and singers, and listens to records, she makes the point that her friend Cordelia "knows how we're supposed to be behaving, now that we're in high school. But I think these things are impenetrable and fraudulent, and I can't do them without feeling I'm acting" (208–09). However, the most striking example of Elaine's constructed identity and the potential for mimetic reproduction is the incident in which she tells Cordelia that she is, in reality, a vampire.

> "You're not," says Cordelia, standing up, brushing off the snow. She's smiling uncertainly.
> "How do you know?" I say. "How do you *know*?"
> "You walk around in the daytime," Cordelia says.
> "That's not me," I say. "That's my twin. You've never known, but I'm one of a twins. Identical ones, you can't tell us apart by looking. . . . I'm just telling you the truth. You're my friend, I thought it was time you knew. I'm really dead. I've been dead for years." (233)

Cordelia is half-convinced, and while this may be, in part, testimony to Elaine's ability to deceive, it also bespeaks the issue of truth within a mimetic economy. For Kristeva, mimesis is the positing of a subject not according to truth but to verisimilitude (*Revolution* 57), in that the object is constructed rather than existing in any phenomenally real way. Consequently, mimesis may mean that "truth is no longer a reference to an object that is identifiable outside of language; it refers instead to an object that can be constructed through the semiotic network but is nevertheless posited in the symbolic and is, from then on, always verisimilar" (58). In Kristeva's account, the mimetic object, like the vampire beside the real Elaine, is separate, "noted but not denoted" (57). And it is at this point that mimicry poses the question of whether there is a first self behind the second one, or whether in fact there is only one self that has adapted. Lacan raises this point when he writes, "Mimicry reveals something in so far as it is distinct from what might be called an *itself* that is behind" (*Four Fundamental* 99). The connoted object and the real one cannot coincide, just as the sign cannot become the referent. But it is at this point of its reproduction that mimesis begins to subvert the thetic or symbolic order by confusing the boundary between the real and the fictional. As Kristeva points out, "the thetic conditions the possibilities of truth specific to language: all transgressions of the thetic are a crossing of the boundary between true and false" (*Revolution* 58). And mimesis is just such a violation, as "the very status of this verisimilar object throws into question the absoluteness of the break that establishes truth" (58).

The contrast between truth and fiction is clearly evident on the occasions when Elaine and Cordelia rewrite history. In a period of teenage friendship with Cordelia, she and Elaine play with words in what becomes "a full-blown game" (230) that renders the Smeaths as being ridiculously bland and boring, and Grace unpopular. The constructedness of these personalities through discourse is evident when Elaine acknowledges that they are manufactured: "Anything can be said about them, invented about them. They're defenceless, they're at our mercy" (230). And the fraudulent nature of the girls' "base treachery" is highlighted when we are reminded that "She [Grace] was adored, by all of us. But she is not any more. And in Cordelia's version, now, she never was" (231). Elsewhere, Elaine feels decidedly uncomfortable with the spurious nature of their construction: "A wave of blood goes up to my head, my stomach shrinks together. . . . It's as if I've been caught stealing, or telling a lie. . . . There's the same flush of shame, of guilt and terror, and of cold disgust with myself" (253). Some time later, when Cordelia is composing the kind of friendship she would have liked to have had, Elaine finds it difficult to sustain a permanent image of her friend: "Cordelia's face dissolves, re-forms: I can see her nine-year-old face taking shape beneath it" (252). This may be seen to reveal the arbitrary nature of the mimetically constructed object and support Kristeva's assertion that while mimetic discourse must posit an object, "this 'object' is merely a result of the drive economy of enunciation; its true position is inconsequential" (*Revolution* 57).

Of course, no single character better portrays the fictional status of the mimetically constructed object than does Cordelia. Kristeva makes the point that mimesis "pluralizes denotation" (*Revolution* 59), and this is evident in the array of Cordelias that exist: "But which Cordelia? The one I have conjured up, the one with the roll-top boots and the turned-up collar, or the one before, or the one after? There is never only one, of anyone" (*CE* 6). She is unrelenting as a child, insecure as a teenager, sophisticated as a young adult, broken later in life. But she is, above all, unrecognizable. As children, playing snow angels, "For a moment she looks like someone I don't know, a stranger . . ." (185). Even for an adult Elaine drinking wine and looking out of a window at a bar, Cordelia's identity has a distinctly illusory quality: "On the other side of the glass, Cordelia drifts past; then melts and reassembles, changing into someone else. Another mistaken identity" (263). And, back in Toronto after many years away, Elaine mistakes another woman for her long-lost friend: " 'Cordelia,' I say, turning. But it's not Cordelia. It's nobody I know" (313).

The deceptiveness in which Cordelia is shrouded exists partly because "She can counterfeit anything" (358). The conversation in which Cordelia recounts the various Shakespearean personae she has performed illustrates the fact that fiction is a principle that structures not only her life in the theatre but her existence in a wider context. After all, on seeing Cordelia in one of the better phases, Elaine recognizes that "she has reinvented herself" (301). None of which is at all surprising as, even as a child, she had a way of talking that seemed like "an imitation of something" (72).

While Cordelia's shifting character is partly a conscious deliberation on her own part, it is undeniable that the various versions of Cordelia exist according to Elaine's construction of them. In the opening pages of the novel, Elaine assembles a number of images. One Cordelia is a bag lady in a worn coat and knitted hat; another is unconscious in hospital, brain-dead; a third is trapped in an iron lung, aware but immobile. These reproductions are indicative of the fact that mimetically constructed objects are enunciations; they are nothing more than compositions spoken by a posited subject. This, in turn, brings to the fore the role of the other in the construction of the self.

For Lacan, the signified as well as signifying subject is indebted to the other: "The Other is the locus in which is situated the chain of the signifier that governs whatever may be made present of the subject — it is the field of that living being in which the subject has to appear" (*Four Fundamental* 203). It is precisely because the subject is constructed in and through discourse that it needs the intervention of alterity, and this is well illustrated by the fact that the adult Elaine longs to see Cordelia in order to explain her own life: "There are things I need to ask her. Not what happened . . . I need to ask her why" (411). And while Elaine recognizes this as being her own desire, and the fact that she herself will be placed as other by another, she sees the interaction as being a reciprocal need: "She will have her own version. I am not the centre of her story, because she herself is that. But I could give her something you can never have, except from another person: what you look like from outside. A reflection. This is the part of herself I could give back to her" (411).

This role of the other in the mimetic construction of the self is most clearly evident in the specular experiences through which Elaine, at Cordelia's insistence, glimpses her self: "Cordelia brings a mirror to school. It's a pocket-mirror, the small plain oblong kind without any rim. She takes it out of her pocket and holds the mirror up in front of me and says, 'Look at yourself! Just look!' " (158). Elsewhere, this kind of experience is marked by the "structural reversal" (Lacan, "Some Reflections" 15) that defines an ego-identity based upon a body image that is by necessity reversed and distorted when reflected back to the subject by way of a mirror: "Cordelia takes her sunglasses out of her shoulder bag and puts them on. There I am in her mirror eyes, in duplicate and monochrome, and a great deal smaller than life-size" (303). Always, however, the presence of the other is in the background, interrupting the narcissistic duality by impinging upon the image that will represent the self: "I dream that I'm trying on a fur collar, in front of the mirror on my bureau. There's someone standing behind me. If I move so that I can see into the mirror, I'll be able to look over my own shoulder without turning around. I'll be able to see who it is" (250).

Occasionally, this identification of the self through the other will overpower the delineation between them. Elaine goes from a position of vulnerability in her relationship with Cordelia to one of control and domination. In this, she comes perilously close to losing her specificity altogether, through a kind of merging that no longer respects the boundaries between them: "I'm not afraid of seeing Cordelia. I'm afraid of being Cordelia. Because in some way we changed places, and I've forgotten when" (227). The fact that the interreflective relationship of the two characters is marked by a power struggle may be seen to be indicative of what Lacan sees as being an integral part of specular identity construction: aggressive relativity. It is this "drama of primordial jealousy" ("Mirror" 5) that forms the dialectic that will, from the mirror-phase onwards, define social interaction. Lacan connects aggressivity to Hegel's master-slave dialectic ("Subversion" 308) and to the death drive ("Some Reflections" 16), both of which feature in sublimated forms in Elaine and Cordelia's relationship.

Cordelia's savage bullying and manipulation culminate in Elaine's near death through freezing. This is rivalled only by the years of intimidation through which Elaine gains control of their friendship in later life. In one incident in which Elaine has managed to unnerve her friend through her skilful use of words, she recognizes her victory: "I'm surprised at how much pleasure this gives me, to know she's so uneasy, to know I have this much power over her. . . . I have a denser, more malevolent little triumph to finger: energy has passed between us, and I am stronger" (233). Thus, Lacan's stipulation that resentment, competitiveness, revenge, persecution, and war are personality states that have as their origin the aggressivity that structures mirror-stage identification ("Aggressivity" 16–17, 19, 21) is well illustrated in Elaine and Cordelia's friendship. It is, perhaps, this rivalrous struggle to the death that structures the original organization of the ego in connection with the other that may explain Cordelia's ability to make Elaine feel as if she does not exist. As Elaine herself says to Cordelia in her thoughts, "You made me believe I was nothing" (199). But as Lacan writes, "in a universe of discourse nothing contains everything, and here you find again the gap that constitutes the subject" ("Of Structure" 193). Hence, the word "nothing" by which Elaine signifies herself is in fact metaphorically representative of the absence that constitutes her as subject: "*What do you have to say for yourself?* Cordelia used to ask. *Nothing*, I would say. It was a word I came to connect with myself, as if I was nothing, as if there was nothing there at all" (41).

This highlights the paradoxical nature of the mimetic imaging of the self, dependent as it is upon presence predicated upon absence and an other who constitutes it yet threatens it with annihilation. It is true that the conflict with the other is a matter of life and death: "The struggle that establishes this initial enslavement is rightly called a struggle of pure prestige, and the stake, [is] life itself . . ." (Lacan, "Subversion" 308). However, as symbolic murder that will allow for signification, it is potentially constitutive as well as destructive for subjective existence: "it is not enough to decide on the basis of its effect — Death. It still remains to be decided which death, that which is brought by life or that which brings life" (308). Furthermore, it is a situation in which there are no clear-cut lines between enemy and victim and no distinct position of assailant. As Lacan notes, "The aggressiveness involved in the ego's fundamental relationship to other people is certainly not based on the simple relationship implied in the formula 'big fish eat little fish', but upon the intrapsychic tension we sense in the warning of the ascetic that 'a blow at your enemy is a blow at yourself' " ("Some Reflections" 16).

It is no coincidence then that Elaine needs to resolve her struggle with Cordelia if she is ever to settle into her own identity. In the closing pages of the novel, she does just this by acknowledging the connection between them while maintaining a separation: "I know she's looking at me. . . . There is the same shame, the sick feeling in my body, the same knowledge of my own wrongness, awkwardness, weakness; the same wish to be loved; the same loneliness; the same fear. But these are not my own emotions anymore. They are Cordelia's; as they always were" (419). The conflict may still be there, but there is no longer any need to fight: "I am the older one now, I'm the stronger. If she stays here any longer she will freeze to death; she will be left behind, in the wrong time. It's almost too late. I reach out my arms to her, bend down, hands open to show I have no weapon. *It's all right*, I say to her. *You can go home now*" (419). Hence, Elaine's ensnarement within a mimetic economy has led to a negotiation with alterity that signals a resolute subjective stance.

Lacan sees mimicry as the device that comes into play in "the struggle to the death" (*Four Fundamental* 107). However, he also names it as structuring "sexual union" in that "In both situations, the being breaks up, in an extraordinary way, between its being and its semblance, between itself and that paper tiger it shows to the other" (107). With this, mimetic discourse becomes an issue of sexual difference, which for Lacan revolves around what he calls "the lure" (100). In his account, mimetic activity has a certain "sexual aim" that is based upon "disguise" and "masquerade" (100). Elaine's construction of a self-image by way of clothing and makeup may be seen to be exactly this kind of masquerade. Her account of trying on frocks in a department store fitting room is indicative of her attempt to construct a suitable image for her exhibition and highlights the camouflaging involved: "I slip it on, zipper and hook it, turn this way and that, in front of the mirror which is as usual badly lit. If I ran a store like this I'd paint all the cubicles pink and put some money into the mirrors: whatever else women want to see, it's not themselves . . ." (44). Like her adolescent use of cosmetics to make her mouth "tough, crayon-red, shiny as nails" (4), her attempt to "squint into the mirror, preparing my face" (19) is demonstrative of a mimetic economy reliant upon costumes. It is, however, one that is sexually specific. At this point, one is reminded of Lacan's belief that "It is no doubt through the mediation of masks that the masculine and the feminine meet in the most acute, most intense way" (*Four Fundamental* 107).

With this, Elaine's masquerading, rather than being an individual stance, may be seen to be a general function of femininity. Indeed, a number of incidents connect this specific form of mimicry to a position specified according to gender. A young Elaine finds it very difficult to be a little girl, saying: "Playing with girls is different and at first I feel strange as I do it, self-conscious, as if I'm only doing an imitation of a girl" (52). Her friend Carol, by contrast, is an expert. She is precious and ladylike and she is a sissy. Together with Grace Smeath, the three of them cut up department store catalogues, constructing their own domestic worlds with figures that are "always women" (53). But in this piecemeal approach to creating their own homes, there is a particular duplicity involved in their self-appraisal: "Grace and Carol look at each other's scrapbook pages and say, 'Oh, yours is so good. Mine's no good. Mine's awful.' They say this every time we play the scrapbook game. Their voices are wheedling and false; I can tell they don't mean it, each one thinks her own lady on her own page is good. But it's the thing you have to say, so I begin to say it too" (53).

This pastiche of frying pans and bed linen is more than a childish game. It signals Elaine's initiation into a new realm: "Something is unfolding, being revealed to me. I see that there's a whole world of girls and their doings that has been unknown to me . . ." (54). Of course, what Elaine is being initiated into is, in fact, the realm of post-oedipal desire. For Freud, the feminine stance is one of three possible outcomes of a castration that initiates the oedipal complex in the little girl: "The discovery that she is castrated is a turning-point in a girl's growth. Three possible lines of development start from it: one leads to sexual inhibition or to neurosis, the second to change of character in the sense of a masculinity complex, the third, finally, to normal femininity" ("Femininity" 160). But Irigaray sees Freudian femininity as being a "masquerade," and the assumption of a system of values that is inherently alien "and in which she can 'appear' and circulate only when enveloped in the need/desires/ fantasies of others, namely men" (*This Sex* 134).

The alienating effect of adopting the feminine mask is well illustrated throughout Elaine's life. She quite simply finds boys more straightforward and less dangerous, not surprising in light of the fact that her best "friends" are terrorizing her. In fact, she herself acknowledges that "My relationships with boys are effortless, which means that I put very little effort into them. It's girls I feel awkward with, it's girls I feel I have to defend myself against; not boys" (237).

Apart from being hard work, she finds collective activity with girls confining: ". . . I wouldn't be caught dead in a girls' school. The idea fills me with claustrophobic panic: a school with nothing in it but girls would be like a trap" (215). And this continues into later life when she finds consciousness-raising groups threatening because "Women collect grievances, hold grudges and change shape. . . . Women know too much, they can neither be deceived nor trusted" (378–79). As a child, she shows unflinching allegiance to boys such as her brother, even remaining loyal to Mr. Smeath as he conspires with her at the Sunday dinner table. And she is appreciated by those with whom she sides: "I have more cards from boys than Carol has, more than Cordelia and Grace have collected. . . . I hug my knowledge, which is new but doesn't surprise me: boys are my secret allies" (163). However, it is important to note that she is speaking of Valentine's Day cards, a situation that hints at the second aspect of Irigaray's account of femininity: the desire of men.

For Grosz, masquerade is artifice designed to make oneself an object of desire; and Freudian femininity is little more than strategies of seduction and coquetry to this effect (*Jacques Lacan*). Indeed, camouflage and travesty geared at attracting the male gaze are evident in Carol's first pubescent experience with makeup: "When we go down to the kitchen for a glass of milk, her mother says, 'What's that on your face, young lady?' Right in front of us she scrubs Carol's face with the dirty dishcloth. 'Don't let me catch you doing such a cheap thing again!'. . . 'Making a spectacle of yourself,' as if there's something wrong in the mere act of being looked at" (163–64). In some ways, this foreshadows the activity of other ladies who are playing their part in a mimetic sexual economy. Through Cordelia's older sisters, Elaine learns that "the curse" when "blood comes out between your legs" (93) is connected to other strange acts, like waxing legs and wearing brassieres. Being ladylike means assuming a specific kind of persona, one that she encounters as a young adult at the Toronto College of the Arts:

> What they wear is cashmere twin sets, camel's-hair coats, good tweed skirts, pearl button earrings. They wear tidy medium-heel pumps and tailored blouses, or jumpers, or little weskits with matching skirts and buttons. . . . They discuss clothes, or talk about the boys they are going out with. . . . Their eyes during these conversations look dewy, blurred, pulpy, easily hurt, like

the eyes of blind baby kittens; but also sly and speculative, and filled with greed and deceit. (276)

The other girl in her class quickly exchanges one feminine persona for another. Suzie "has a little breathless voice and a startled little laugh; even her name is like a powder-puff," and she manages to make even a retribution "come out like a cat rubbing against a leg, an admiring hand on a bicep" (282). However, before too long, Suzie deteriorates into yet another feminine persona, the nagging frump, "slumping like a middle-aged woman" (319). After she suffers an ill-fated abortion, the posturing necessary to entrap a man becomes clear: "The pink nightie brings it home to me: she is none of the things I've thought about her, she never has been. She's just a nice girl playing dress-ups" (320).

This connection of pantomime with adult sexual desire is the point at which a mimetic economy becomes a post-oedipal dynamic. In fact, Lacan has shown how the contribution of the oedipal complex to the repression of libidinal desires and the first sublimation that constitutes reality revolves around mimesis.[1] The oedipal identification with a parent of the same sex inhibits the sexual function by repressing the desires through the agency of the superego. However, it preserves the function by way of "misconception," by maintaining in consciousness an ego-ideal image of future satisfaction of desires. Thus, the complex is dependent not only upon the unconscious but on "misunderstanding" and a certain duplicity: "the imago itself appears under two structures whose disparity defines the first sublimation of reality" (Lacan, "Oedipus Complex" 196). The parental object of identification is no longer the object of desire, and "the identification of the mimetic has become propitiatory" (196), whereby the object separates from the subject in a new dialectic of love and fear that is, in fact, a step toward the construction of reality. In this way, the original object of desire seems to have been conjured away; and in an act of narcissistic defence, the subject establishes the object in a new reality. Both the object and its newly found position within a representative economy are predicated upon mimesis: "The object . . . normally comes to fill the frame of the double where the ego first identifies itself, and through which it still can confuse itself with the other" (196).

Thus, the mimetically constructed image of future satisfaction of desires is what allows for the relinquishing of desires at that particular juncture. Meanwhile, the mimetic economy posits the newly emerged object as effigy, and opens the way for the discursive construction of a reality now based on the metonymy of post-oedipal desire. This juncture of femininity as masquerade with oedipal desires and the necessary redirection of them may be seen to be evidenced in Elaine's concept of fathers. In her eyes, fathers do play some particular role, and it is sexually specific in its shadowy and cryptic nature, which is highly suggestive: "fathers and their ways are enigmatic. . . . All fathers except mine are invisible in daytime; daytime is ruled by mothers. But fathers come out at night. Darkness brings home the fathers, with their real, unspeakable power. There is more to them than meets the eye. And so we believe the belt" (164).

A short while later, Elaine's mother miscarries. While "the splotch of blood" (166) connects it to all other matters feminine, the point to note is that it effects a separation between mother and daughter. This interruption in their relationship may be seen to symbolize the shift in the oedipal gaze consequent to the father's intervention: "My mother comes back from the hospital and is weaker. . . . It's as if she's gone off somewhere else, leaving me behind; or forgotten I am there" (166). Later, the adult interactions that are subsequent to this kind of symbolic separation from the maternal are imaged in those around Elaine or those with whom she will actually become involved. However, time and time again, the mimetic quality of this kind of interaction is evident.

Carol's mother and father, for example, are a conventional married couple who epitomize the domestic and marital economy. What is striking is the way in which their lives are somehow duplicate:

they sleep in two little beds, exactly alike, with matching pink chenille bedspreads and matching night-tables. These beds are called twin beds . . . it's strange to think of Mr. and Mrs. Campbell lying in them at night, with different heads — his with a moustache, hers without — but nevertheless twin-like, identical, under the sheets and blankets. It's the matching bedspreads, the night-tables, the lamps, the bureaus, the doubleness of everything in their room, that gives me this impression. (51)

Similarly, her brother Stephen seems to undergo a change when he awakens to his attraction for the opposite sex. His harbouring of a secret desire for Bertha Watson seems to accompany a weakening of his identity in which he is reduced to an imitation of his former self: "I'd like to know how she's done it, this trick with my brother that's turned him into a stupider, more nervous identical twin of himself" (103). Away from feminine wiles, his singular self can still be glimpsed. Washing the dishes together, Elaine sees him as if unchanged: "on some of these dish-drying nights he reverts to what I consider to be his true self" (218).

Cordelia also exhibits the artifice evident in relations between the sexes. She is overwhelming for the boys of their age because she approaches them playing adult games of desire. Elaine describes her as being too "studied and overdone" (243). Cordelia flatters them, emulating predetermined scripts: "Her attempts at conversation with them are a performance, an imitation. . . . She's mimicking something, something in her head, some role or image that only she can see" (243–44). What is evident here is that she is copying a femininity that is in itself a figment of discursive and mimetic construction. This double take — Cordelia imitating what is already an imitation — places her in a position of being twice removed within the mimetic economy. Perhaps this can be seen to be indicative of Mary Anne Doane's contention that women speaking or appropriating discourse is "the greatest masquerade of all" ("Woman's Stake" 223) because the female body does not permit the representation of lack. In her account of woman, "she can only mime representation" because "she has nothing to lose, nothing at stake" (222).

The inability of the female form to be castrated is something Stephen Heath also focuses upon. He sees it as a "negative relation to the symbolic," in which the female experience of castration is based upon simulation: "she passes from loss of an imaginary part of herself — the doubling, the partition — to loss of an organ that can only be a superimposition on that other loss which it then continues to figure" ("Difference" 68). As a consequence of this, women are subject to a specific form of division: "woman fails symbolic castration which catches up in her, problematically, an imaginary partition (in the sense of a dividing up, a separating out) that is specifically feminine" (68). Naming the dual nature of female genitalia, the duality of the relation to the mother, and the "doubling-loss of herself as one" through menstruation and childbirth, Heath concludes that "woman's order is that of the double" (68), and, quoting Cixous, he writes: "rather than castration anxiety the woman knows the anxiety of partition" (68–69).

Given, then, that women have a relationship with the symbolic order that heightens intrasubjective division and privileges mimesis, it is no surprise that Elaine's relationships with men rely heavily upon a mimetic and representative economy. Elaine characterizes her affair with Josef as one that lacks actuality: "Women were not real to Josef, any more than he was real to me. . . . The reason I've never dreamed about him was that he belonged already to the world of dreams . . ." (365). A kind of lack of actuality also characterizes Jon. His work creating special effects for movies makes him an artisan of discursive construction. Looking at his workbench, Elaine notices that "there's part of a face, with the skin blackened and withered, made to fit over the actor's real face" (18). His love of reproducing effigies signals a kind of theatricality that also characterized their marriage, as their interactions increasingly begin to resemble one-act plays: "I see these things as scenarios, to be played through and discarded, perhaps simultaneously. None of them precludes the others. In real life, the days go on as usual" (370).

The simulated quality of the marriage in which they mimicked roles that seemed appropriate is evident long after they divorce and are living separate lives. At their daughter's graduation, they continue to mime: "we acted like responsible, grown-up parents. . . . We even dressed the way we knew Sarah wanted us to: I had on an outfit, matching shoes and all, and Jon wore a suit and an actual tie" (17). The fact that "he looked like an undertaker" (17) may be seen to illustrate the highly alienating nature of the role thrust upon him as a consequence of the marital economy. Josef, too, suffers at the hands of desire, becoming for Elaine a "Life Drawing" hanging on a gallery wall: ". . . Josef preserved in aspic and good enough to eat" (365). However, Josef is himself "duplicitous" and thinks "women are helpless flowers, or shapes to be arranged and contemplated" (318). The posturing to which Elaine is subject through their relationship is evident in his attempts to construct exactly the kind of image he desires: "Josef is rearranging me. 'You should wear your hair loose,' he says, unpinning it. . . . 'You look like a marvellous gypsy' " (304). Her complicity is marked by the dynamics of desire that underpin the situation: "He presses his mouth to my collarbone, untucks the bedsheet he's draped me in. . . . I stand still and let him do this. I let him do what he likes. . . . He places me against the twilight of the window, turns me, stands back a little, running his hand up and down my side. . . . I feel my knees begin to give, my mouth loosen" (304). This connection of sexual desire and the feminine role with the dynamics of representative and mimetic construction culminates in a situation in which Elaine becomes little more than an effigy. Wearing the new purple dress Josef has chosen for her, with its tight bodice, low neckline, and full skirt, Elaine recognizes herself as nothing more than a reproduction: ". . . I catch a glimpse of myself, without expecting it, in the smoked-mirror wall of the elevator as we go up, and I see for an instant what Josef sees: a slim woman with cloudy hair, pensive eyes in a thin white face. I recognize the style: late nineteenth century. Pre-Raphaelite. I should be holding a poppy" (304).

Her seeing herself through another's eyes is exactly the dynamic of specular misrecognition that marks the mirror-phase construction of subjectivity. It illustrates not only male desire as a dynamic of alterity through which feminine identity is constructed, but the disparity between the mimetically constructed object and its supposed referent. On both a symbolic and a sexual level, then, the post-oedipal economy is marked by posturing and imitation. Nowhere is this more evident than in Elaine's own summation of the fact that, in being involved with Jon and Josef, she is immersing herself in a series of "deceptions" (316). Hiding Josef from her parents and Jon from all of them, she is engaged in a kind of "treachery" of two-timing: "I sneak around, heart in my mouth, dreading revelations; . . . I evade and tiptoe" (316). The ultimate effect of this immersion within the dynamics of desire is her own division; and one is reminded of Heath's point that women are "divided up in the order of the double" ("Difference" 68) when we read of Elaine's splitting: "my life is now multiple, and I am in fragments" (CE 316).

Elaine being modelled in the image of the Pre-Raphaelite heroine may be seen to be a clever inversion of the part she herself plays as an artist and painter. Lacan has made clear the fact that "pictorial creation" (*Four Fundamental* 108) is the function of a mimetic economy, saying: "the facts of mimicry are similar, at the animal level, to what, in the human being is manifested as art, or painting" (100). His analysis depends upon the function of the *"trompe-l'oeil"* (111), which is that which is designed to make the spectator think the objects represented are real. This is pertinent for Elaine who prefers paintings that hide the processes of their formation. For this reason, she has a decided aversion to oil paintings: ". . . I have come to dislike their thickness, their obliteration of line, their look of licked lips, the way they call attention to the brushstrokes of the painter. . . .What I want instead is pictures that seem to exist of their own accord" (326).

This desire for the simulation of what is phenomenologically real is connected to her own reproductions of domestic and marital reality through her admission that her paintings are somewhat like her earlier mimetic experiences with the scrapbook and the "Eaton's Catalogue" (327). Jon's dismissal that "a picture of something recognizable" is mere "illustration" evokes the accusation that she "might as well be a photographer" (327). However, the photographer never deals with true reality, but with specular images that are inverted, illusory, and counterfeit: "When the pictures come back from being developed, the negatives come too. I hold them up to the light: everything that's white in the real picture is black in the negative" (55). The quality of unreal reality that marks the photographic medium may be seen to be illustrative of Elaine's occupation as one who trades in images and artifice. However, it further elucidates the falsification inherent in her profession as a painter. As Lacan notes, "The point is not that painting gives an illusory equivalence to the object, . . . the point is that the *trompe-l'oeil* of painting pretends to be something other than what it is" (*Four Fundamental* 112).

While the system of construction (brush strokes, light and dark patches, perspectives) that marks the painting in its composition resembles an object, it denies that it is doing so and therefore falsifies its own phenomenological and ontological status. Painting is not the outward appearance of some thing (the semblance of an object); it is not the exterior surface of an object, as the *trompe-l'oeil* would like to have the spectator believe. Painting is the resemblance to or simulation of that object; the constructed image pretends to *be* the object, and mimics it. But in this denial of its processes of formation, the painting falsifies not only the represented object but itself.

Lacan states that "if one wishes to deceive a man, what one presents to him is the painting of a veil, that is to say, something that incites him to ask what is behind it" (*Four Fundamental* 112). This illustrates the double entendre that is painting: namely, the two layers of semblance and resemblance, or of ontological reality and discursively constructed meaning, which become confused and ambiguous. Such confusion surfaces in one of the paintings in Elaine's exhibition called "Picoseconds." Here, in comparison with the landscape, her parents are well defined: "They are painted in another style: smooth, finely modulated, realistic as a snaphot" (405). However, the symbols underneath them undermine their apparent and self-evident existence: "By their obvious artificiality, they call into question the reality of landscape and figures alike" (406). This dialectic of realism and artificiality culminates in a questioning of the very existence of the artistically constructed object. As Lacan notes, the painting may pretend to be the object: "the picture is the appearance that says it is that which gives the appearance" (*Four Fundamental* 112). However, it is diametrically opposed not to principles of construction but to the phenomenologically real object or referent: "The picture does not compete with appearance, it competes with what Plato designates for us beyond appearance as being the Idea" (112).

Elaine eventually relinquishes the idea of painting real objects, saying: "Until now I've always painted things that were actually there, in front of me. Now I begin to paint things that aren't there" (337). She does nevertheless reproduce entities that are undeniably objects — a silver toaster, a glass coffee percolator, a wringer washing machine. However, they seem to exist in their own right, without the directive of the subject's intention that usually defines the object: "I know that these things must be memories, but they do not have the quality of memories. They are not hazy around the edges, but sharp and clear. They arrive detached from any context; they are simply there, in isolation, as an object glimpsed on the street is there" (337).

The lack of subjective intentionality within these manufactured objects bespeaks the very purpose of art as a form of mimesis, and it questions Elaine's role as subject and painter/creator of a discursively constructed, illusory reality. The painting may appear to function as an object in its own right, somewhat like a clear pane of glass through which to view the object. However, it is really a discursively constructed image that comes into existence only through a conscious intention on the part of the artist. For Lacan, the moment at which we differentiate between the two is the moment at which we shift our stance and realize that our perspective has not changed, as it would have had the image been phenomenologically real: "At the moment when, by a mere shift of our gaze, we are able to realize that the representation does not move with the gaze and that it is merely a *trompe-l'oeil* . . ." (*Four Fundamental* 112). This functions as a recognition of our previous misrecognition: "it appears at that moment as something other than it seemed, or rather it now seems to be that something else" (112); and for Lacan this is precisely what "captures our attention and delights us," that which "attracts and satisfies us in *trompe l'oeil*" (112).

Such a moment exists for Elaine when the Mrs. Smeath who exists in one of her paintings is revealed as being captured and held within the confines of the frame: "I look away from Mrs. Smeath, and there is another Mrs. Smeath, only this one is moving. She's just inside the door and heading towards me. . . . It's as if she's stepped down off the wall, the walls" (352). Elaine is thoroughly mesmerized — a reaction that Lacan predicts. However, even more poignant is the misrecognition that marks the effects of Elaine's gaze, for the Mrs. Smeath of the painting reassembles as her daughter Grace, who in turn becomes an unknown observer: "But of course this can't be Mrs. Smeath . . . And it isn't. . . . It's Grace Smeath. . . . But I look again, more closely: this woman is not Grace. She doesn't even look like Grace. . . . This woman is a stranger" (352–53). Her misrecognition further heightens the sense of multiplicity that characterizes Mrs. Smeath's existence at the hands of Elaine's brush and canvas. There are, in fact, "many of her" (404): sitting, standing, flying, with and without her rubber plant, or her husband.

The synthetic nature of these Mrs. Smeaths, made, as they are, in imitation of the natural product, is dependent upon the illusion of the image. This signals a reliance upon the specular rivalled only by Elaine's own dubious self-imaging through painting. The self-portrait entitled "Cat's Eye" displaces the idea of the self by placing Elaine's head in the right foreground rather than making it the central focus within the frame. What holds pride of place is a large mirror through which a different, decentred perspective of the same self is afforded: "in the centre of the picture . . . a pier-glass is hanging. . . . In it, a section of the back of my head is visible; but the hair is different, younger" (408). The discrepancy between the frontal image of an aging Elaine and the reflected image of a younger woman hints at a kind of specular alienation, evident also in the "defacing" (20) of the photograph that advertises her exhibition. Here a stranger has drawn a moustache and goatee on top of what is otherwise a faithful reproduction of herself. Elaine characterizes this as an act of vandalism that robs her of her identity: "it was taking away someone's face" (20). And it may be seen in relation to the fact that, while Elaine may create a toaster, percolator, and washing machine through her painting, she affords these objects a certain status while losing her own: "I have no image of myself in relation to them" (337).

Barthes makes the point that while the portrait is assumed to be the most natural of reproductions, it "is not a realistic representation, a related copy, an idea such as we might get from figurative painting; it is a scene made up by blocks of meaning, at once varied, repeated" (61). His contention that the portrait is by definition "subject to a linguistic structure" and resembles "the semantic space" (61) is illustrated by the fact that both Elaine's self-portrait and photograph are positioned within the social domain. As a symbolic construction, it is subject to intervention by an other, either at the level of content, such as in "Cat's Eye," where Elaine's image is tempered by the figures of Grace, Cordelia, and Carol, or at the structural level of form, as is evidenced by the graffiti. As a symbolic form, the self-portrait is undeniably a construction of the self, a fact that Elaine recognizes: "I have achieved, finally, a face that a moustache can be drawn on. . . . This is an accomplishment. I have made something of myself, something or other, after all" (20).

Elaine's constitution of the self, while metaphorically represented by the self-portrait and photograph, is actually effected through her dynamics of painting others and objects external to her self. This is because by doing so, she establishes herself as a gazing subject: "I put light into them . . . I have said, *Look*. I have said, *I see*" (404). This may be seen to illustrate Lacan's belief that the scopic drive is the channel through which subjective identity may emerge: ". . . I emerge as eye, assuming, in a way, emergence from . . . the function of *seeingness (voyure)*" (*Four Fundamental* 82). For Merleau-Ponty, the gaze is a subjective stance in that it is the juxtaposition of simultaneous points in one direction (255), and the organization of objects that is "motivated": "the gaze is that perceptual genius underlying the thinking subject which can give to things the precise reply that they are awaiting in order to exist before us" (264).

Such intentionality is evident in Elaine's fascination with the washing machine. She finds gazing upon it satisfying in that it externalizes the dynamics in which she orders objects around her: "I watch it, hands on the edge of the tub, chin on my hands. . . . The water turns grey and I feel virtuous because of all the dirt that's coming out. It's as if I myself am doing this just by looking" (122). Elaine's imagined control of the external world by way of her look illustrates Merleau-Ponty's definition of the gaze as being "the involvement of our body in the typical structures of the world" (310). Lacan further develops the symbolic function of the gaze as being a matter of castration (*Four Fundamental* 77) and desire (85), and the very constitution of the subject: "The subject is strictly speaking determined by the very separation that determines the break of the *a*, that is to say, the fascinatory element introduced by the gaze" (118). However, the gaze, as the function in which the subject is suspended, is marked by a number of structural features. The first is what Lacan calls "the pre-existence to the seen of a given-to-be-seen" (74), whereby the subject who looks is himself or herself looked at. This "gratuitous showing" (76) determines not only the dynamics of the scopic drive but of subjectivity itself: "This is the function that is found at the heart of the institution of the subject in the visible. What determines me, at the most profound level, in the visible, is the gaze that is outside" (106). Consequently, the subject himself or herself becomes a "picture" or "photograph" (106), and is positioned as screen upon which an image may be projected. This makes the external world "all-seeing" (75), for while the subject sees only from one vantage point, he or she is viewed from all sides (72). Furthermore, the gaze that circumscribes the subject remains hidden and does so without necessarily showing itself. In Lacan's words, "The gaze I encounter . . . is, not a seen gaze, but a gaze imagined by me in the field of the Other" (84).

Both of these aspects characterize Elaine's experience of the preexisting gaze. As a child, she observes her parents in their bedroom one night in an incident reminiscent of the primal scene: "I see my parents. . . . It's disquieting to look at them, in through the window, and know that they don't know I can see them. It's as if I don't exist; or as if they don't" (68). Her acknowledgement of the fact that her own existence as well as that of those around her depends upon a mutual showing foreshadows her later understanding that, even if apparently absent, the gaze of the other is necessary for an identified self. After the exhibition, a now adult Elaine is drunk and depressed and conscious of herself still being on show, even in an empty room. She is, in fact, always being exhibited: "[I am] making a spectacle of myself. I feel it's a spectacle, even though no one's watching" (414). This illustrates Lacan's contention that "we are beings who are looked at, in the spectacle of the world" (*Four Fundamental* 75). However, equally as significant is the fact that this incident illustrates the dynamic that Lacan has described as the process by which "I see myself seeing myself" (81). In her hazy awareness of being entangled in relations of seeing and being seen, Elaine is touching upon the very structure of her own subjective identity. The momentary detachment through which she can see herself seeing is epitomized in her actually holding in her hand a marble "eye," which in this context symbolizes the omnipotent look: "The cat's eyes really are like eyes, but not the eyes of cats. They're the eyes of something that isn't known but exists anyway; like the green eye of the radio; like the eyes of aliens from a distant planet" (62–63).

At this point, the view of the other as omnipresent is quietly unsettling, but eventually it becomes a source of tangible anxiety.

Going to the theatre as a child reveals the mutual reciprocity of the gaze to be tinged with unease. There is some confusion as to who is on show and for whom, largely because Cordelia is disguised in a weasel's costume, and, since there is a number of such animal characters, the return gaze of those up on stage is uncontainable: "Knowing she's there but not knowing where is the worst thing. She could be anywhere" (127). Some time later, the reciprocated look is positioned firmly as a point of conflict. Elaine's painting "Half a Face," which draws upon the technique of the theatrical mask, features Cordelia "looking out with that defiant, almost belligerent stare of hers" (227). The eyes in the painting are described as having "sabotaged" even the artist: "They aren't strong eyes; the look they give the face is tentative, hesitant, reproachful. Frightened. Cordelia is afraid of me, in this picture. I am afraid of Cordelia" (227).

This description seems to illustrate the fact that the relationship between the picture and the spectator via the artist is one of exchange that has a certain warring quality. So too does Elaine's decision to name one of her paintings "An-Eye-For-An-Eye" (352). As Lacan notes, the painter "gives something for the eye to feed on, but he invites the person to whom this picture is presented to lay down his gaze there as one lays down one's weapon. This is the pacifying, Apollonian effect of painting" (*Four Fundamental* 101). Thus, we are brought to another structural feature of the gaze: the fact that it is marked by a certain hostility or "aggressivity" (118). In Lacan's account, this appears to be due to two factors. The first is that the desire of the other as expressed through the gaze is directed toward the subject in the form of an "appetite of the eye that must be fed" (115). Through the separation effected by the gaze in its function as *objet a*, the detached subject is left "hanging," and becomes, for the other, "the possession that gives satisfaction" (116). However, further to the subject being positioned as image for the other to consume, there is a certain threat implicit when the subject becomes aware of himself or herself as viewing as well as viewed. At this point, there is a danger of "vanishing" (83): "When carried to the limit, the process of this mediation, of this reflecting reflection, goes so far as to reduce the subject apprehended by the Cartesian meditation to a power of annihilation" (81).

This danger inherent within the subject being brought face-to-face with his or her gaze may be seen to be responsible for Elaine's shifting identity due to her "eye-problems": "too close to the mirror and I'm a blur, too far back and I can't see the details. . . . Even when I've got the distance adjusted, I vary. I am transitional; some days I look like a worn-out thirty-five, others like a sprightly fifty" (5). However, while this illustrates the aggressive intentions that exist intrasubjectively in a scopophilic drive that is autoerotic, even more striking is the conflict that marks Elaine's relationship with others. Elaine's childhood relationship with Cordelia, and to a lesser extent with Carol and Grace, is characterized not only by aggression but by entrapment through looking. Initially, this manifests itself as their focusing upon others: "Cordelia and I are in the habit of looking closely" (6); and it is mutual: "She can outstare anyone, and I am almost as good" (4). However, eventually the gaze becomes aimed solely at Elaine: "Cordelia circles me warily. I catch her eyes on me, considering, as we walk home from school" (192). Further to this, the dynamic eventually becomes invested with collective strength. In church with Grace, Elaine feels decidedly uncomfortable because "she's watching me" (125). Not long after, she feels endangered by her other friend because "everything I do, is heard and seen by Carol and will be reported later" (127).

Elaine's protection is a kind of aloofness that she can cultivate by stepping consciously into a role of alterity. When she takes the eye of the other into her own hands, she can reduce people to "bright animated dolls" (141) who no longer seem real and no longer affect her own emotional state. This allows her a sense of empowerment: "I keep my cat's eye in my pocket, where I can hold onto it. It rests in my hand, valuable as a jewel, looking out through bone and cloth with its impartial gaze. With the help of its power I retreat back into my eyes" (155). Hidden, much like the omnipotent gaze outside oneself, this talisman is a secret weapon that Cordelia knows nothing about: "She doesn't know what power this cat's eye has, to protect me. Sometimes when I have it with me I can see the way it sees" (141). And it allows Elaine to save herself in the battle: "I am alive in my eyes only" (141).

While much of the war between the young girls is fought in an underhand fashion, occasionally the combat surfaces in a more direct way. When Elaine overhears Mrs. Smeath's harsh condemnation of her as being sinful and deserving of punishment, she confronts her in a contest of stares as well as wills. The older woman steps straight into the firing line, "into my line of vision" (180), and the battle has begun: "If my eyes could shoot out fatal rays like the ones in comic books I would incinerate her on the spot. . . . As if she can feel my stare she turns and sees me. Our eyes meet" (180). For Elaine, as indeed for Lacan, the bitter struggle becomes one to the death, symbolized by the mythical "evil eye." For Lacan, "The evil eye is the *fascinum*, it is that which has the effect of arresting movement and, literally, of killing life" (*Four Fundamental* 118). For Elaine, who has imagined Mrs. Smeath going through the wringer of a washing machine, bones cracking and flesh oozing amid pools of blood, the look is also wicked and deadly: "Her bad heart floats in her body like an eye, an evil eye, it sees me" (180). Through this, the aggressive intention of the other now becomes externalized and expressed in a conflict of authority that Lacan describes as an articulation between two terms that act in an antinomic way (*Four Fundamental* 109). In light of this, this conflict of the eyes is a final reminder that much of Elaine's interaction with herself and with others is structured by various dynamics of looking and being looked at, and that in this intersubjective mode, the gaze endangers as well as positions the subject.

Lacan has defined the origin of mimicry as the inscription of the subject in the picture (*Four Fundamental* 99). This bespeaks the relationship between imitation and the formation of identity, a theoretical premise that has accounted for Elaine's interaction with herself and with others, the passage of time, the construction of personae, the role of the gaze, and the potential place textual practice has in the construction of a self-image. With this, Elaine's identity has been shown to be a function of a mimetic economy. With this also, her identity has been shown to be subject to the division of dissemblance, image, effigy, and masquerade.

[1] The following account of the oedipal complex is drawn from Lacan's "The Oedipus Complex" (196).

CHAPTER SIX

The Robber Bride:

The SPLIT SUBJECT, *the* OTHER, *the* OBJECT, *and* AGGRESSIVITY

Of all the novels, *The Robber Bride* (RB) most fully explores the role of the other in the constitution and continuance of the self. The plot is driven almost exclusively by a struggle for supremacy between the characters as it enacts a bitter battle between protagonist and antagonists: siege and conquest on the part of the merciless Zenia and strategies of defense from the embittered and embattled Tony, Roz, and Charis. Even secondary characters are in some way implicated: either they are directly involved as players or pawns in the primary chain of events or they are shown to have played a part in earlier incidents that may not show immediate impact upon the present but have had formative value as infantile experiences of struggle.

In accordance with this, my account sees *The Robber Bride* as above all an exploration of the aggressivity that demarcates the subject. Implicit in this is the belief that there are three important aspects by which this rivalry functions within the novel. The first of the ways in which aggressivity is made manifest is through forms of intersubjective rivalry and competition between individuals expressed within social and symbolic forms — those dynamics that are perhaps the most obvious within the narrative and have the greatest dramatic impact. The second is rivalry in its intrasubjective aspect: relations with the other as they are internalized within the individual, the earliest advent of alterity as the relativity that structures the subject and propels him or her into a communal existence.

The third is to do with the subject's positionality, his or her location in the external world. It is the corporeal reality of aggressivity, the rivalrous ordering of the body and of space. Effected by the natural dimension of subjectivity — the fact that the subject is a function of his or her material existence — it is this that gives inter- and intrasubjective struggle both a tangible and metaphoric effect.

Thus, motivated by the desire to fully explicate the dynamics of aggression that are responsible not only for the narrative but for characterization in a way in which all three aspects will be accounted for and reveal their distinct yet interrelated functions, my account draws together the work of Hegel, Merleau-Ponty, and Lacan in a specific theoretical juncture appropriate for this text. Hegel's formulation of the development of self-consciousness gives priority to the self as it interacts with the world by focusing upon the other as an immediate object of perception. In this, his work provides the most suitable model for explaining the intersubjective dynamics of the novel, the interpersonal relations between characters that appear to proceed along the very (developmental) lines Hegel speaks of.

Thus, using the phenomenological account as the point of entry for my analysis, my analysis begins by outlining what Hegel names as the appetitive aim: relations of consumption that are the first of three stages the subject undergoes in the development of a self-conscious stance. Of importance here is the fact that the other is cast in the role of object while the subject now in pursuit becomes focused and directed away from itself. From this, the more formative relation of recognition may proceed and a second phase that is by definition more dynamic as it allows for a counterattack in the face of an onslaught from the mighty.

Hegel's work on the developing relation between the I and the other as the subject seeks to assert itself is perfectly suited to explaining dynamics within the narrative that otherwise would not gain full thematic significance. With this in mind, I seek to explore the character traits of the protagonist in a way that does more than relegate her to the position of villain. Thus, Zenia's predatory nature, her tendency to objectify, her lack of empathy, and her infamous success are contextualized within a scheme of object relations that are neither arbitrary nor unique. Similarly, the battles between Zenia and the three women are now able to be discussed with the significance they deserve — as imaging the crucial battle for recognition that each and every individual must undergo if he or she is to reach subjective maturity.

It is in this context of according the incidents status as representing the fundamental types of struggle that underwrite the very notion of subjectivity that aspects of the warfare between the women are discussed in light of specific Hegelian dynamics. The motif of slavery and bondage that Hegel uses to describe the patterns of behaviour that are established between victim and vanquished provides the theoretical framework within which a number of character traits may be interpreted. With this, certain elements (such as the women's apparent weakness) now become explicable, not as defects of personality as such but as definable elements within a necessary configuration of relations between subjects and their objects/others. With this, the idiosyncracies of each woman's experience may be respected in a way that does not detract from a meaning that is more collective and in which they share not only wounds but an increasing awareness in the development of their identity.

The significance of Hegel's schemata is that rivalry is shown to be a structure that regulates behaviour between two given subjects. It similarly accounts for the other-now-object who is situated in a unique position within this scheme. With this, the part played by the men in the novel is contextualized in a way that explains their apparent passivity. Furthermore, this paves the way for discussing the sexual connotations and a consideration of objectification as a function of the materiality of the subject.

At this point, the work of Merleau-Ponty becomes important as it best theorizes the corporeal aspect of objective thought. Furthering the phenomenological focus, my account turns to a discussion of the body and the ways in which it is used as a tool in the power play now characterizing the self. This approach is well justified in terms of *The Robber Bride*, in which the villainous actions are executed almost entirely through seduction, and relations of love and sex are shown to be a structured form of aggressive intent.

If the body is a medium for intersubjective rivalry, then no less can be said of the natural world in which the subject imposes his or her will. For the connection between the subjective, the somatic, and the spatial is made clear not only by Merleau-Ponty but in the novel itself where significant attention is given to the dynamics of location and a geographical situation that reflects aggressive intent. Thus, what follows is a discussion of certain incidents that would be underemphasized if they were seen purely to be reflective of the character's emotional state. Instead, they become metaphors of how the self and other relate to each other and to the object in space.

Merleau-Ponty's notion of the way in which object relations become social or intersubjective finds expression within *The Robber Bride* not only in images of the body in space but in the other aspect he names as being of cultural significance: language as a medium of dialogue. With this, the otherwise anomalous or extraneous aspects of the narrative (such as Tony's secret language and reference to historical discourse) find significance as part of the symbolic structure of aggressive, objective thought.

While phenomenological accounts of rivalry and relations with the other have a necessary focus upon the subject's response to the external world, a differing focus is needed to elucidate the internal mechanisms specific to the psyche defined by the aggressive intent. Calling upon psychoanalysis, then, I draw from the work of Lacan to theorize the delicate shift from the inter- to intrasubjective so well illustrated within the text. In the light of aggressivity as a fundamental structure of subjectivity and the earliest introduction of alterity to the developing self, my account turns to a discussion of multiple identity, which characterizes protagonist and antagonists alike. Thus, Zenia's counterfeit personality, along with her construction of images and tales of Roz's childhood marked by imitation and duplicate selves, are interpreted in the light of the Lacanian model of mirror-phase alienation. But if aggressive relativity operates as a form of rupture through self-image, it is no less of a break when it finds expression in libidinal terms. Hence, aggressivity, as it is expressed within the network of familial relations, is a distinct type of rivalry that deserves attention in analysis of the text.

For this reason, I descry the nature of the relationship between Roz and her parents as a particular dynamic of oedipal resolution, and in this way, an episode from early childhood that is seemingly incidental gains significance in terms of the overall theme of the book. Furthering the examination of the oedipal expression of aggressivity, Charis's infantile experiences of rape and incest are discussed as instances of illicit desire. What differentiates my account, however, from one that utilizes a more conventional notion of power is that in this interpretation Lacanian theory is able to provide a precise explanation for every aspect of her response. Thus, the splintering of self that marks the entire experience and the unusual imagery used to describe it become perfectly intelligible when read in the light of the archetypes of corporeal, fragmentary aggression.

At this point in my analysis, the figure of Charis has taken precedence, and in this lies a certain irony given she is somewhat of a caricature in the text. Yet with discussion of her transitivistic tendencies in light of the boundaries of identification that position the subject precariously between being the subject and object of perception, we are brought to a type of ambiguity in which lies the crux of the tale. For now the true nature of interaction between individuals and the communal aspects of the subject's phenomenological and psychic world may be brought to the fore as the novel is seen to conclude by illustrating the third of Hegel's phases, in which the development of self-conscious identity takes on a universal and more enlightened tone. Here the subject surpasses the limitations of purely objective thought and comes to accept and acknowledge the other in a more expansive embrace. With this, Hegel's model is used to interpret a conclusive ending that mirrors the global concerns imaged in the resolution of the tale: the women reconcile their past with a future that promises to be less troubled, Zenia has found some sort of peace, and there is some understanding of their mutual interrelatedness within a shared world.

* * *

The Robber Bride is the story of three middle-aged women who, despite the different directions their lives have taken, are united in a common goal: the struggle against one woman who has at various times become arch-rival for each one of them, robbing them of someone they loved through a play of treachery, deceit, and a contest of wills. Through Roz, Charis, and Tony's interaction with the villainous Zenia, who comes to epitomize power, brutality, and belligerence, the novel explores the aggressivity that characterizes the subject's encounter with alterity and the role of the other in the constitution of the self.

Zenia is described as being "Brilliant, and also fearsome. Wolfish, feral, beyond the pale" (154). A list of her activities reads like a catalogue of horrors, as she manipulates, blackmails, exploits both financially and emotionally, abuses hospitality, earns trust and then betrays, then, in the end, steals the lovers and husbands of her opponents. She lives by her own maxim that fear is "the only thing that works" and that neither love nor respect is a strategy worth pursuing (218). But while Zenia exemplifies in the extreme the kind of battles fought between individuals, her behaviour may be seen to represent the type of rivalry that underwrites each and every subject — the instinct for self-preservation by which the subject "sinks or swims." As she herself asks, "what if you'd been on the *Titanic*, going down? Would you have elbowed and shoved, or stood back and drowned politely? What if you were starving, in an open boat, and one of the others died? Would you eat him? If so, would you push the others overboard so you could keep him all to yourself?" (152).

In Hegel's phenomenological account of the subject, contestation plays an inevitable and necessary role in the formation of selfhood. In his *Philosophy of Mind*,[1] Hegel outlines the important process whereby a general consciousness within the psyche gives way to a more directed "self-consciousness." Self-consciousness is the more "truthful" and developed state of mind in which the self is conscious of itself; the ego is able to appraise the self in what is the development of an "I." Self-consciousness has a certain "finitude," the vested interests of self-identification that take the form of relations with the other, or, to use the more precise Hegelian term, relations with the "object." The self-conscious awareness of the object is integral in this growing awareness of self, and it involves a distinct transition with three identifiable developmental stages.

The first of these stages is what Hegel calls "appetitive self-consciousness," an "impulse" directed toward the object in which the self seeks only to satisfy itself. Here the self comes to know itself in the object only through its appetite for that object: it negates the independent existence of the object, takes possession of it, and "satisfies itself by consuming it" (*Philosophy* 168). Appetitive self-consciousness is an "absolute" activity in which the self is related to the object only through its own immediacy. It posits a certitude of the self effected by a nullification of the object. It is a relation in which the object must perish, and thus "appetite in its satisfaction is always destructive, and in its content selfish" (169). It is in no way a formative relation, and despite its ferocity and apparent success, it is doomed to a kind of endless repetition, for the hunger is again generated at the very moment of its satisfaction. It is "an objectification which never absolutely attains its goal but only gives rise to the progress *ad infinitum*" (169).

Ultimately, self-consciousness is unable to supersede the object through this negative relation of appetite,[2] and so eventually the certainty of viewing the object purely in consumptive terms gives way to a truer account of the object. The result is a new conceptualization of the object, one that acknowledges the autonomous existence of that object, a new relation (the second of the phases) that Hegel terms "the process of Recognition." Here we no longer speak of the relation of a self-consciousness and an object but an interaction of two self-consciousnesses. For the object, now equally independent and self-contained, is no longer an object existing primarily for desire, but an "other" that the self-consciousness cannot readily utilize for its own purposes. As Hegel himself writes, "experience makes it [self-consciousness] aware that the object has its own independence" (*Phenomenology* 109), with the result that there is now a reciprocity emerging from the "double movement of the two self-consciousnesses" (112).

While there is a kind of equality generated by this acknowledgement of the object's newly found status, it is important to note that the interaction is still marked by inequality, for in this mutual recognition of selves one is the recognized and one is the recognizer. It is even more important to note that this new dynamic results in what Hegel terms "the play of Forces" (112) and a twofold action on the part of self and other whereby each seeks to destroy or overpower the other. It is this "life and death struggle" that Hegel goes on to describe in one account as "lordship and bondage,"[3] and in another as the relation of "master" with "slave."[4]

The Robber Bride, with its separate though intersecting tales of Tony, Charis, and Roz's altercations with the wicked Zenia, may be seen to fully explicate the servitude and struggle that characterizes both of Hegel's phases in the development of self-consciousness. The "utterly selfish destruction" (Hegel, *Philosophy* 169) of the appetitive ego that characterizes the first stage is evident in the fact that Zenia has the power to "obliterate" (*RB* 147) any opponent. Her ability to slay her adversary is taken for granted, and the impending destruction of a target like West is fully anticipated: "Tony is convinced that Zenia could indeed wreak havoc. One contemptuous flick of her hand could splatter him all over the sidewalk" (200). That this is more than mere bravado is proven not only by the rampage of destruction that has occured earlier in the women's lives but by the immediate sense of annihilation the women experience on Zenia's arrival. Roz speaks of herself as barely alive: "There is no *her* . . . she might as well not be here. . . . She has never felt so non-existent in her life" (440); so does Tony: "In the presence of Zenia she feels more than small and absurd: she feels non-existent" (147). And this response is something they all share: "Tony senses them all fading in the glare that spreads out from her" (38).

Similarly, the endless repetition of desire that marks the "incessant renewal of appetite" (Hegel, *Philosophy* 169) in the first stage is obvious in no less than five of Zenia's character traits. First is the fact that she wants only to possess: ". . . Zenia likes challenges. She likes breaking and entering, she likes taking things that aren't hers" (325). Second, she pursues her opponents constantly: ". . . Zenia likes hunting. She likes hunting anything. She relishes it" (42). Third is her total objectification of men, so that they become little more than "target practice": "She probably has a row of men's dicks nailed to her wall, like stuffed animal heads" (325). Fourth is her unrelenting power over them: "What is her secret? How does she do it? Where does it come from, her undeniable power over men? How does she latch hold of them, break their stride, trip them up, and then so easily turn them inside out?" (441–42). And last is the fact that she is a "man-eater" (455) who unabashedly consumes the other purely for her own satisfaction: "She'll just take one bite out of him and throw him away"(215).

Descriptions of West as a broken, desolate man after having been discarded by Zenia, the disappearance of Billy, and the suicide of Mitch, who by this time is sick, old, weak, and battle weary,[5] attest to the inevitability of the outcome: the fact that in this phase of aggression, the object will perish.[6] However, the second of Hegel's phases is marked by a more active struggle between subjects rather than the passive and immediate consumption of the object. It is in this context that the conflicts between Zenia and the three women take on the greatest significance as they image the relation of two self-conscious subjects pitted in fierce battle against each other in the process of recognition.

What goes on between the women is no less than warfare, and it is described metaphorically as such. We are told quite simply that "Roz is going to war" (118) and that "the personal is military" (45); Tony's career as a historian proves fruitful for comparisons of her encounter with Zenia to the battles of antiquity, battles in which "for the hundredth, for the thousandth time, one man prepares to kill another" (44). Tony's own actions are described as a kind of military manoeuvre — *"Forward! Charge! Fire!"* (39) — and they culminate in her taking a gun to her final meeting with Zenia. And Zenia is repeatedly characterized as the dangerous opponent in a number of different forms of "knife play": "It's not as if Zenia has a gun. Still, Tony can sense the contemptuous ultramarine gaze drilling through the back of her flimsy little dotted-rayon dress like a laser" (40); "Zenia is a street fighter. She kicks hard, she kicks low and dirty, and the only counterploy is to kick her first, with metal cleats on your boots" (119); "[Roz] has a flash of Zenia, wearing black fringed gloves with gauntlets, blowing the smoke off her six-shooter, sliding it back into her holster" (430).

While Tony, Roz, and Charis eventually prove themselves worthy opponents, for the most part Zenia seems to wield the greatest power. The lord and bondsman metaphor that Hegel uses to describe the journey to self-certainty aptly images just such a situation in which the combatants are unequal though opposed. While it is a relation of two self-conscious subjects in recognition of each other, their consciousnesses take differing and complementary "shapes": one is the independent consciousness that exists purely for itself, while the other is the dependent consciousness whose essential nature is to live or exist for another.

All of Zenia's relationships with the three women are characterized by an initial lack of resistance on their part and this relegates them to a position of bondage. Zenia's ability to manipulate and play upon their emotional vulnerabilities combines with their acquiesence in complying with her demands. Tony, we are told, feels "grateful" when she dutifully gives Zenia money: "pattering off to her room, locating her little cheque book, writing out her little cheque. Offering it up" (140). The otherwise assertive Roz is so touched by being "chosen" (422) that she embarks upon the "save-poor-Zenia project" (427) with no heed to her own protection: "Roz opens her heart, and spreads her wings, her cardboard angel's wings, her invisible dove's wings, her warm sheltering wings, and takes her in" (424). Meanwhile, the unsuspecting Charis invests all her own energy into healing Zenia, and, feeding her a steady diet of love, goodwill, scented baths, and vegetable juices, allows her to move into her already financially impoverished home. The effect of her act of charity, however, is to relegate herself to a position of weakness: ". . . Charis's astral body falls to its knees, raising imploring hands to the astral body of Zenia . . ." (229).

Hegel succinctly makes the point that the lord in this relationship is "the sheer negative power for whom the thing is nothing. Thus, he is the pure, essential action in this relationship . . ." (*Phenomenology* 116). This is borne out by the fact that Zenia is seen to be advancing, while the role of the women is to sit quietly and prepare for her spirited attacks: "How long before Zenia descends on them, with her bared incisors and outstretched talons and banshee hair, demanding what is rightfully hers?" (222). However, Hegel describes even more aptly the experience of the bondsman, saying "[it] has trembled in every fibre of its being, and everything solid and stable has been shaken to its foundations" (*Phenomenology* 117). This "absolute melting-away of everything stable" (117) Hegel speaks of is best articulated in Tony's reaction on seeing her antagonist once again:

> Tony felt safe this morning, safe enough. But she doesn't feel safe now. Everything has been called into question. Even in the best of times the daily world is tenuous to her, a thin iridescent skin held in place by surface tension. She puts a lot of effort into keeping it together, her willed illusion of comfort and stability, the words flowing from left to right, the routines of love; but underneath is darkness. Menace, chaos, cities aflame, towers crashing down, the anarchy of deep water. She takes a breath to steady herself and feels the oxygen and car fumes rushing into her brain. Her legs are wavery, the facade of the street ripples, tremulous as a reflection on a pond, the weak sunlight blows away like smoke. (40)

While this is a moving account of the terror experienced by the powerless, it is reinforced by the fact that the fear proves not to be excessive. For in submitting to Zenia's merciless ways, the women divest themselves of privacy, money, even their loved ones, effecting for themselves the destruction of their own lives. As Hegel states, for the bondsman, "his consciousness is not this dissolution of everything stable merely in principle; in his service he *actually* brings this about" (*Phenomenology* 117).

What marks Hegel's account of the dynamic between lord and bondsman is the fact that it is operative via an external object. That is, the lord positions him- or herself in relation "to a *thing* as such" that becomes, in Hegel's own words, an "object of desire" (115). This is clearly evident in Zenia's use of men whom she readily objectifies as possessions: "In no time at all . . . Zenia has reclaimed West, in the same way she might reclaim any piece of property belonging to her, such as a suitcase left at a train station" (212). However, Hegel clearly states that the real target is the bondsman, not the object, and thus the object is merely the means to an end: "The lord relates himself mediately to the bondsman through a being (a thing) that is independent, for it is just this which holds the bondsman in bondage; it is his chain from which he could not break free in the struggle . . ." (*Phenomenology* 115). Aware of the hold the object has upon the bondsman, the lord is then able to truly effect his or her control: "since he is the power over this thing and this again is the power over the other (the bondsman), it follows that he holds the other in subjection" (115).

Nowhere is this more obvious than in Tony's own appraisal of the true intentions of her foe: "Now Zenia is back, and hungry for blood. Not for West's blood: West is an instrument merely. The blood Zenia wants to drink is Tony's . . ." (220). However, interestingly enough, while the lord uses the object as a kind of intermediate agency, Hegel makes the point that the bondsman also relates "negatively" to the thing and "takes away its independence" (*Phenomenology* 116). In this, paradoxically, the bondsman begins to mirror his or her oppressor,[7] and the lord is able to take full advantage of a situation that the bondsman has created. All three women infantilize their men and consistently protect them, and by allowing them never to take responsibility for their actions, relegate them to a state of dependence. In this sense, the men are doubly objectified and particularly prone to the wiles of Zenia, and this may explain their characterization as mere pawns in a game that they never fully understand.[8]

That Zenia attacks her rivals by seducing the men whom they love is not coincidental given the nature of the battle for recognition. For as Hegel notes, the objectification that is an integral part of this intersubjective rivalry exists because the subject has "an immediate existence, natural and corporeal" (*Philosophy* 171). With this, the other is made an object through the materiality of his or her existence. As Merleau-Ponty states, all perceptions of the subject are set against a background of nature, and objective thought has a sensory function: "every object will be, in the first place and in some respect, a natural object, made up of colours, tactile and auditory qualities, in so far as it is destined to enter my life" (347). Given the organic conditions of human existence and the fact that the subject can only experience sensory perception through his or her own consciousness, Merleau-Ponty asks how it is that we experience alterity: "how can the word 'I' be put into the plural, . . . how can I speak of an *I* other than my own, how can I know that there are other *I*'s, how can consciousness which, by its nature, and as self-knowledge, is in the mode of the *I*, be grasped in the mode of the Thou" (348). The answer lies in the formation of what Merleau-Ponty terms the "cultural object," whereby the object existing in nature is moulded to the human action that it serves. In this, "behaviour patterns" settle into nature and are "deposited" in the form of a cultural world. In this account, the prototypical object invested with such intentionality is in fact the human body: "The very first of all cultural objects, and the one by which all the rest exist, is the body of the other person as the vehicle of a form of behaviour" (348).

Throughout the interpersonal warfare described in *The Robber Bride*, relations of the body are indeed paramount. As Charis says of herself, "it was her body that got her into this," a body that she characterizes as "the malign contagion of the material world" (228).[9] Indeed, very early in the novel, the natural world — space and corporeality — is imaged as the underpinning of aggressive relativity: "The Z floats on the page as if scrawled on a wall, as if scratched on a window, as if carved in an arm" (45). And we are reminded of the significance of the body by the fact that Zenia dons her "flesh dress" (57) to commit her acts of aggression, a dynamic emphasized by her strategic reliance upon feminine artifice, and the contextualization of her actions within a feminine setting.[10]

Zenia's manipulation of her own body through makeup and masquerade succinctly brings to the fore the point that Merleau-Ponty makes: that the body, while an entity of nature, takes on the function of cultural object, at which point it is imputed with purpose and intent. The intentionality or patterns of behaviour imbued in the object at this point are relations of intersubjectivity or, to use Merleau-Ponty's words, "the close presence of others" (348). And while this may be inevitable, it is a relation that is beset with adversity, for the existence of other people is "a difficulty" and "an outrage" (349) for objective thought. The reasons for this are similar to the points raised by Hegel: the fact that in the formation of the "I" there is no place for a plurality of consciousnesses;[11] that in protection of the self the ego resists acknowledging another on equal terms;[12] and the fact that the self or "constituting consciousness" tends to objectify the other in its own field of perception: "The body of another . . . is an object standing before the consciousness which thinks about or constitutes it. Other men . . . are merely pieces of mechanism worked by springs . . ." (Merleau-Ponty 349). The result is the kind of power play Hegel speaks of, the fact that "The *cogito* of another person strips my own *cogito* of all value . . ." (Merleau-Ponty 353), and in this Merleau-Ponty's account begins to resemble that of his counterpart Hegel.[13] The point of interest, however, is that this account raises the issue of intentionality as it is expressed within the corporeal world of space: "we need to know how . . . an intention, a thought or a project can detach themselves from the personal subject and become visible outside him in the shape of his body, and in the environment which he builds for himself" (Merleau-Ponty 348–49).

It seems then that intentionality is intersubjective and because of this it is rivalrous, and since intentionality is reflected in the materiality of existence, what will be reflected in space is the battle between subjects. This is an important point for analysis of *The Robber Bride* since relations with the body and its surrounds are to do with power and the intent of the other. Charis, for example, describes the effects of her altercation with Zenia in somatic terms: "she feels thinner — lighter and more porous. It's as though energy has been drained out of her, energy and substance, in order for Zenia to materialize . . . she's taken a chunk of Charis's own body and sucked it into herself" (78). And Tony's descriptions show that the battle between subjects is inscribed in the physical world in a way that orders space according to rivalrous intent. Her house, we are told, is normally "her stronghold," but when Zenia appears it begins to lose its stability: "In the waning light the house is no longer thick, solid, incontrovertible. Instead it looks provisional, as if it's about to be sold, or to set sail. It flickers a little, sways on its moorings. Before unlocking the door Tony runs her hand over the brickwork, reassuring herself that it exists" (43). Some time later, her own feelings of powerlessness are imaged by distinct metaphors of spatial and physical dislocation: "She feels as if she's being dragged along on a rope, behind a speeding motorboat, with the waves sloshing over her . . . or as if she's racketing downhill on a bicycle, with no hands and no brakes either. She's out of control . . ." (155–56). And later still, when the battle is in full swing, her house becomes "too fragile" (221) as she imagines complete material destruction: "She thinks about how the house would look if she or anyone else were to blow it up. Study, bedroom, kitchen, and hall, suspended in fiery mid-air. Her house is no protection for her, really" (221).

These descriptions (like others[14]) illustrate both of the functions of the cultural object made significant in Merleau-Ponty's account: the imputing of body and space with subjective intention, and that intention being one of power and struggle. In addition, the displacement of intent from the subject to his or her "landscape" or the "instruments" of the external world (Merleau-Ponty 348) is evident in the novel in the episodes when relations with the other are reflected in object relations in space. Roz finds that after Mitch leaves, space becomes empty with his absence, and what she is left with is "blanks" (431) — "the empty man-shaped outline left by Mitch" (454). On the other hand, at other times Mitch remains, "taking up the same amount of room" (443) although he has long gone from the house.[15] She finds it difficult sleeping in the middle of their bed because Mitch is still "beside her" as a "blank shape" or an "outline" and hence "she can't bring herself to occupy the whole space" (443). The alternate filling and then vacating of space is evident also in the young Tony's ability to distinguish between "full silences and empty ones" (162) according to the state of her mother's mind. "Just because there's a silence it doesn't mean that nothing is going on" (162), we are told, as even emptiness may be full with intent.

Similarly, there is a tendency in the novel for objects to be imprinted with social relations, to the point where they are personified in their own right. The spinet and the lute that West once played are held "captive" in Tony's living room so that they become emblematic of her lost lover (218). This is a dynamic reminiscent of Tony's early life when she regarded her mother's clothes as hostages that would ensure a safe return. In a different vein, Charis's inability to territorialize or possess others means that for her "Objects have a life of their own, and the ones in her house move around at night" (58). This brings to mind Merleau-Ponty's mention of the situation in which "the spontaneous acts through which man has patterned his life should be deposited, like some sediment, outside himself and lead an anonymous existence as things" (348). The significance of this is that the cultural world — what Merleau-Ponty terms "civilization" — is making itself self-evident and unavoidable. By this, the subject is being given a kind of locality and is being positioned as a "being-in-the-world" (351), a dynamic that is extremely important for, like Hegel, Merleau-Ponty stipulates that while objective thought is inevitable, ultimately it must be transcended so as to allow the subject to recognize other people and perspectives. Merleau-Ponty makes clear the fact that this will mean a radical change in perception: "Clearly this involves a profound transformation of the notions of body and consciousness" (351); however, he provides the solution: "We must therefore rediscover, after the natural world, the social world . . . as a permanent field or dimension of existence . . ." (362). This is best done through "the experience of dialogue": "There is one particular cultural object which is destined to play a crucial role in the perception of other people: language" (354).

For Merleau-Ponty, dialogue is an inevitable part of the subject's corporeal nature[16] and a collaboration of "consummate reciprocity" (354) that overcomes the self-centered nature of objective thought. It is the supreme way in which alienation at the hands of a rival may be overcome for it makes alterity accessible to the self.[17] The necessary function of signification in mediating the conflict of selves is inferred throughout the novel by references to history and the telling and retelling of battles.[18] Tony's interpretation of her own life in terms of historical discourse illustrates the role such representation plays in the formation of identity, and the fact that it invokes the materiality of struggle is made clear by Charis's sensitivity to the referent: "for Charis the words are pictures and then screams and moans, and then the smell of rotting meat, and of burning, of burning flesh, and then physical pain, and if you dwell on it you make it happen" (74). Furthermore, language is shown to be a way of either creating or destroying a rival, as proven by the fact that once Zenia has been murdered her existence becomes purely a matter of narrative.[19] But perhaps most telling is the simple assertion made very early in the novel that "war is what happens when language fails" (45) — a statement that affirms the necessity of sublimating inter-subjective conflict into words.

While Merleau-Ponty makes it clear that intersubjectivity through dialogue is, in the end, unavoidable,[20] through the figure of Tony the desire to withdraw from communication is illustrated in her construction of her own language. Her formulation of "another language, an archaic language" (21) that no one else can understand is, on the surface, an innocuous pastime based on reversing the letters in a word: "Gnilrad ym ho, / Gnilrad ym ho, / Gnilrad ym ho, / Enitn(e)melc, / Reverof(e)nog dna tsol er(a)uoy, / Yrros lufdaerd, / Enitn(e)melc" (136). It takes on a more ominous tone, however, when we are told that it is "dangerous" for her as it carries the potential for collapse: "It's her seam, it's where she's sewn together, it's where she could split apart" (22). With this, we are brought to the final point Merleau-Ponty makes in concluding his discussion of otherness and the self. It is "the problem of the existential modality of the social," the question of how the self can remain open to phenomena that were constructed by the self but then proceed to threaten that self: *"how the presence to myself . . . which establishes my own limits and conditions every alien presence is at the same time depresentation . . . and throws me outside myself"* (363).

Thus, while both the body and language in their role as cultural objects function as intersubjective, symbolic structures for the expression of rivalry, they carry the potential to initiate an entirely different realm of aggressive relativity: the conflict that occurs within a single self. This is made clear by Tony's admission that "the effort of tracking Zenia" is "fusing her neurons, rearranging the molecules in her brain": "She has the sensation that she's growing hair, little prickles of it pushing out through the skin of her legs like the quills of a porcupine, hanks of it shoving through in tufts around her ears. . . . A hairy white devil is what she's becoming, a fanged monster" (468). While Tony admits that the growth of an unfamiliar self is a necessary internal transformation, her further statement that "every weapon is two-edged" foreshadows the fact that her encounter with Zenia will result in a splintering of selves: "she has another self, a more ruthless one, concealed inside her. She is not just Tony Fremont, she is also *Tnomerf Ynot*, queen of the barbarians, and, in theory, capable of much that Tony herself is not quite up to" (469). In this context, the secret language becomes important once more, as it introduces the second self who is to become a contender in the battle:

> As a child, Tony kept a diary. Every January she would write her name in front of it, in block letters:
> TONY FREMONT
> Then under it she would write her other name:
> TNOMERF YNOT.
> This name had a Russian or Martian sound to it, which pleased her. It was the name of an alien, or a spy. Sometimes it was the name of a twin, an invisible twin. . . . (160)

While this other self is named as "stronger" and more "daring" (160) and thus the side of Tony that will take on the enemy, it is important to note that the division is an infantile phenomenon that predates the actual battle with Zenia. Furthermore, at the same time as imaging this other self in light of her present (adult) predicament, she characterizes her own otherness as a biological entity that is the predecessor to any consciousness of self.[21] From this may be inferred an important point: that any manifestation of aggressive intention between subjects necessarily draws upon a pre-existing, rivalrous division within the self. As Lacan states, "the structural effect of identification with the rival . . . can only be conceived of if the way is prepared for it by a primary identification that structures the subject as a rival with himself" ("Aggressivity" 22).

With this we are brought to Lacan's psychoanalytic account of aggressivity as *"an experience that is subjective by its very constitution"* (9). Here Lacan draws upon Hegel's schema of the ways in which subjects will eventually relate to each other, but emphasizes the intrasubjective element of rivalry that is one of the earliest dynamics of division and displacement. At this point, aggressivity becomes a founding and structural principle of subjectivity. As Lacan himself states: "the ego appears to be marked from its very origin by this aggressive relativity" (19).

There are a number of aspects to Lacan's formulation of "the drama of primordial jealousy" ("Mirror Stage" 5) that become significant when considering dynamics of aggression in *The Robber Bride*. First and foremost is Lacan's point that while aggressivity will eventually be deflected into "socially elaborated situations" (5), it is, in the first instance, a matter of the specular rather than the social I. By this, what is meant is that the origins of rivalry lie not in the identification with others as such but with the introduction of an imago of the self that is introjected at the moment of specularization. This is "the phenomenon of recognition" (Lacan, "Aggressivity" 18), but it differs from that spoken of by Hegel or Merleau-Ponty for it refers to the infant's encounter with his or her own image in the mirror. As such, it is a function of the earliest advent of otherness (before aggressive relations have been structured into any symbolic form) and involves the specific form of misrecognition for which Lacan's account of the mirror-stage has come to be known. In Lacan's own words, what we are dealing with is "the notion of an aggressivity linked to . . . the structures of systematic *méconnaissance* and objectification that characterize the formation of the ego" (21).

Tony touches upon the foreignness inherent within assumed images of the self when she says of herself that "she was disguised as herself, one of the most successful disguises" (142). Zenia, the "double agent" (213) who admits that " 'you can be whoever you like' " (193), also provides multiple accounts of herself, none of which appear to be true. She is either of White Russian background, the daughter of a Romanian gypsy, born in Berlin and witness to the Nazi holocaust, or of Greek orthodox ancestry.[22] She uses numerous names,[23] changes her appearance endlessly and with great effect,[24] and, as Roz finds out, "the question of whether Zenia is real or not" (432) is difficult to solve.

Zenia is by far the most "manufactured" of the characters who show that "When you alter yourself, the alterations become the truth

. . ." (118). However, the more interesting example of the subject alienated through self-image is Roz, whose behaviour well illustrates the fictitious and illusory nature of assumed guises. Her memories of childhood are dominated by the conscious creation of an identity: "she imitates. She picks up their accents, their intonations, their vocabulary . . ." (401); and this makes her a kind of "pastiche" (402): "she adds layers of language to herself, sticking them on like posters on a fence, one glued over the top of the next, covering up the bare boards" (401). The result is a number of differing identities, dependent upon whether she is attending Catholic or Jewish school, is hiding or admitting her father's background, is poor or rich, is "Rosalind Greenwood instead of Roz Grunwald" (369). The social aspect of this identification with the image of the counterpart is made clear by the fact that she is competing with her peers, and heightened by the painful stories of her rejection by them and her inability to fit into social circles. However, most poignant is her own awareness of the facade — the fact that "once upon a time Roz was not Roz" (369) — and her consequent estrangement both in terms of herself and those around her: "She's an oddity, a hybrid, a strange half-person. . . . She finds herself in a foreign country. She's an immigrant, a displaced person" (399).

The unusual characterization of herself as a migrant, the fact that "her father's ship has come in" but she's the one "just off the boat" (399), refers, on one level, to the fact that it is her father who has been responsible for her "new clothes . . . and a new name" (398). On another level, however, it may be seen to refer to a deeper identification with her father, one in which she chooses the paternal over and above her early life with her mother. Indeed, it is made quite clear that the arrival of her father signals an interruption of her relationship with her mother: "Now Roz's life has been cut in two. On one side is Roz, and her mother, and the rooming house, and the nuns and the other girls at school. . . . That's the side where there are mostly women, women who have power, which means they have power over Roz. . . . On the other side is her father . . ." (386). Feeling forced to choose, Roz is blatant about whom she prefers, saying, "he was the one she adored" (394); however, the oedipal connotations of the choice become more overt in her response to finding her parents hugging and kissing: "[she] is full of disgust at her mother for being so soft [she feels] sorrow and jealousy and the rage of banishment" (386). Her feeling that she is being "pushed off to the edge" (386) by her mother's desire for her father brings to the fore the fact that aggressivity plays a role in the constitution of the subject via the function of the oedipal complex. As Lacan states, the necessary repression operates through a specific emotional movement involving rivalry: "aggression against the parent in regard to whom the child's sexual desire places him as a rival" ("Oedipus Complex" 192).

Roz's revulsion at the sight of her mother's desire initiates the expected oedipal response: an impulse to castigate her mother and a new awareness of the paternal: "To punish her mother for such betrayals Roz turns away from her. She turns to the uncles, when they are there, and also, and especially, to her father" (386). At this point, rivalry becomes tinged with infantile desires as it begins to image the oedipal drama in this new negotiation of relativity. Perched on her father's knee — the "safe place" (386) from which to regard her mother — Roz expresses her new acceptance of paternal authority through competition with her mother: " 'Make yourself useful,' her mother snaps, and once Roz would have obeyed. But now her father's arms hold her tight, 'I didn't see her for so long,' he says. And her mother clenches her lips and says nothing, and Roz watches her with gloating triumph and thinks it serves her right" (386–87).

Roz's mother now "abdicates" (386) from her previous position of power, and this implies a resolution of the struggle that will allow the daughter the necessary access to paternal desire. Lacan makes the point that this is to be effected through identification with the mother, so that "a *secondary identification* by introjection of the *imago* of the parent of the same sex" ("Aggressivity" 22) is a normal part of the dialectical relationship. While we have no reason to suspect that Roz fails to undergo the appropriate transfer of desires, elsewhere in the novel this "identificatory reshaping of the subject" (22) has drastic consequences for the developing identity of the oedipal subject. The total renunciation on the part of Tony's mother, her refusal to contend for the desires of either her husband or her daughter, may be seen to symbolize a withdrawal from the oedipal struggle with the result that Tony is unable to sublimate her longing for the maternal.[25] Meanwhile, Tony, while still a child, is positioned as the only female presence in what should be a connubial setting. Even more destructive is the withdrawal of Charis's mother who, also effecting an abdication of sorts, leaves her daughter to become a surrogate wife in illicit sexual relations with her uncle.

The effects of struggle within an oedipal context and rivalrous intentions that are incestuous are poignantly illustrated in Charis's traumatic encounters with her uncle Vern. These incidents, while providing dramatic counterpoint to the other images of sexual battle in the novel, illustrate a number of important points that feature in Lacan's account of aggressive relativity. The general notion that the consequences of aggressivity amount to a kind of psychic displacement is evidenced by the fact that Charis, "once-Karen" (250), is no longer one with herself: *"You can't win this fight. . . .* Finally she changed into Charis, and vanished, and reappeared elsewhere, and she has been elsewhere ever since" (47). Further description of this "banished" self as "that cowed, powerless face Charis used to see in the mirror looming up to her own face" (265) invokes the specular aspect of alienation as a function of aggressive relativity. More specifically, however, Lacan's statement that *"Aggressivity in experience is given to us as intended aggression and as an image of corporal dislocation . . ."* ("Aggressivity" 10) is succinctly illustrated in the descriptions of the rape: "he falls on top of Karen and puts his slabby hand over her mouth, and splits her in two. He splits her in two right up the middle and her skin comes open like the dry skin of a cocoon, and Charis flies out" (300–01).

Lacan speaks of certain images that function as structural forms or "vectors" of aggressive intentions ("Aggressivity" 11). These take the form of "imagos of the fragmented body" that surface in the form of the symptom when "a certain level of aggressive disintegration" ("Mirror Stage" 4) has occurred within the individual. Lacan names these images as being those of "disjointed limbs" (4), "mutilation," "devouring," "dismemberment," the "bursting open of the body" ("Aggressivity" 11) — images that seem especially pertinent given that the rape is described as being "like an animal eating another animal" (301). Young Karen is being brutalized at the hands of another and it is "as if she's drowning" or "hooked through the neck" (301), and these metaphors are reinforced by the implication that she is in some way being disembowelled.[26] An otherwise incongruous image, the fact that "she flies over to the window" takes on significance as an imago of the fragmented body in light of Lacan's reference to "growing wings" ("Mirror Stage" 4) as being a common image of aggressive disintegration. However, just as significant as the reference to the body is the fact that this other self "flies" to a position where she can, in effect, observe herself. By this, Karen looks down upon herself in a complete state of detachment: "After the third time Karen knows she is trapped. All she can do is split in two; all she can do is turn into Charis, and float out of her body and watch

Karen, left behind with no words, flailing and sobbing" (302). This is a specific form of dissolution whereby the self becomes an object for itself, and as such it is an important dynamic within the experience of aggression. As Lacan notes, the aggressive reaction can take a number of "belligerent forms," from "a lesional one" (which is a physical intrusion) to "a profanatory one" (which is the violation of intimacy), and each of these "retains the original organization of the forms of the ego and of the object" ("Aggressivity" 17). These forms of aggression, however, can affect the structure of the ego and its object, "even to the spatial and temporal categories in which the ego and the object are constituted" (17). The result may well be "a perspective of mirages" or an event that "suspends the workings of the ego/object dialectic" (17).

Just such a confusion of subject and object expressed in spatial and temporal terms is evident in Charis's experience of being raped. In observing herself, we are told, "Charis can see right through things, through the sheets, through the flesh to the bone . . ." (301). This is significant in that it takes aggression into the perceptual and phenomenological realm of space, an example of *"a notion of aggressivity as one of the intentional co-ordinates of the human ego, especially relative to the category of space"* (Lacan, "Aggressivity" 25). In this context, it is interesting to note her earlier attempts at escaping by sleepwalking "out through the French windows, or in the kitchen, shaking the back door handle" (300),[27] and the use of spatial metaphors to objectify the detached self.[28]

While the spatial and corporeal dimension of aggressivity are important aspects of the incident, even more significant is the fact that this x-ray vision, her looking "out through the cloth, right through the pattern of pink and orange roses" (301), may be seen to be an act of transitivism, under normal circumstances an infantile phenomenon whereby the child has not yet asserted his or her own boundaries and draws no distinction between itself and its physical surroundings.[29] This tendency to see the world in undifferentiated terms, the fact that "she wasn't sure where the edges of her body ended and the rest of the world began" (72), comes to be a characteristic of her personality, as we later learn that even as an adult "everything — even the water, even the stones — is alive and aware, and her along with it" (231). In Lacan's account of aggressivity, transitivism is an early stage in "objectifying identification" ("Aggressivity" 17) that marks the history of the genesis of the ego. It gives equal significance to the act of "attack and counter-attack" and

232

as such places the subject in a "state of ambiguity" because "his ego is actually alienated from itself in the other person" ("Some Reflections" 16). In this context, Charis's fondness for "the illusion of being able to walk through a solid barrier" (234) may be connected to her apparent lack of self-preservation, the fact that "she doesn't like to intrude on the selfhood of others" (252) nor does she herself want to be fully present as a subject. At school she perfects the art of becoming invisible so that "When the teacher looked at her the look went right through, to whoever was sitting behind her" (294). Unlike Roz and the other girls at McClung Hall, who were "solid and uncomplicated," Charis, we are told, is "slippery and translucent and potentially clinging, like soap film or gelatin or the prehensile tentacles of sea anemones. If you touched her, some of her might come off on you. She was contagious" (139). This overidentification with the other and inability to assert her own boundaries leaves her vulnerable to attack: "She herself is so penetrable; sharp edges stick into her, she bruises easily, her inner skin is puffy and soft, like marshmallows" (243). Similarly, others and objects gain undue influence in her life: "Charis is a screen door, an open one at that, and everything blows right through" (243).

While Charis's transitivistic personality may be seen to illustrate a form of alienation due to the blurring of relations between subject and object, she should not be discounted too readily as being weak or powerless. Indeed, Lacan encourages us to "re-examine certain notions that are sometimes accepted uncritically, such as the notion that it is psychologically advantageous to have a strong ego" ("Some Reflections" 16). This is because "In actual fact, the classical neuroses always seem to be by-products of a strong ego ... of all men, the real neurotics have the best defences" (16). This may explain why even though "as soon as Uncle Vern touches her she splits in two" (302), and he and Aunt Vi are her guardians and so "they are in control" (303), she is inexplicably stronger and he "is afraid of her now" (303).[30]

What then is responsible for this apparent contradiction, this coexistence of power with powerlessness? The answer lies in the transformation of consciousness that the adult Charis, many years later, perfects into an art of healing; the state of mind in which "The *I* must be transcended. The self must be cut loose. It must drift" (249). Through her experience of teaching yoga, Charis is able to help others without concern for their ego or her own: "Charis feels energy flowing out of her, through her fingers, into the other bodies. . . . [T]he faces are not important to her, because the face is the individualism, the very thing Charis wants to help these women transcend" (249–50). With this we are brought to what Hegel has termed "the suppression of immediate self-hood" and "the subjuga-tion of the slave's egotism," which, far from being a sign of weakness, is the beginning of what he goes on to call "true human freedom" (*Philosophy* 175). Freedom is attained in the battle for supremacy but is, on the part of the victim, a rising above the self-centered desires of the I in true acceptance of the other or the object. This, for Hegel, is true liberation, the ultimate transcendence, the supreme state of the human spirit: "the slave . . . in the service of the master, works off his individualist self-will, overcomes the inner immediacy of appetite, and in this divestment of self and in 'the fear of his lord' makes 'the beginning of wisdom' — the passage to universal self-consciousness" (175). This, then, is Hegel's third phase in the struggle for recognition and development of the self and with it lies the ultimate explication of the characters and the resolution of the novel.

Universal self-consciousness as defined by Hegel is "the affirmative awareness of self in an other self" (*Philosophy* 176), what he otherwise calls the ". . . 'I' that is 'We' and 'We' that is 'I' " (*Phenom-enology* 110). In *Philosophy of Mind*, he describes it thus: "the violent diremption of mind or spirit into different selves which are both in and for themselves and for one another, are independent, absolutely impenetrable, resistant, and yet at the same time identical with one another, hence not independent, not impenetrable, but, as it were, fused with one another" (177). The beginning of precisely this kind of fusion is seen when Charis's other self begins to surface but instead of looking like Karen, she changes appearance; her eyes darken, her skin pales, until little by little "she looks like Zenia": "She walks towards Charis and bends, and blends into her, and now she's inside Charis's body. . . . She forgets about Karen, she forgets about herself. Everything in her has been fused together" (306). This is perhaps what elsewhere in the novel has been described as "a continuous ebb and flow, a blending, a shift of territories" (130); however, in this context, the corporeal nature of simultaneous division and fusion is evoked as the different selves move "inside their shared body" (307) and a new life is conceived.[31]

What makes this form of union a supreme state of transcendence rather than a step back into transitivism is the fact that with this new awareness the subject manages to retain his or her liberty while functioning in a state of mutual coexistence. As Hegel writes, it is a matter of "the unity of the different independent self-consciousnesses which, in their opposition, enjoy perfect freedom and independence" (*Phenomenology* 110). Given the earlier phases in Hegel's scheme of developing consciousness and the rivalrous intentions that mark both objective thought and relations with the other, how then is this "true freedom" to be achieved, on what grounds does it depend? Hegel makes clear the fact that this new consciousness is to be based upon autonomy, "that free self-consciousness, for which the other self-consciousness confronting it is no longer, as in the second stage, unfree but is likewise independent" (*Philosophy* 176). However, how is this to be effected when the subjects are locked in battle with each other as indeed they are in the novel? Hegel writes, ". . . I am only truly free when the other is also free and is recognised by me as free" (171), and clearly this has not been the case for our protagonists given their inability to release Zenia from their grasp. As we are told in the beginning, they've continued to meet regularly years after their various altercations and "She's here at the table all the same. . . . She's here, we're holding her, we're giving her the air time. We can't let her go" (34).[32] This illustrates the difficulty in effecting a shift in consciousness once patterns of objective, aggressive thought have been established. But while we are given the focalizing perspective of the three women and thus our sympathy lies with them, we have no reason to assume that Zenia is not likewise trapped in a repetitive stance. Hegel outlines the ways in which the master or bondsman remains imprisoned although he or she is powerful,[33] but in light of *The Robber Bride* what is most pertinent is his assertion that neither master nor slave can be free as long as they are "imprisoned in their immediacy, in their natural being" (*Philosophy* 171). Indeed, it is just this that excludes them from one another and in doing so prevents them from being free, and so the subject needs to cease to heed his or her own natural existence or tolerate the natural existence of others. On the contrary, "he should in his individual, immediate actions stake his own life and the lives of others to win freedom" (171).

In this context, Hegel's contention that "Only through struggle . . . can freedom be won . . ." (172) gives new significance to the struggles between the women. In the closing pages of the novel, we are told "wherever else Zenia had been in her life, she has also been at war. An unofficial war, a guerilla war, a war she may not have known she was waging, but a war nevertheless" (545). The placatory tone with which this is now said is accompanied by a final admission that rather than being an aberrant occurrence, conflict is, in fact, the way of the world: "Who was the enemy. . . . Where was her battlefield? Not in any one place. It was in the air all around, it was in the texture of the world itself . . ." (545). With this, the women's battles become neither arbitrary nor negative but a necessary stage in the development of both victor and vanquished, and the conflicts no longer function merely as dramatic devices but as a meaningful thematic that now allows for significant resolution. Similarly, Zenia's disregard for her own body, which eventually results in her destruction, now becomes symbolic of a bid for freedom and, in its own way, life affirming. As Hegel claims, "man demonstrates his capacity for freedom only by risking his own life and that of others. . . . [T]he *absolute* demonstration of freedom in the fight for recognition is death" (*Philosophy* 172).

Perhaps it is only through death that Zenia can leave behind "the colourful show of the sensuous here-and-now" (Hegel, *Phenomenology* 110) and be free finally to commune with the world: "She's a scattering of dust, blown on the wind like spores; she's an invisible cloud of viruses, a few molecules, dispersing" (*RB* 535). For it is at this point that Zenia can reach her own universality as each of her contenders is now able to do as Hegel prescribes: to recognize the other and know him or her to be free (*Philosophy* 176). In order for such "real universality" to be achieved, however, there must be relations structured by reciprocity, here defined as being a recognition of the other based upon the recognition of one's own self in that other. As Hegel maintains, "true freedom . . . consists in my identity with the other" (171) and a shared existence "so far as each knows itself recognized in the other freeman" (176). This is the subject "aware of itself in its objectivity" (176) and for that reason finally made universal, or, in other words, the dynamic that Lacan describes by saying: "The aggressiveness involved in the ego's fundamental relationship to other people is certainly not based on the simple relationship implied in the formula 'big fish eat little fish', but upon the intra-psychic tension we sense in the warning of the ascetic that 'a blow at your enemy is a blow at yourself' " ("Some Reflections" 16).

The reciprocity of universal self-consciousness has earlier been foreseen by Charis's "new-age" philosophy and the "cosmic insight" that "If everyone is part of everyone else, then she herself is a part of Zenia. Or the other way around" (64). This is further emphasized by Charis's desire to embrace elements from the external world ("the garden earth," "the Bible," "her grandmother's presence" [484]) and to incorporate aspects of her friends into her own personality: "What she wanted was to absorb the positive aspects of her friends, the things that were missing in herself. From Tony she wanted her mental clarity, from Roz her high-decibel metabolism and her planning abilities" (484). But even more perceptive is her understanding that, of all people, Zenia is a part of herself: "she has part of Zenia inside herself, the only part that's necessary to her" (309).

While the characterization of Charis as a New Age eccentric provides comic relief in the novel, the mutual recognition of self and other that underlies her homespun philosophy is reflected in other ways throughout the tale. Roz, for instance, admits to a deep-seated identification with her rival, saying: "she would like to be someone else. But not just anyone. Sometimes — for a day at least, or even for an hour, or if nothing else was available then five minutes would do — sometimes she would like to be Zenia" (457). This surely explains her otherwise contradictory response to Zenia's death after having hated her for so long: "The funny thing is, she actually feels sad. Now figure that out! Zenia was a tumour, but she was also a major part of Roz's life. . . . She feels something else she never thought she would feel, towards Zenia. Oddly enough, its gratitude" (542–43). Meanwhile, Tony illustrates succinctly Hegel's point that "in being reflected into myself, I am immediately reflected into the other person" (*Philosophy* 176), when she turns a specular gaze upon Zenia: "Tony looks at her, looks into her blue-black eyes, and sees her own reflection: herself, as she would like to be" (193). And Hegel's continuation of the same point, his statement that, "conversely, in relating myself to the other I am immediately *Self*-related" (*Philosophy* 177), is evident in Tony's description of Zenia as "her unborn twin" (220), the person who best expresses a side of her usually hidden,[34] and the fact that they are mutually related: ". . . Tony will be Zenia's right hand, because Zenia is certainly Tony's left one" (195).

Mention of the reversed image of the self that is reflected back via the other may be seen to be a subtle reference to the specular as underpinning the subjective warfare between selves. As such, it is significant that it has surfaced sporadically throughout the novel. On first seeing Zenia in the Toxique, Tony asks, "What is she doing here, on this side of the mirror?" (39), while Charis inadvertently predicts the role Zenia will play in their own formation of themselves: *"For now we see through a glass, darkly; but then face to face"* (51–52). For while we are later told that "the mirror was whoever was watching" and that through this game "Zenia devised herself" (535), it has already become quite clear that the women, too, are using their opponent as a way of constructing themselves. Charis may be duelling with the image of her opponent; what she finds, however, is a vision of herself: "Charis goes close and then closer, and she sees the two of them side by side in the mirror. Then Zenia's edges dissolve like a watercolour in the rain and Charis merges into her. She slides her on like a glove, she slips into her like a flesh dress, she looks out through her eyes. What she sees is herself, herself in the mirror, herself with power" (462–63) .

Hegel has written that "In this stage, therefore, the mutually related self-conscious subjects, by setting aside their unequal particular individuality, have risen to the consciousness of their real universality, of the freedom belonging to all, and hence to the intuition of their specific identity with each other" (*Philosophy* 176). It seems precisely this with which the story ends, giving the novel an understated although resolute conclusion. The three women have by now learned to reach out to each other and this is imaged in their holding of hands: ". . . [Charis] takes the hands held out to her, one on either side, and grips them tightly, and in this way they glide in to the Island dock" (545). Zenia, we are told, "will now be free" (544), and they fully understand the mutual existence they shared: "Was she in any way like us? thinks Tony. Or, to put it the other way around: Are we in any way like her?" (546). These final words, then, may be seen to represent what Lacan calls "the re-absorption of man's ego, whether by re-integration into a universal good, or by the effusion of the subject towards an object without alterity" ("Aggressivity" 24), and this concludes "the antinomy" so well theorized by Hegel as being "the starting-point of the ego" (Lacan, "Some Reflections" 16). For Hegel, this state of freedom and universal consciousness lies at the base of true spiritual life and all the qualities we name as virtues — family, fatherland, religion, love, friendship, bravery, honour (*Philosophy* 176). If it is so that this third stage of development is "the substance of ethical life" (177), then aggressivity becomes not only the base from which ego identity is constructed but the foundation of social and communal life. And it is perhaps here that the significance of this story lies, as the story not only of a battle between individuals but of the rivalry constitutive of subjective identity in light of the other and the object in the external world.

¹ The following account is taken from "Self-Consciousness" (Hegel, *Philosophy* 165–78).

² "[I]t is really because of that relation that it produces the object again, and the desire as well" (Hegel, *Phenomenology* 109).

³ I refer here to "Self-Consciousness" in *Phenomenology of Spirit.*

⁴ I refer here to "Self-Consciousness" in *Philosophy of Mind.*

⁵ West is left disoriented, careless, "sucked dry of any will of his own" (203). Billy quite simply disappears. The once handsome and distinguished Mitch (the man who was himself a sexual predator) is described before his death as being "rumpled like a park-bench drunk, his skin is grey from travel, dark hollows ring his eyes. He's lost weight, his flesh is loose, his face is starting to cave in, like some old guy without his false teeth . . ." (439).

⁶ Note also that Roz's son Larry is characterized as passive and a potential victim at the hands of women: ". . . Larry has an exiled look to him, the look of a lost traveller. . . . [A] man who can be wrecked by women" (96).

⁷ "[W]hat the bondsman does is really the action of the lord" (Hegel, *Phenomenology* 116).

⁸ While all three men are characterized as passive victims, West provides the most striking example. He is described at various times as "frangible" (10), "a pushover" (45), "an innocent" (128), "hypnotized" (212), a "zombie" (212), "occupied territory" (215), "like a dog summoned by a supersonic whistle, inaudible to human ears" (220).

⁹ It is also noteworthy that at this point Charis speaks of her own body as an object, saying: "Although she treats her body with interest and consideration, paying attention to its whims, rubbing lotions and oils into it, feeding it with selected nutrients, it doesn't always repay her" (228).

¹⁰ Fathers are absent or ambiguous in what is named as being "the real world of women" (129). The divorced Mrs. Morley with her various "accoutrements" (390) is the epitome of the feminine persona, and she joins numerous others — Tony's mother with her ever-painted mouth, Charis's daughter Augusta with her sling-back high heels and painted nails, the prostitutes "stuccoed with makeup" (153), and the girls at McClung Hall with their pyjama parties, haircurlers, and gossip. Meanwhile, "the Zenias of this world are abroad in the land, plying their trade, cleaning out male pockets, catering to male fantasies" (456). Like the Robber Bride, they lurk in mansions in the dark forest, "preying upon the innocent, enticing youths to their doom in her evil cauldron" (342).

¹¹ "In so far as I constitute the world, I cannot conceive another consciousness, for it too would have to constitute the world and, at least as regards this

other view of the world, I should not be the constituting agent" (Merleau-Ponty 350).

¹² "[I]n so far as the other resides in the world, is visible there, and forms a part of my field, he is never an Ego in the sense in which I am one for myself. In order to think of him as a genuine *I*, I ought to think of myself as a mere object for him, which I am prevented from doing . . ." (Merleau-Ponty 352).

¹³ Merleau-Ponty refers to the Hegelian concept of a life-or-death struggle: "With the *cogito* begins that struggle between consciousnesses, each one of which, as Hegel says, seeks the death of the other" (355); and the necessity of recognition: "Once the other is posited, once the other's gaze fixed upon me has, by inserting me into his field, stripped me of part of my being, it will readily be understood that I can recover it only by establishing relations with him, by bringing about his clear recognition of me . . ." (357).

¹⁴ See, for example, Tony's reaction on realizing that West is with Zenia: "Tony's arms and legs are coming detached from the rest of her, and sounds are slowing down" (149); Tony contemplating sexual intercourse: "the thought of giving another person that much power over her makes her flinch" (205), "She is too small, and West is too big. She would be shredded" (206); and Charis's reaction to Zenia insinuating Billy's infidelity: "Her entire body has gone slack, as if her bones have melted" (263).

¹⁵ This is the case also for Tony when, as a young child, her mother leaves: "Although Anthea was gone, she was still there, sitting at the table with them. She was there more than ever" (178).

¹⁶ "In so far as I have sensory functions, a visual, auditory and tactile field, I am already in communication with others taken as similar psycho-physical subjects" (Merleau-Ponty 353).

¹⁷ Merleau-Ponty writes: "If I am dealing with a stranger who has as yet not uttered a word, I may well believe that he is an inhabitant of another world in which my own thoughts and actions are unworthy of a place. But let him utter a word . . . and already he ceases to transcend me: that, then, is his voice, those are his thoughts and that is the realm that I thought inaccessible" (361).

¹⁸ See, for example, the opening paragraphs of chapter 17.

¹⁹ "She will only be history if Tony chooses to shape her into history. . . . The story of Zenia is . . . a rumour only, drifting from mouth to mouth and changing as it goes" (535).

²⁰ This is firstly because the social world predates any one subject: "before any voluntary *adoption of a position* I . . . [am] already *situated* in an intersubjective world" (Merleau-Ponty 355); and secondly, because even by refusing to speak to the other, the subject is acknowledging and asserting the presence of that other: "The refusal to communicate, however, is still a form of communication" (361).

[21] Tony characterizes this other self as an unborn twin: "when Tony grew up and learned more about left-handedness she was faced with the possibility that she might in fact have been a twin, the left-handed half of a divided egg, the other half of which had died" (160).

[22] Note also that one of the secondary characters, Shanita, constructs herself in a similar fashion. In chapter 9, we are told that she "changes her story. Sometimes she's part Chinese and part black, with a West Indian grandmother, . . . but there are other grandmothers too, one from the States and one from Halifax, and one from Pakistan and one from New Mexico, and even one from Scotland. . . . [B]ut sometimes she's part Ojibway, or else part Mayan, and one day she was even part Tibetan. She can be whatever she feels like, because who can tell?" (66).

[23] "Tony once said that Zenia probably had a different name every year. Roz said, No, every month, she probably subscribed to the Name-of-the-month Club" (489).

[24] "Zenia is no longer a small-titted person with two implants, she's a big-breasted knockout. The same goes for the nose job. . . . Like a renovated building, Zenia is no longer the original, she's the end result" (118).

[25] "Anthea was her own absence. She hovered just out of reach, a tantalizing wraith . . . endowed with a sort of gauzy flesh by Tony's longing for her" (179).

[26] "[H]er body is made of something slippery and yellow, like the fat in a gutted hen" (301).

[27] This in turn is reminiscent of her earlier experience of sleepwalking after having been beaten by her mother, as it is described in chapter 34.

[28] See, for example, anecdotes of Karen kept in storage in a suitcase underneath a bed, or being like a leather bag that has been thrown into the waters of Lake Ontario (304).

[29] Lacan gives the following example: "The child who strikes another says that he has been struck; the child who sees another fall, cries" ("Aggressivity" 19).

[30] "When she looks at him with her stone eyes it's as if she's reaching in through his ribs and squeezing his heart so it almost stops. He says he has a heart condition, he takes pills for it, but they both know it's a thing she's doing to him" (303).

[31] At this point, one is reminded of Kristeva's work on pregnancy and the splitting of the maternal subject in essays such as "The Maternal Body," "Motherhood According to Giovanni Bellini," and "Stabat Mater."

[32] See also the admission that "It's Charis who needs her to be here, it's Charis who won't cut her free" (57).

[33] "The master confronted by his slave was not yet truly free . . . it is only when the slave becomes free that the master, too, becomes completely free"

(Hegel, *Philosophy* 177), and "the slave rises above the selfish individuality of his natural will, and his worth to that extent exceeds that of his master who, imprisoned in his egotism, beholds in the slave only his immediate will and is only formally recognized by an unfree consciousness" (175).

34 ". . . Zenia is doing Tony's rebelliousness for her" (195).

AFTERWORD

This study has involved a detailed analysis of six of Margaret Atwood's novels. It has been inspired by the fact that each of the novels in question is identifiably about a definitive person. Atwood's use of protagonist and focalizing perspective support the reader's sense that in reading each novel we are getting to know an individual. Thus, the first contention of this book has been that the self — the identity, consciousness, or psyche of the protagonist — should be the focal point of analysis. However, not only is there a self that dominates each narrative, but a self that is, uniformly and consistently, divided. There is no exception to this rule: in each of the six novels, all the protagonists and many of the peripheral characters are fractured, disintegrating, alienated, or displaced. Thus, the second principle underlying this book has been a conviction that it is not only the self that is the perspective through which the novels should be read and examined, but it is the divided self that should be the focus for study.

Having maintained that the divided self is the key to understanding Atwood's novels, my next question has been: what is the best way to understand the divided self? It is at this point that I have contended that psychoanalytic and phenomenological theories are most apt, as they offer an in-depth analysis of human consciousness and the psyche, and allow for a greater complexity than any political agenda or critical imperative would otherwise allow. Traditional psychoanalytic models explain the ways in which the psyche functions, while phenomenology contextualizes the individual within a world regulated through perception. The more contemporary poststructuralist focus of recent psychoanalytic and phenomenological theory adds the issue of discursivity to the debate. The result is that the self and its attendant divisions now become a function of decentred subjectivity; that is, the self is split owing to signification and enunciative positioning, the interplay of Imaginary demands and symbolic desires, the process of specular identity formation, the drama of familial relations, and the requirements of social organization. The outcome is a more theoretically precise account of the divided self or split subject, and a systematic examination of the ways in which it features in Atwood's novels.

What, then, has been the result of this analysis? First and foremost is a detailed reading of each of the six novels explaining the ways in which each protagonist's existence is marked by division and the ways in which that division has been effected. This has been achieved by taking into account the narrative development, characterization, and use of symbol in each novel. As a consequence, an identifiable focus upon the split self has not precluded a holistic interpretation inclusive of the major aspects of each novel. Further to this, the distinctive characteristic of each novel, that which differentiates it from the others — be it setting, thematic focus, or plot — has been taken as the point of entry for analysis. Hence, there have come to light differing perspectives on split subjectivity in accordance with the different ways in which it has featured in each novel.

While the analysis has been underwritten by a commitment to respecting the specificity of each novel, and thus each text has been appraised on its own terms and each protagonist dealt with separately, interpretation in light of psychoanalytic and phenomenological theories has proved to be a cogent way of accounting for familiar motifs of Atwoodian characterization and general and recurrent trends within the novels. Lacan's model of the mirror-phase, for example, is well suited to explaining why it is that each protagonist at some point gazes upon herself in a mirror but has a problematic relationship with her own reflection. Similarly, a Freudian formulation of the oedipal complex and familial configuration accounts for the various identifications (or lack thereof) that then affect the protagonists' relationships with men. Theories of the pre-oedipal phase are appropriate for explaining how it is that a number of the protagonists struggle with femininity or are haunted by their mother. Each and every protagonist experiences some form of unconscious regression, be it daydream, hallucination, textual practice, or irrational behaviour, and this common psychopathology is best explained by way of psychoanalytic formulations of the symptom.

A number of quite specific dynamics recur, allowing for connections between texts. Aggressivity, for example, is an overriding feature of Elaine Risley's relationship with her friend Cordelia, yet the tension of rivalry is also well illustrated in Elizabeth and Lesje's battle over Nate. On a similar note, the Hegelian master-slave dynamic features in *The Edible Woman*, where Marian MacAlpin consumes and is herself consumed, while in *The Robber Bride* such power plays form the basis of the entire narrative. Spatial positioning is an overt and determining feature of Rennie Wilford's story, yet we also witness Elizabeth Schoenhoff struggle to find her place in the world and Joan Foster negotiate spatiality in the light of her relationship with the maternal. Textual practice as a negotiation of enunciative and hence subjective position is most overt in *Cat's Eye* where the protagonist is an artist, yet similar dynamics are evident in *Lady Oracle* and are illustrated by way of Joan's authorship of Gothic romances. Even the ancillary figures bear resemblances to each other. Duncan's role in *The Edible Woman*, for example, has been linked to the agency of the phallic signifier, while in *Lady Oracle* Fraser Buchanan takes the position of discursive intermediary between experience and representation. While in this book I have chosen not to focus upon such connections between texts, a more systematic cross-referencing would be possible and signals a potential for future and further applications of this approach.

While this book has resulted in a close reading and new interpretation of six of Atwood's novels, I would argue that the methodology — an interweaving of psychoanalytic and phenomenological theories and a consequent application of these theories to the texts — has provided a model through which Atwood's work may be read. While Atwood's poetry and short fiction has been outside the scope of this book, it may in fact be true that this methodology could also apply to these other forms and be able to explain characterization and thematic and narrative concerns in the rest of Atwood's work.

APPENDIX

The Handmaid's Tale AND *Surfacing*

This appendix addresses the fact that *The Handmaid's Tale* and *Surfacing* have been placed outside the critical parameters of this study. This is because neither novel lends itself to the methodology; not because a framework of psychoanalytic and phenomenological theories is in any way partial, but because these two texts are significantly and fundamentally different in form from the other six novels. While psychoanalytic and phenomenological theories could be applied to them, examination in these terms would provide a limited interpretation; hence, they are best suited to other forms of critical analysis.

An analysis of *The Handmaid's Tale* in light of psychoanalytic and phenomenological theories could focus upon the Gileadean social structure, and its attempt to deprive the individual of subjective identity. Implicated would be the fact that naming and certain forms of symbolic exchange are forbidden; pregnancy as a biosocial program whereby the act of childbirth becomes a biological function that no longer involves agency; and the role of "The Eye" as the gaze experienced by the self in the field of the other. While discussion of the novel in these terms would provide insight into certain issues, it is my contention that such an analysis would not account for *The Handmaid's Tale* in its entirety. That is, such a reading would illuminate certain aspects of the novel rather than provide a holistic interpretation that could account for plot, characterization, theme, and setting. Analysis in these terms would constitute only a partial reading of the text.

This decision is based upon a number of factors. The first of these is the undeniably political focus of *The Handmaid's Tale*, the fact that equal emphasis is given to the state, nature, and status of the society as is given to the thoughts, emotions, and consciousness of the protagonist. The fact that, to the reader, what happens to Gilead is as important as what happens to Offred (although the reader's sympathy may lie with the latter) imputes to the text a didactic element of social commentary not felt as keenly in any of the other novels.

Second, what differentiates this novel from the others is its play with reality. *The Handmaid's Tale* is marked by its futuristic setting, yet Gilead incorporates aspects of the contemporary world (its North American location, technological developments, conservative and reactionary political movements, and the like). It is this identification of past and present with the future that is partly responsible for the novel's implicit prophetic warning. That is, while a novel such as *Bodily Harm* makes a political statement, the islands of St. Antoine and St. Agathe already exist contemporaneously with the reader, and as such are a kind of fait accompli for the reader who at this point is largely powerless to change the situation. By comparison, the reader of *The Handmaid's Tale* realizes — with relief — that Gilead has not yet happened. However, the implication is that awareness and appropriate political action are needed to ensure that Gilead never does happen.

This anxiety is further heightened by the inconclusive ending. By contrast, the protagonist of *Bodily Harm* is able, in the end, to board a plane and leave under the jurisdiction of her own, fairer government. As readers, we are given the opportunity to muse upon her safe return home and a happier state of existence. No such indulgence is possible in reading the final pages of *The Handmaid's Tale*; Offred's betrayal, incarceration, or death at the hands of the regime are every bit as likely as her precarious escape to England, and once more we are reminded that the protagonist's individual fate is not the most important issue.

These issues of narrative development and setting mark *The Handmaid's Tale* as being a qualitatively different text when set beside Atwood's other novels. It is, in fact, of a different genre, and should rightly be considered as being dystopian in nature. Further to this, however, the subject matter is conspicuous in its concern with women; and it is in part its obvious commentary upon reproductive rights, the position of women in society, the nature of sexuality, economic and social disempowerment, the division of labour, and the like, that make the novel as arresting as it is. This, in conjunction with the focalizing voice of the female protagonist, makes Gileadean society misogynistic, and the novel a feminist dystopia.

Not surprisingly, all these judgements are well supported in critical work on the novel to date. A number of critics comment upon the juxtaposition of fantasy and reality in the text.[1] Critics also note the political focus of the work.[2] For at least one critic, this ideological and "definite philosophical and socio-political outlook" (Malak 11) together with a reality that is not distorted beyond recognition are "the salient dystopian features" (10) of the work. The positioning of the novel within a tradition of dystopic writing is common critical practice.[3] However, for many, what Atwood adds to the genre is an identifiably feminist focus.[4] As one critic points out, "What distinguishes Atwood's novel from those dystopian classics is its obvious feminist focus" (Malak 11). And indeed there is a broad consensus of opinion concerning the feminist nature of the work.[5]

Thus, given the literary context, thematic concerns, and use of setting in *The Handmaid's Tale*, it is my contention that analyses either in terms of feminist issues or in light of the novel functioning as an example of dystopic literature or both are the most appropriate ways of accounting for this novel. Even the aspects that could benefit from a psychoanalytic and phenomenological slant would need to be supplemented by a feminist perspective. The issue of the gaze provides a good example. For while the gaze is a dynamic of the scopic drive that situates the subject in the external world, "the motifs of vision" are, as Glenn Deer points out, "an important part of the presentation of the politics of sexual control" (228). By this, Deer means that in Gilead vision has a power structure whereby the observer dominates the object of sight, and the regulation of vision expresses the subjugation of the Handmaids to the Commanders in a relation of master to slave. In this sense, the issue of the gaze would benefit from analysis in psychoanalytic and phenomenological terms but would be incomplete without the necessary perspective of sexual difference. Of course, psychoanalysis and feminism are by no means incompatible. Indeed, a merging of the two disciplines has been shown to provide a fruitful account of the novel. Michele Lacombe's work on the dynamics of signification in the Gileadean symbolic order and the narrative agenda of sexual oppression is a seminal piece, and Lucy M. Freibert's account of the novel introduces "French feminist principles" to analysis of *The Handmaid's Tale* (Freibert 285). My own approach, however, intentionally does not privilege feminist over other types of psychoanalytic theory.

* * *

An analysis of *Surfacing* in light of psychoanalytic and phenomeno-logical theories could interpret the dichotomy between head and body evident within the novel as being the dichotomy between a subjective position and presubjective experience, the conscious and the instinctual, or, to use Kristeva's terminology, the symbolic and the semiotic. This would involve contrasting the paternal realm of logic, intellect, and discourse with a more primordial existence, which, given its associations with childbirth and the reclamation of pregnancy, could then be interpreted in light of Kristevan notions of the asymbolic chora. In this context, the protagonist's awakening could be seen to be effected through a regression to this maternal chora, resulting in the knowledge that, while an enunciative position is necessary, what is also needed is a new acknowledgement of the semiotic, maternal forces upon which it is founded.

While such an analysis would be functional in terms of accounting for the dichotomy that plagues the protagonist's mind, it does not adequately address the issue that sets this novel apart from the others: the fact that in *Surfacing* the process undergone is as impor-tant as the protagonist herself. In *The Edible Woman*, *Lady Oracle*, *Life before Man*, *Bodily Harm*, *Cat's Eye*, and *The Robber Bride*, the consciousness of the protagonist is paramount and the detail with which we witness the workings of her mind — be it conscious thought processes, patterns of logic, or irrational associations — overrides whatever narrative changes may be occurring. However, in *Surfacing*, there is a certain anonymity that makes the protagonist less distinctive. Meanwhile, her course of action takes over as focus. Furthermore, it does so with a sense of inevitability, with the result that the series of changes she undergoes seems predetermined. It is my contention that these impressions are not coincidental, but are appropriate given that, once looked at closely, the development of the protagonist, the plot, and the narrative structure of *Surfacing* conform to the genre of the romance quest.

Drawing upon Northrop Frye's seminal work on genre and modes of fiction, it may be said that, in writing *Surfacing*, Atwood has both conformed to and subverted the classical expectations of romance, so that the novel moves both within and against that genre. The first point to be made is that *Surfacing* exhibits the processional and sequential form definitive of romance. Joseph Campbell identifies three stages of the journey — "the Departure," "the Initiation," and "the Return" — and these are clearly echoed in Atwood's choice of a three-part narrative structure. Frye also mentions the significance of the threefold structure; however, he names four stages in the most complete romantic form, namely the quest. These four phases are also clearly evident in the novel.[6]

The issue of narrative strategy is rudimentary, as it not only defines the coordinating principle of the work but gives *Surfacing* its distinct quality. No other of Atwood's novels concludes so clearly featuring all three elements of the questing hero: an awakening, the reception of knowledge and insight that is of specific social consequence, and an unambiguous return to society with the added responsibility that the heroine is under obligation to pass this knowledge on to others. As Campbell notes, in "The Crossing of the Return Threshold" phase the hero is faced with a problematic situation: he must reenter society and confront a world peopled by those who are destined not to understand. The questing hero faces the danger that the boon brought back from the transcendent world will be rationalized and thus lose significance, and given that the return with knowledge may involve breaking the taboos of social reality, the reentry from the mystic realm into everyday life may indeed be difficult. However, the key to the romance myth, notes Campbell, lies in understanding that, while the two worlds seem distinct, they are in fact superimposed upon each other. In order that they continue to intersect, a "Cosmic Dancer" or "Master of Two Worlds" may be involved. Thus, the fact that our protagonist returns ("I dress, clumsily . . . I re-enter my own time") but does so not by herself but with a "time-traveller" and "primeval one" (*Surfacing* 191) takes on added significance, as perhaps this new child growing inside will be able to pass freely across the division and thus effect real change.

In keeping with the romance mode, characterization is essentially twofold whereby there is a hero/protagonist who faces an enemy/antagonist.[7] As in classical romance, all energy is focused upon this conflict that takes place in the human world characterized by the cyclical movement of nature,[8] with the reader's emotional responses weighted in favour of the protagonist. The protagonist's "power of action" places her firmly within the romantic mode as Frye defines it. That is, the heroine is an ordinary mortal rather than a great leader or a divine figure and the ordinary laws of nature are slightly suspended.[9]

Thematically, *Surfacing* is identifiably "episodic" in that its primary concern with the boundary of consciousness is typical of the genre as it is outlined by Frye. More specifically, *Surfacing* functions as a "poem of revelation" in that it contrasts a "vita nuova" or new insight with traditional, accepted laws of social existence, or, in the words of the protagonist, "new places, new oracles, . . . true vision" (*Surfacing* 145). In keeping with the traditional form, *Surfacing* uses female and divine grace to reach a state of enlightenment. As is typically the case with the episodic form, Atwood emphasizes the separateness of her heroine's personality and vision through her distinct sense of isolation. Further to this, the novel remains an example of "comic" rather than "tragic" romantic fiction. This is because its mode is idyllic rather than elegiac[10] and it resembles the pastoral in that it privileges the rural setting as a place naturally inclined toward spiritual enlightenment. In addition, the fact that the heroine's exploits are not individualized[11] makes the work comic, as does the fact that as a consequence, the natural world is not reduced merely to the physical and the vegetable but is imbued with a magical power all its own.

In *Surfacing*, the emphasis upon adventure usually seen in the romance quest has been replaced by a realism; a realism that makes it the story of an ordinary Canadian woman coming to terms with her present life, her parents, and her past, rather than the tale of dragon-slaying knight-errantry replete with sirens, witches, or magicians.[12] This move away from fantasy and toward verisimilitude may be seen to be a slide into irony[13] — the mode Frye defines as having as its central structural principle the parody of romance. By Atwood's thus applying the romantic conventions to a more realistic content, the protagonist does not journey into a magical land but instead treks into the Canadian bush, she does not travel to Hades but suffers a type of psychological breakdown, and her birth and resurrection provide a more believable kind of awakening.

If, then, parody is one of the ways in which *Surfacing* may be seen to interface with the romantic quest, there are yet other ways in which Atwood may be seen to be subverting the genre. First, there is a distinct rejection of Christianity and organized religion as the philosophy underwriting the quest and eventual enlightenment. Further to this, in Atwood's novel, the hero is not used as a way of projecting the ideals of the dominant intellectual and economic class. In fact, in a clever inversion of the traditional romantic "wish fulfilment" form in which the virtuous hero represents the ideals of the ruling class and the villain a threat to their power, in *Surfacing* the protagonist's new insight actually poses a threat to dominant materialistic, industrialist, and patriarchal values, while the "villains" are those protecting that social order.

Second, there is both idiosyncratic use and inversion of the traditional point of epiphany: the symbolic presentation of the point at which the revelatory world and the cyclical world of nature come into momentary alignment. While it is true that there is no mountaintop oration, this fleeting connection between heaven and earth occurs in the poetic sequence in which the human and the natural, word and thing, become one.[14] However, there is also an inversion of that same motif. According to Frye, an analogous form of the epiphany is the motif of sexual fulfilment, with the climax signifying arrival at the summit of experience. In *Surfacing*, sexual intercourse is significant, but it lacks the necessary element of epiphanic union.[15] In accordance with the resolution of the quest, the motif of sexual fulfilment is eventually reclaimed as an epiphanic moment, as in the third phase the protagonist has intercourse, "keeping the moon on my left hand and the absent sun on my right" (*Surfacing* 161). On this occasion, the climax is heightened even further by the introduction of a distinctly female element: the conception of life itself.

The significance of the feminine in Atwood's reworking of the traditional quest romance should by no means be overlooked. Foremost is her placing of a woman in the key heroic role. This is further emphasized in that the gift of insight with which the heroine will return to society is undeniably female in nature.[16] In terms of narrative strategy, this should not be altogether unexpected. Campbell stipulates that as part of the Initiation phase, the ultimate adventure when all the barriers have been overcome is commonly represented as a meeting with the Queen Goddess of the World.[17] This Goddess is the universal mother who imputes to the cosmos the cyclical attributes of nurture and of death and destruction. However, while this gives the feminine a role within the quest, it answers a specifically masculine demand; for the Goddess is the ultimate, unattainable Woman, the reply to all desire. With her the hero is given the gift of love in what Campbell terms a mystical marriage. By comparison, Atwood's use of the maternal and feminine principle is devoid of any sexual connotations.

Equally subversive is Atwood's inversion of the element Campbell calls "Woman as the Temptress." This is traditionally the point at which Woman becomes the symbol of temptation, enticing the hero whose purity of soul is threatened with defeat. From the princess who sprouts an enormous rear and ends up being cross-eyed with one breast bigger than the other (*Surfacing* 53–57), to Anna's traumatic encounter with the camera as pinup girl, to the "new kind of centerfold" we are left with in the final pages — "face dirt-caked and streaked, skin grimed and scabby, hair like a frayed bath-mat stuck with leaves and twigs" (190) — Atwood cleverly subverts a traditional motif while making a feminist statement about the position of women in the contemporary world. This, in addition to the moral condemnation of behaviours seen to be masculine (violence, exploitation, rationalization) and constant reference to the difficulties of being a woman in contemporary society, results in a kind of "feminization" of romantic convention.

The focus upon sexual difference in a genre otherwise prescribed by tradition, and indeed the adherence to a definitive literary form, makes *Surfacing* unique in comparison with Atwood's other novels. It is thus my contention that the most appropriate critical analysis would be one that takes both of these factors into account.

Of course, some critical work has been directed toward these issues. *Surfacing* is often seen as a quest, although exactly what kind of quest it is remains largely a matter of opinion.[18] As one critic notes, "Margaret Atwood's *Surfacing* has been widely celebrated and criticized as a narrative quest, but the form and aim of the quest are matters of considerable disagreement" (Berryman 51). A smaller but significant number of critics refer to traditional formulations of the romance quest, citing the work of either Campbell[19] or Frye.[20] Significant also is the fact that there has been considerable preoccupation with narrative structure and resolution,[21] and it is my own contention that this bespeaks an allegiance not only to an appraisal of the novel as a romance quest but to an underlying belief that of Atwood's novels, this is like no other. With this, I set it aside, along with *The Handmaid's Tale*, as more apt for other forms of analysis.

¹ Katherine Doud asserts that "hardly anyone thought this scenario was entirely fabricated" (1–2). Anne Tyler maintains it "could be taking place at this moment" (28). Ellen Cronan Rose discusses *The Handmaid's Tale* in light of the industrial pollutants, toxic chemicals, and birth defects that plague today's world. Dorothy Jones begins her analysis by stating that "although *The Handmaid's Tale* is set in a not too distant totalitarian future, it also describes the patriarchal capitalist society in which most of its readers currently live" (31). Ken Norris believes Offred's story "could plausibly become a story of our own immediate future" (357). Stephanie Barbe Hammer sees Gileadean society as "a grotesque mirror image of our own" (46) because the world that Atwood is describing "reflects not a future reality but a present actuality" (44).

² Michael Foley opens his piece with the comment that "*The Handmaid's Tale* deals with the perennial issue of politics, the exercise of power in human society" (50). Lucy M. Freibert agrees, saying "In *The Handmaid's Tale* the context is essentially political . . ." (280). Hammer identifies "the clear existence of a topical political target" (39). Like most critics and reviewers, Amin Malak sees Atwood as cautioning against right-wing fundamentalism and dogmatic theosophies. See also Mary M. Reefer; John Goddard; and Cynthia Burack.

³ Most often the novel is compared to George Orwell's *1984*, Aldous Huxley's *Brave New World*, and Yevgeny Zamyatin's *We*. See, for example, Mary McCarthy; Cathy N. Davidson; Chris Ferns; Robert Fulford; Ken Adachi; Roger Harris; Peter S. Prescott; Jerome Rosenberg, "In a Future"; and Nancy Schieffer.

⁴ See, for example, Barbara Hill Rigney; Charles A. Brady; and Michele Lacombe.

⁵ Roberta Rubenstein states that in *The Handmaid's Tale*, ". . . Atwood develops the themes of selfhood and boundary in more explicitly feminist terms, focusing on such issues as body image, female sexuality and fertility, pornography and exploitation, and the nature and perpetuation of male power in patriarchy" *(Boundaries* 101). Cathy N. Davidson simply states that "unlike her predecessors, she concentrates on what happens to women" (24). Jones speaks of the novel as having "the theme of female resistance within a patriarchal society" (31). For Hammer, ". . . Atwood's narrative focuses specifically on men's domination of women by means of other women, and more generally portrays women's physical and mental imprisonment within a particularly sinister male regime" (39). Similarly, for Foley, "the abiding focus of interest is the subordination of women in Western culture and the role women themselves have played in accepting and enforcing this subordination" (51). See also Eileen Pahl; Teresa Heger; Gayle Greene, "Choice"; Margaret Meek; Barbara Ehrenreich; and Maureen Freely.

6 The initial "agon" or conflict usually consisting of a perilous journey or minor adventure may be seen to be represented by the protagonist's trek into the Canadian wilderness in search of her father, and the further voyaging later disguised as a fishing trip with the others. The "pathos" or death struggle usually imaged as a battle is somewhat muted; however, during the most crucial part of the tale, the protagonist is in danger of being found and taken captive by agents of conventional society, and this danger is expressed through the image of the hunt. The third element, which Frye identifies as being the disappearance of the protagonist, takes the traditional form of the "sparagmos," with the difference that the "tearing to pieces" that this entails is, in this instance, expressed by a disintegration of personality and a loss of social persona. The final element of "anagnorisis" or discovery takes the traditional form of resurrection or rebirth in that the protagonist will give birth not only to a newly reintegrated, enlightened self but to "the child inside me showing through the green webs of my flesh" (*Surfacing* 181).

7 Thus, the characterization is suitably dialectic, with Anna, David, and Joe seen primarily in terms of whether they hinder or support the heroine's development. In addition, Paul, who greets the heroine in his guise as "priest" or "porcelain mandarin" waiting at the fence (*Surfacing* 19), serves as an ancillary character who leads the protagonist into the new world. In the protagonist's own words, "the lake was the entrance for me" (147), and, to use Campbell's terminology, Paul is the "threshold guardian" who stands at the entrance to the realm of magnified power and the unknown, most often represented by an alien land.

8 The cyclical imagery usually associated with this is well represented in the novel by the cycles of time, patterns of eating and of sexual fulfilment, and the like.

9 A suspension of disbelief is necessary to accommodate the ghostly appearance of the protagonist's mother and father and the animism that endows the surroundings with supernatural power.

10 The novel utilizes the motif of escape from society and idealizes a simplified life in the country.

11 The protagonist is an everywoman figure who could in fact be any woman.

12 There is, for example, a certain "domestication" of what Campbell calls "The Road of Trials" — the phase in which the hero has crossed the threshold and must undergo a succession of trials, tests, and ordeals. In *Surfacing*, the daily chores necessary for survival — fishing, gathering vegetables, chopping firewood, steering a canoe — are difficult enough to be tests in themselves.

13 Frye states that the central principle of ironic myth is the application of romantic forms to a more realistic content.

14 "I lean against a tree, I am a tree leaning. . . . I am not an animal or a tree,

I am the thing in which the trees and animals move and grow, I am a place" (*Surfacing* 181).

¹⁵ Anna's desperate whining and fast panic culminates in her having "prayed to nobody" (112). What should be an ultimate experience — a meeting of cosmic proportions — is in this case empty: she communes with nobody and remains alone.

¹⁶ "The power from my father's intercession wasn't enough . . ." (*Surfacing* 153).

¹⁷ Campbell also stipulates that there is a phase of Atonement with the Father who separates the hero from the maternal and embodies contradictions such as good/evil, pleasure/pain, and life/death. While the similarities with the father figure in *Surfacing* are evident, it is interesting to note that the rivalry between hero and Father for mastery of the universe that usually complicates the process is, in Atwood's female version, absent.

¹⁸ Francine du Plessix Gray sees the novel as a female religious quest and the literary expression of feminist theology. Charles Berryman, himself committed to the idea that the narrator reenacts a mythological pattern of ritual rebirth and descent, sees *Surfacing* as the archetypal story of Persephone inspired by a number of factors: Atwood's time as a student of Northrop Frye, aspirations for a rebirth of Canadian literature, an interest in the liberation of women, and contemporary ecological concerns for the natural world. Sue Thomas sees *Surfacing* as a "mythic reconception of grail legends" (73). By this she means that Atwood alludes in characterization, plot, imagery, symbol, and language to "various grail motifs" (73) that are reconceived in feminist terms and thus draw together the psychological, cultural, and mythic levels of the narrator's experience as a woman. Annis Pratt's feminist archetypal analysis sees the protagonist as undergoing a "rebirth journey" that is a "form of transformation of personality" (140). Pratt outlines seven phases, a number of which resemble the stages of the romantic quest. However, the process she outlines is a psychological one in that it is a journey into the individual psyche, the goal of which is to integrate body and head in one personality as the heroine plunges down into unconscious materials and is empowered by absorbing the archetypal symbols.

¹⁹ Josie Campbell, for example, writes that "its total structure and meaning are informed by the mythic heroic quest, demonstrated in Joseph Campbell's *The Hero with a Thousand Faces*" (169). However, while her own analysis draws heavily upon Campbell's formulation, most critics mention it only in passing. Rubenstein, for example, refers to Campbell's work in a footnote while discussing the protagonist's inner journey ("*Surfacing*"). Peter Klovan describes the protagonist by saying "her general movement from hostility to reconciliation illustrates a central feature of the romance quest as described by Joseph

Campbell" (3). In general, the problem is, as Josie Campbell notes, that "critics mention only briefly Atwood's indebtedness to Campbell, viewing the mythic pattern as merely a minor element of the novel, almost as if they fear to unravel the sometimes knotty mythic figures and patterns to be found in the work. As a result, much that is crucial to the novel's meaning remains unexplored" (169).

[20] Arnold and Cathy Davidson categorize *Surfacing* as "a romance in the high old style" (40) in their reference to Frye's *Anatomy of Criticism*. They also identify an agon, pathos, and anagnorisis, demonstrating that the structure of the quest may be traced in the novel, with the difference that they see the novel as having "a conclusion that is almost anti-mythic" (38). By this they mean that the ending is uncertain because the protagonist has no society in which to report back her success, and no society will be saved by her success.

[21] This issue of the conclusion has sparked considerable debate, both in terms of its position within the genre and in general discussion of the novel. Pratt contextualizes the debate in light of the issue of sexual difference, pointing out that while the male questor will have far less difficulty as a transformed personality in reintegrating into his culture, in the case of the woman hero, the return will be problematic as her adventures will increase her chances for death, madness, and accusations of social deviance, and her elixir will be devalued and seen as a threat to civilization. She also makes the point that quite often the returning female hero is depicted as passing on her boon to a younger apprentice since she is unlikely to be able to affect a broad sector of her society. Pratt does, however, see *Surfacing* as ultimately optimistic, and "unique" in that "the hero seems wholly transformed and wholly determined to 'surface' in her full powers back into the world of culture" (156). Jerome H. Rosenberg makes the point that the actions of Atwood's heroine are similar to those of the classical journey as described by Campbell, but he feels that in *Surfacing* Atwood "truncates the myth" because the heroine does not return with an elixir that restores the world ("Woman" 128). This, for Rosenberg, is in full keeping with the artistic and literary parameters of the work, with the heroine constrained by psychological and social influences yet envisaging the possibility of something better.

WORKS CITED

Adachi, Ken. "Atwood Takes a Chance and Wins." *Toronto Star* 13 Oct. 1985: E1.

Atwood, Margaret. *Bodily Harm.* 1981. London: Virago, 1986.

——. *Cat's Eye.* 1988. London: Virago, 1990.

——. *The Edible Woman.* 1969. London: Virago, 1980.

——. *The Handmaid's Tale.* 1985. London: Virago, 1987.

——. *Lady Oracle.* 1976. London: Virago, 1987.

——. *Life before Man.* 1979. London: Virago, 1982.

——. *The Robber Bride.* Toronto: McClelland, 1993.

——. *Surfacing.* 1972. London: Virago, 1977.

Bachelard, Gaston. *The Poetics of Space.* Trans. Maria Jolas. Boston: Beacon, 1969.

Barthes, Roland. *S/Z.* Trans. Richard Miller. New York: Hill, 1974.

Berryman, Charles. "Atwood's Narrative Quest." *Journal of Narrative Technique* 17. 1 (1987): 51–56.

Brady, Charles A. "Puritan Anti-Utopia Envisioned." *Buffalo News* 23 Feb. 1986: E6.

Brooks, Peter. "The Idea of a Psychoanalytic Criticism." *Critical Inquiry* 13 (1978): 334–48.

Burack, Cynthia. "Bringing Women's Studies to Political Science: The Handmaid in the Classroom." *NWSA Journal* 1.2 (1988–89): 274–83.

Campbell, Joseph. *The Hero with a Thousand Faces.* Princeton, NJ: Princeton UP, 1968.

Campbell, Josie. "The Woman as Hero in Margaret Atwood's *Surfacing.*" McCombs 168–79.

Carrington, Ildikó de Papp. " 'I'm Stuck': The Secret Sharers in *The Edible Woman.*" *Essays on Canadian Writing* 23 (1982): 68–87.

Chodorow, Nancy. "Mothering, Object-Relations, and the Female Oedipal Configuration." *Feminist Studies* 4.1 (1978): 137–58.

Davey, Frank. "*Lady Oracle*'s Secret: Atwood's Comic Novels." *Studies in Canadian Literature* 5 (1980): 209–21.

——. *Margaret Atwood: A Feminist Poetics.* Vancouver: Talonbooks, 1984.

Davidson, Arnold, and Cathy Davidson. "The Anatomy of Margaret Atwood's *Surfacing.*" *Essays on Canadian Writing* 10.3 (1979): 38–54.

Davidson, Cathy N. "A Feminist '1984.'" *Ms* Feb. 1986: 24–26.

Deer, Glenn. "Rhetorical Strategies in *The Handmaid's Tale*: Dystopia and the Paradoxes of Power." *English Studies in Canada* 18.2 (1992): 215–33.

Doane, Mary Anne. "Caught and Rebecca: The Inscription of Femininity as Absence." Penley 196–215.

——. *The Desire to Desire: The Woman's Film of the 1940's.* Indianapolis: Indiana UP, 1987.

——. "Woman's Stake: Filming the Female Body." Penley 216–28.

Doud, Katherine. "A Woman's Place: Future: Handmaid's Tale." *Kalamazoo Gazette* [MI] 15 Feb. 1987: G1–2.

du Plessix Gray, Francine. "Nature as the Nunnery." McCombs 131–34.

Ehrenreich, Barbara. "Feminism's Phantoms." *New Republic* 17 Mar. 1986: 33–35.

Feldstein, Richard, and Henry Sussman, eds. *Psychoanalysis and . . .* New York: Routledge, 1990.

Felman, Shoshana. "Turning the Screw of Interpretation." *Literature and Psychoanalysis: The Question of Reading: Otherwise.* 1982. Ed. Felman. Baltimore: Johns Hopkins UP, 1989. 94–207.

Ferns, Chris. "The Value/s of Dystopia: *The Handmaid's Tale* and the Anti-Utopian Tradition." *Dalhousie Review* 69.3 (1989): 373–82.

Fiske, John. *Reading the Popular.* Boston: Unwin, 1989.

Foley, Michael. " 'Basic Victim Positions' and the Women in Margaret Atwood's *The Handmaid's Tale.*" *Atlantis: A Women's Studies Journal* 15.2 (1990): 50–58.

Freely, Maureen. "Picking up the Pieces." *Observer* [London, Eng.] 16 Mar. 1986: 25.

Freibert, Lucy M. "The Artist as Picaro: The Revelation of Margaret Atwood's *Lady Oracle.*" *Canadian Literature* 92 (1982): 23–33.

——. "Control and Creativity: The Politics of Risk in Margaret Atwood's *The Handmaid's Tale.*" McCombs 280–91.

Freud, Sigmund. "Anxiety and Instinctual Life." Freud, *New Introductory Lectures* 113–44.

——. "The Archaic Features and Infantilism of Dreams." Freud, *Introductory Lectures* 235–49.

——. "The Development of the Libido and the Sexual Organizations." Freud, *Introductory Lectures* 362–82.

——. "The Dissection of the Psychical Personality." Freud, *New Introductory Lectures* 88–112.

——. "The Ego and the Id." *The Ego and the Id and Other Works.* Trans. and ed. James Strachey. London: Hogarth, 1961. 12–66. Vol. 19 of *The Standard Edition of the Complete Psychological Works of Sigmund Freud.* 24 vols. 1966–74.

——. "Female Sexuality." Freud, *On Sexuality* 371–92.

——. "Femininity." Freud, *New Introductory Lectures* 145–69.

——. "Instincts and Their Vicissitudes." Freud, *On the History* 117–40

——. *Introductory Lectures on Psychoanalysis.* Trans. James Strachey. Ed. James Strachey and Angela Richards. Pelican Freud Library 1. Harmondsworth, Eng.: Penguin, 1975.

——. "The Libido Theory and Narcissism." Freud, *Introductory Lectures* 461–81.

——. *New Introductory Lectures on Psychoanalysis.* Trans. James Strachey. Ed. James Strachey and Angela Richards. Pelican Freud Library 2. Harmondsworth, Eng.: Penguin, 1975.

——. "On Narcissism: An Introduction." Freud, *On the History* 73–102.

——. *On Sexuality: Three Essays on the Theory of Sexuality and Other Works.* Trans. James Strachey. Ed. Angela Richards. Pelican Freud Library 7. Harmondsworth, Eng.: Penguin, 1977.

——. *On the History of the Psycho-Analytic Movement: Papers on Metapsychology and Other Works.* Trans. and ed. James Strachey. London: Hogarth, 1957. Vol. 14 of *The Standard Edition of the Complete Psychological Works of Sigmund Freud.* 24 vols. 1966–74.

——. "The Paths to the Formation of Symptoms." Freud, *Introductory Lectures* 404–24.

——. "Resistance and Repression." Freud, *Introductory Lectures* 327–43.

——. "Revision of the Theory of Dreams." Freud, *New Introductory Lectures* 35–59.

——. "Three Essays on the Theory of Sexuality." Freud, *On Sexuality* 45–169.

——. "Totem and Taboo." *Totem and Taboo and Other Works.* Trans. and ed. James Strachey. London: Hogarth, 1955. 1–162. Vol. 13 of *The Standard Edition of the Complete Psychological Works of Sigmund Freud.* 24 vols. 1966–74.

Frye, Northrop. *Anatomy of Criticism: Four Essays.* Princeton, NJ: Princeton UP, 1957.

Fulford, Robert. "Atwood Puts Her Own Generation's Experience to Work." *Toronto Star* 28 Dec. 1985: H5.

Givner, Jessie. "Names, Faces and Signatures in Margaret Atwood's *Cat's Eye* and *The Handmaid's Tale.*" *Canadian Literature* 133 (1992): 56–75.

Godard, Barbara. "My (m)Other, My Self: Strategies for Subversion in Atwood and Hébert." *Essays on Canadian Writing* 26 (1983): 13–44.

Goddard, John. "Lady Oracle." *Books in Canada* Nov. 1985: 6–8, 10.

Goodwin, Ken. "Revolution as Bodily Fiction — Thea Astley and Margaret Atwood." *Antipodes: A North American Journal of Australian Literature* 4.20 (1990): 109–15.

Grace, Sherrill. *Violent Duality: A Study of Margaret Atwood.* Montreal: Véhicule, 1980.

Greene, Gayle. "Choice of Evils." *Women's Review of Books* July 1986: 14–15.

——— . *"Life before Man*: 'Can Anything Be Saved?' " *Margaret Atwood: Vision and Forms.* Ed. Kathryn Van Spanckeren and John Garden Castro. Carbondale: Southern Illinois UP, 1988. 65–84.

Grosz [Gross], Elizabeth [E.A.]. "The Body of Signification." *Abjection, Melancholia and Love: The Work of Julia Kristeva.* Ed. John Fletcher and Andrew Benjamin. London: Routledge, 1990. 80–103.

——— . *Jacques Lacan: A Feminist Introduction.* Sydney: Allen, 1990.

——— . "Lacan, the Symbolic, the Imaginary and the Real." *Working Papers in Sex, Science and Culture* 1.1 (1976): 12–32.

——— . "Language and the Limits of the Body: Kristeva and Abjection." *Futurefall: Excursions into Post-Modernity.* Ed. Grosz, et al. Sydney: Power Institute, 1987. 106–17.

——— . *Sexual Subversions: Three French Feminists.* Sydney: Allen, 1989.

Hammer, Stephanie Barbe. "The World as It Will Be? Female Satire and the Technology of Power in *The Handmaid's Tale." Modern Language Studies* 20.2 (1990): 39–49.

Harris, Roger. "Atwood's Anti-Utopia Is a '1984' for Women." *Star Ledger* (Newark, NJ) 9 Feb. 1986, sec. 4: 12.

Heath, Stephen. "Difference." *Screen* 19.3 (1978): 51–112.

——— . "Notes on Suture." *Screen* 18.4 (1977–78): 48–76.

Hegel, G.W.F. *Phenomenology of Spirit.* 1952. Trans. A.V. Miller. Oxford: Oxford UP, 1977.

——— . *Philosophy of Mind.* 1971. Trans. William Wallace and A.V. Miller. Oxford: Oxford UP, 1990.

Heger, Teresa. "Atwood Fashions Another Feminist Novel." *Daily Iowan* [Iowa City] 24 Apr. 1986: B8.

Hengen, Shannon. " 'Your Father the Thunder/Your Mother the Rain': Lacan and Atwood." *Literature and Psychology* 32.3 (1986): 36–42.

Hutcheon, Linda. *The Canadian Postmodern: A Study of Contemporary English-Canadian Fiction.* Oxford: Oxford UP, 1988.

——— . "From Poetic to Narrative Structures: The Novels of Margaret Atwood." *Margaret Atwood: Language, Text, and System.* Ed. Sherrill E. Grace and Lorraine Weir. Vancouver: UBC P, 1983. 17–32.

——— . "Reading Atwood's *Life before Man*: Structural Form through Psychic Verisimilitude." *Comparison* 12 (1981): 41–58.

Irigaray, Luce. "And the One Doesn't Stir without the Other." *Signs* 7.1 (1981): 60–67.

——— . "Is the Subject of Science Sexed?" *Cultural Critique* 1 (1985): 73–88.

——— . *This Sex Which Is Not One.* Trans. Catherine Porter with Carolyn Burke. Ithaca: Cornell UP, 1985.

——— . "Women, the Sacred and Money." *Paragraph* 8 (1986): 6–18.

Iser, Wolfgang. *The Implied Reader: Patterns of Communication in Prose Fiction from Bunyan to Beckett.* Baltimore: Johns Hopkins UP, 1974.

Jacobus, Mary. *Reading Woman: Essays in Feminist Criticism*. New York: Columbia UP, 1986.

Jones, Dorothy. "Not Much Balm in Gilead." *Commonwealth* 11.2 (1989): 31–43.

Klein, Richard. "In the Body of the Mother." *Enclitic* 7.1 (1983): 66–75.

Klovan, Peter. " 'They Are Out of Reach Now': In Margaret Atwood's *Surfacing*." *Essays on Canadian Writing* 33 (1986): 1–28.

Kristeva, Julia. *Desire in Language: A Semiotic Approach to Literature and Art*. Ed. Leon S. Roudiez. Trans. Thomas Gora, Alice Jardine, and Roudiez. New York: Columbia UP, 1980.

— . "Father, Love and Banishment." *Literature and Psychoanalysis*. Ed. Edith Kurzweil and William Phillips. New York: Columbia UP, 1983. 389–99.

— . "Four Types of Signifying Practice." *Semiotext(e)* 1.1 (1974): 65–74.

— . "From One Identity to an Other." Kristeva, *Desire* 124–47.

— . "Histoires D'Amour — Love Stories." *Desire*. Ed. Victor Burgin, et al. Spec. issue of *ICA Documents* (1984): 18–21.

— . "The Maternal Body." *M/F: A Feminist Journal* 5–6 (1981): 158–63.

— . "Motherhood According to Giovanni Bellini." Kristeva, *Desire* 237–70.

— . "Phonetics, Phonology and Impulsional Bases." *Diacritics* 4.3 (1974): 33–37.

— . "Place Names." Kristeva, *Desire* 271–94.

— . *Powers of Horror: An Essay on Abjection*. Trans. Leon S. Roudiez. New York: Columbia UP, 1982.

— . *Revolution in Poetic Language*. Trans. Margaret Waller. New York: Columbia UP, 1984.

— . "Stabat Mater." *The Kristeva Reader*. Ed. Toril Moi. Trans. Leon S. Roudiez. Oxford: Blackwell, 1986. 160–86.

— . "The Subject in Signifying Practice." *Semiotext(e)* 1.2 (1974): 19–26.

Lacan, Jacques. "The Agency of the Letter in the Unconscious or Reason since Freud." Lacan, *Écrits* 146–78.

— . "Aggressivity in Psychoanalysis." Lacan, *Écrits* 8–29.

— . "Desire and the Interpretation of Desire in *Hamlet*." *Yale French Studies* 55–56 (1977): 11–52.

— . "The Direction of the Treatment and the Principles of Its Power." Lacan, *Écrits* 226–80.

— . *Écrits: A Selection*. Trans. Alan Sheridan. New York: Norton, 1977.

— . *The Four Fundamental Concepts of Psycho-Analysis*. 1978. Trans. Alan Sheridan. Ed. Jacques-Alain Miller. New York: Norton, 1981.

— . "The Freudian Thing, or the Meaning of the Return to Freud in Psychoanalysis." Lacan, *Écrits* 114–45.

— . "The Function and Field of Speech and Language in Psychoanalysis." Lacan, *Écrits* 30–113.

— . "The Mirror Stage as Formative of the Function of the I as Revealed in Psychoanalytic Experience." Lacan, *Écrits* 1–7.

——. "The Oedipus Complex." *Semiotext(e)* 10 (1981): 190–200.

——. "Of Structure as an Inmixing of an Otherness Prerequisite to Any Subject Whatever." *The Languages of Criticism and the Sciences of Man: The Structuralist Controversy.* Ed. Richard Macksey and Eugenio Donato. Baltimore: Johns Hopkins, 1970. 186–200.

——. "On a Question Preliminary to Any Possible Treatment of Psychosis." Lacan, *Écrits* 179–225.

——. "The Signification of the Phallus." Lacan, *Écrits* 281–91.

——. "Some Reflections on the Ego." *International Journal of Psychoanalytic Analysis* 34 (1953): 11–17.

——. "The Subversion of the Subject and the Dialectic of Desire in the Freudian Unconscious." Lacan, *Écrits* 292–325.

Lacombe, Michele. "The Writing on the Wall: Amputated Speech in Margaret Atwood's *The Handmaid's Tale*." *Wascana Review* 21.2 (1986): 3–20.

Laplanche, J., and J.B. Pontalis. *The Language of Psycho-Analysis.* Trans. Donald Nicholson-Smith. New York: Norton, 1973.

Laplanche, Jean, and Serge Leclaire. "The Unconscious: A Psychoanalytic Study." *Yale French Studies* 48 (1972): 118–75.

Lefebvre, Henri. *The Production of Space.* Trans. Donald Nicholson-Smith. Oxford: Blackwell, 1991.

Lévi-Strauss, Claude. *The Elementary Structures of Kinship.* Trans. James Harle Bell. Boston: Beacon, 1969.

Lorsch, Susan E. "Androgyny and the Idea of the Double: Margaret Atwood's *The Edible Woman*." *Dalhousie Review* 63.3 (1983): 464–74.

Lynch, Denise E. "Personalist Plot in Atwood's *Bodily Harm*." *Studies in the Humanities* 15.1 (1988): 45–57.

Maclean, Susan. "*Lady Oracle*: The Art of Reality and the Reality of Art." *Journal of Canadian Fiction* 28–29 (1980): 179–97.

Malak, Amin. "Margaret Atwood's *The Handmaid's Tale* and the Dystopian Tradition." *Canadian Literature* 112 (1987): 9–16.

Mansbridge, Francis. "Search for Self in the Novels of Margaret Atwood." *Journal of Canadian Fiction* 22 (1978): 106–17.

McCarthy, Mary. "Breeders, Wives, and Unwomen." *New York Times Book Review* 9 Feb. 1986: 1.

McCombs, Judith, ed. *Critical Essays on Margaret Atwood.* Boston: Hall, 1988.

McMullen, Lorraine. "The Divided Self." *Atlantis* 5.2 (1980): 53–67.

Meek, Margaret. Rev. of *The Handmaid's Tale*, by Margaret Atwood. *School Librarian* 35.3 (1987): 278.

Mellard, James M. *Using Lacan Reading Fiction.* Urbana, IL: U of Illinois P, 1991.

Merleau-Ponty, Maurice. *Phenomenology of Perception.* 1962. Trans. Colin Smith. London: Routledge, 1989.

Mitchell, Juliet. *Psychoanalysis and Feminism.* 1974. Harmondsworth, Eng.: Penguin, 1976.

Mulvey, Laura. "Visual Pleasure and Narrative Cinema." Penley 55–79.

Mycak, Sonia. "Divided and Dismembered: The Decentred Subject in Margaret Atwood's *Bodily Harm*." *Canadian Review of Comparative Literature* 20.3–4 (1993): 469–78.

Nodelman, Perry. "Trusting the Untrustworthy." *Journal of Canadian Fiction* 21 (1977–78): 73–82.

Norris, Ken. " 'The University of Denay, Nunavit': The 'Historical Notes' in Margaret Atwood's *The Handmaid's Tale*." *American Review of Canadian Studies* 20.3 (1990): 357–64.

Oudart, Jean-Pierre. " 'La suture': The Tutor-Code of Classical Cinema." Trans. Daniel Dayan. *Film Quarterly* (fall 1974): 22–31.

Pahl, Eileen. Rev. of *The Handmaid's Tale*, by Margaret Atwood; and *The Good Mother*, by Sue Miller. *Harvard Women's Law Journal* 10 (1987): 335–40.

Patterson, Jayne. "The Taming of Externals: A Linguistic Study of Character Transformation in Margaret Atwood's *The Edible Woman*." *Studies in Canadian Literature* 7.2 (1982): 151–67.

Patton, Marilyn. "Tourists and Terrorists: The Creation of *Bodily Harm*." *Papers on Language and Literature* 28.2 (1992): 150–73.

Penley, Constance, ed. *Feminism and Film Theory*. New York: Routledge, 1988.

Pratt, Annis. "Surfacing and the Rebirth Journey." *The Art of Margaret Atwood: Essays in Criticism*. Ed. A.E. Davidson and C.N. Davidson. Toronto: Anansi, 1981. 139–57.

Prescott, Peter S. "No Balm in This Gilead." *Newsweek* 17 Feb. 1986: 70.

Ragland-Sullivan, Ellie. *Jacques Lacan and the Philosophy of Psychoanalysis*. Urbana, IL: U of Illinois P, 1987.

——. "The Magnetism between Reader and Text: Prolegomena to a Lacanian Poetics." *Poetics* 13 (1984): 381–406.

——. "Seeking the Third Term: Desire, the Phallus, and the Materiality of Language." *Feminism and Psychoanalysis*. Ed. Richard Feldstein and Judith Roof. Ithaca: Cornell UP, 1989. 40–64.

Rainwater, Catherine. "The Sense of the Flesh in Four Novels by Margaret Atwood." *Margaret Atwood: Reflection and Reality*. Ed. Beatrice Mendez-Egle and James M. Haule. Edinburgh, TX: Pan American UP, 1987. 14–28.

Rao, Eleonora. *Strategies for Identity: The Fiction of Margaret Atwood*. New York: Lang, 1993.

Reefer, Mary M. "Political Novel Deprives Women of Identities." *Kansas City Times* [MO] 23 Feb. 1986: C5–6.

Rigney, Barbara Hill. "Dystopia." *Canadian Literature* 111 (1986): 143–44.

Rose, Ellen Cronan. "The Good Mother: From Gaia to Gilead." *Frontiers: A Journal of Women's Studies* 12.1 (1991): 77–97.

Rose, Jacqueline. "Paranoia and the Film System." Penley 141–58.

Rosenberg, Jerome. "In a Future World, New Puritans Rule and Women Suffer." *Philadelphia Inquirer* 9 Feb. 1986: 1, 8.

—. "Woman as Everyman in Atwood's *Surfacing*: Some Observations on the End of the Novel." *Studies in Canadian Literature* 3 (1978): 127–32.

Rubenstein, Roberta. *Boundaries of the Self: Gender, Culture, Fiction.* Urbana, IL: U of Illinois P, 1987.

—. "Pandora's Box and Female Survival: Margaret Atwood's *Bodily Harm*." *Journal of Canadian Studies* 20 (1985): 120–35.

—. "*Surfacing*: Margaret Atwood's Journey to the Interior." *Modern Fiction Studies* 22.3 (1976): 387–99.

Rubin, Gayle. "The Traffic in Women: Notes on the 'Political Economy' of Sex." *Towards an Anthropology of Women.* Ed. Rayna R. Reiter. London: Monthly Review, 1975. 157–210.

Schiefer, Nancy. "A Baleful Look at the Folly of Self-Righteousness." *London Free Press* [London, ON] 1 Nov. 1985: A17.

Silverman, Kaja. *The Acoustic Mirror: The Female Voice in Psychoanalysis and Cinema.* Bloomington: Indiana UP, 1988.

Skura, Meredith Anne. *The Literary Use of the Psychoanalytic Process.* New Haven, CT: Yale UP, 1981.

Stovel, Nora Foster. "Reflections on Mirror Images: Doubles and Identity in the Novels of Margaret Atwood." *Essays on Canadian Writing* 33 (1986): 50–67.

Stow, Glenys. "Nonsense as Social Commentary in *The Edible Woman*." *Journal of Canadian Studies* 23.3 (1988): 90–101.

Thomas, Sue. "Mythic Reconception and the Mother/Daughter Relationship in Margaret Atwood's *Surfacing*." *Ariel* 19–20 (1988): 73–85.

Tyler, Anne. "Margaret Atwood's Chilling New Tale of Future America." *Chicago Sun-Times* 2 Feb. 1986, show sec.: 28.

Wilson, Sharon R. "Turning Life into Popular Art: *Bodily Harm*'s Life-Tourist." *Studies in Canadian Literature* 10.1–2 (1985): 136–45.

Winnicott, D.W. "Transitional Objects and Transitional Phenomena." *International Journal of Psychoanalysis* 34.2 (1953): 89–97.

INDEX